"*Flawless Consulting* is not just a practical, useful, and inviting book for practitioners. It's all those things, but it's also a book about some of the most vexing issues we face when consulting to organizations—issues of resistance, truth, doubt, vulnerability, and accountability. If you find yourself giving advice to people making choices, then this book is a must-have for you. Buy it today, use it tomorrow."

**Jim Kouzes,** award-winning coauthor of the best-selling *The Leadership Challenge* and *The Truth About Leadership*; Dean's Executive Professor of Leadership, Leavey School of Business, Santa Clara University

"Consulting at its best is about action and interaction, relationships and results. In a highly readable guide that is both inspirational and practical, Peter Block leads consultant and client together through a proven approach to realize their future."

**Samuel R. Strickland,** chief financial and administrative officer, Booz Allen Hamilton

". . . surpasses the high standards of relevance, clarity, and wisdom characteristic of previous versions. . . . Whether one's consulting experience spans five years or fifty, there is a great deal in this new edition to prompt us to reflect upon our own practice and to discuss with colleagues."

**Roger Harrison,** independent consultant and author of *Consultant's Journey: A Dance of Work and Spirit* and *The Collected Papers of Roger Harrison*

"Peter Block has written a masterful third edition of his masterpiece, *Flawless Consulting*. A powerful message that emerged gradually in editions one and two comes clearly to the surface in this latest edition. Important additions to edition three are the strength-based strategies that many are beginning to use . . . in solving seemingly intractable problems in health care and other industries. They are featured in a new Chapter Twelve and form a common thread that runs through this entire path-breaking book."

**Jon C. Lloyd, MD, FACS,** senior associate, Positive Deviance Initiative; clinical advisor, Plexus Institute

". . . shows why the earlier versions of the book are deeply valued by those who have read them. The updates in this edition . . . showcase the premises of the book. *Flawless Consulting* is at the head of the class for those wanting to master the complexities of consultation."

**Larry Browning,** professor, Department of Communication Studies, University of Texas at Austin; adjunct professor of management, Bodø Graduate School of Business, Bodø, Norway

"My company uses this book as our primary guide to consultant skills. Interestingly, our most experienced consultants value the insights from *Flawless Consulting* the most. It has made a big difference in how we think about and work with clients."

**Tønnes Ingebrigtsen,** CEO, mnemonic

"Every new story and fresh insight in this third edition of *Flawless Consulting* abounds with sagely wisdom for anyone learning the art of influence without power. With the warm, gentle voice of a trusted friend, Peter guides, nudges, and inspires."

**Arvinder S. Dhesi,** group talent director, Aviva

"This new edition of *Flawless Consulting* is highly germane to educators at all levels who are serious about helping bring about true educational reform. Teachers and students can drop their roles and engage one another authentically with discovery and dialogue about mutual expectations. Peter also helps us restore a sense of sanity in following what we know makes sense. I highly recommend this new edition for my colleagues in the education profession."

**David W. Cox,** professor of education, Arkansas State University

"Peter Block did it again! With this edition of *Flawless Consulting* he demonstrates why he continues to inspire millions of change leaders around the world. We practice with more impact because of Peter's teachings."

**Louise van Rhyn,** change activist and nation builder, South Africa

". . . very special as it has equipped me to be an enabler of transformation by making our clients and us work like real partners that build the capacity of both to work for the well-being of all stakeholders."

**Anil Sachdev,** founder and CEO of Grow Talent Company and the School of Inspired Leadership, Gurgaon, India

"Peter Block's masterpiece *Flawless Consulting* in 1980 informed my point of view on developing organizations. This book is the capstone—you can't afford not to read it."

**Phil Harkins,** CEO, Linkage Inc.

". . . invaluable insights to the evolution and usefulness of *Flawless Consulting*. In this practical guide, one thing that stands out for me is Peter's emphasis on the importance of consulting from the view of possibilities over problems."

**Marcia Mendes-d'Abreu,** vice president, Human Resources, Ontario Teachers' Pension Plan

# FLAWLESS CONSULTING

The Instructor's Manual for the third edition of
*Flawless Consulting* is available free online. If you would
like to download and print out a copy of the Manual, please visit:
www.wiley.com/college/block

THIRD EDITION

# FLAWLESS CONSULTING

## A GUIDE TO GETTING YOUR EXPERTISE USED

### PETER BLOCK

Illustrated by Janis Nowlan

JOSSEY-BASS
A Wiley Imprint
www.josseybass.com

Published by Pfeiffer
An Imprint of Wiley
989 Market Street, San Francisco, CA 94103-1741
www.pfeiffer.com

For additional copies/bulk purchases of this book in the U.S. please contact 800-274-4434.

Pfeiffer books and products are available through most bookstores. To contact Pfeiffer directly call our Customer Care Department within the U.S. at 800-274-4434, outside the U.S. at 317-572-3985, fax 317-572-4002, or visit www.pfeiffer.com.

Pfeiffer also publishes its books in a variety of electronic formats. Some content that appears in print may not be available in electronic books.

**Library of Congress Cataloging-in-Publication Data**
Block, Peter.
    Flawless consulting: a guide to getting your expertise used / Peter Block;
illustrated by Janis Nowlan. — 3rd ed.
        p. cm.
    Includes index.
    ISBN 978-0-470-62074-8 (hardback)
        1. Business consultants.    I. Title.
    HD69.C6B57 2010
    001—dc22

                                                                    2010034719

Acquiring Editor: Matthew Davis
Marketing Manager: Brian Grimm
Director of Development: Kathleen Dolan Davies
Developmental Editor: Leslie Stephen
Production Editor: Michael Kay/Susan Geraghty
Printing    10 9 8 7 6 5 4 3 2 1

Editor: Beverly H. Miller
Editorial Assistant: Lindsay Morton
Manufacturing Supervisor: Becky Morgan
Printed in the United States of America

*To Dorothy, with love . . .*

## ALSO BY PETER BLOCK

# CONTENTS

The last time I revised this book was in 1999 when we were millennium-minded. On the one hand, we feared business would be shutting down because the computer world was going to abort and refuse to grow one year older. On the other side was the belief that the new millennium would mark the beginning of a new consciousness for peace and well-being.

Well, neither really happened. Our dependency on computers and technology has only intensified, and a decade into the millennium, we are at war, still addicted to fossil fuels, and concerned whether the economic system we have grown used to is still relevant. This means that living with a vulnerable present and an uncertain future is going to be a permanent condition.

This situation bodes well for the world of consulting. The more complexity, confusion, and uncertainty in our lives, the more we realize we cannot go it alone or keep doing what we have been doing. The demand for help and advice should keep growing.

The profound uncertainty of our lives, both personally and at work, also results in more and more people functioning in a consultative stance. The essence of this stance is that of wanting to have influence when you do not have direct control. This challenge is true not just for consultants; it is true for people who used to be in charge: bosses, teachers, preachers, doctors, sergeants, mayors, and, not least of all, parents. Permanent vulnerability and uncertainty demand a level of relatedness based on listening, authenticity, and not knowing. This is what makes command-and-control behavior increasingly obsolete. Not all of us get this, but sooner or later, we are going to develop our capacity for deeper relatedness and partnership or we will be looking for a new job sooner than our careful planning might have indicated.

In response to the wider need for a consultative stance, I have added in this edition two examples of how consulting skills can be useful, actually transformative, in a broader context than strictly for people in a support or consulting role. I have picked two sectors of society where the call for change and reform has been shouting in our ears for decades with little to show for it: health care and education. These are also service industries, which is where most of us work these days.

Both of these fields are in the throes of the language of reform. But most reform efforts are more about improvement rather than rethinking something more fundamental. The health care "reform" is mostly about cost control, who pays, and increasing the pressure on standardization. There is no reform in that conversation, just better or different management. Real reform in health care will come from changing our relationship with our service provider and having service providers change their relationship with each other. In consulting terms, we need more balanced contracting, more joint discovery, and a new dialogue. This is starting to occur, and Chapter Twelve presents a great example from a very special surgeon, Paul Uhlig.

Like health care, the current conversation about education reform is also not reform; it is just more controls and imposed standards masquerading as reform. True reform will shift our thinking about the culture of the classroom, accountability of the learner, and the relationship between teacher and student. An example of this from an amazing high school teacher, Ward Mailliard, is in Chapter Eighteen.

Looking at the face of reform in these two arenas gives us clues on ways to achieve changes for leadership in other areas, such as business, government, religion, and human services.

In addition to living with permanent uncertainty, we are living increasingly virtual lives. Many of our relationships are long distance. We are part of virtual teams spread too far to ever be in the same room together. We are more and more dependent on electronic interaction. We speak to friends by writing on an electronic wall, and we substitute webinars for seminars. Soon we will be able to hold all our conversations, be entertained, find a life partner, and visually be with our family all on a handheld device.

Despite the growth of the virtual world, our days are still occasionally populated with live human beings and when we are in the room with others, we need to get to the point and make the most of it. Playing roles, being vague, speaking in generalities, and getting to the point in the last five minutes waste the uniqueness of having all our senses available when we are face-to-face. We want to take advantage of real meetings to become personally connected in ways powerful enough to overcome the distancing and isolating effects inherent in an electronic connection. Thus, the need for authenticity and directness about sensitive issues outlined in this book increases. There is a discussion in

Chapter Six about ways to make virtual relationships as useful as possible. If you do not want to read that far, text me and I will compress it and send to your drop box, assuming you give me the key.

Another revision in this edition is in the chapters on the feedback phase and on implementation. Giving feedback is part of every consulting or support effort, but almost every meeting is one where ideas or analyses are presented with the intent of improving or shifting a person's or organization's strategy or operation. We still spend way too much time making our point, often our PowerPoint, without realizing that the purpose of most meetings is not to make a point, or express ideas, or to sell something but to move something forward. That is why I have broadened the idea of a feedback meeting to include any meeting that has the intent of producing action. The action does not move forward when one person is talking and a group of people are listening. It is dialogue, interaction, doubts, and commitments that move the action forward. This sounds so simple and remains so rare that I explore it in more detail in Chapters Fifteen and Seventeen.

One other addition relates to the shift occurring in the organizational world from a primary focus on needs and deficiencies to a focus on possibilities, gifts, and strengths. The belief is that more change occurs

when we focus on the future and our capacities rather than try to make sense of the past or even the present and look so much at problems and what is wrong. In Chapter Twelve, I give some examples of where this is occurring and offer some thoughts on what this means for consulting work.

## THE DESIGN OF THE BOOK

I am somewhat neurotic about meeting rooms—how they are arranged, the light, the color, the art, the movement: all the things that bring aliveness into our experience. In the same way, I believe the design of a book is as important as its content. Ideas should be accessible and written in everyday language. The pages should invite readers in with white space, large type for aging eyes, and images, in this case, drawings, to break up patterns and give the eye more places to go.

Along these lines, one of my concerns about the first revision was that the book became too thick. It was heavy to hold, hard to travel with, exhausting to contemplate finishing. Worried about this, I turned to the Internet to provide the vehicle to do something about it. In this edition, I have taken all the content that did not seem right to the point and moved it to the Flawless Consulting Web site: www .flawlessconsulting.com. Icons throughout the book guide you to expanded content that is relevant to the material you are reading. It also gives me a way to update ideas as they evolve. I hope this works. If it doesn't work for you or if you do not have access to the Internet, let me know, and I will provide more hard copy. If enough of you want more hard copy, I have got me another book, so that's not so bad either.

## WHAT IS STILL TRUE

What needs reaffirmation in this edition of the book is that teams and personal relationships are still critical to technical and business success. The value of teams and relationships is now more widely accepted than it was in the past, at least intellectually. We may not be any better at working together, but at least we know it matters and want to create more cooperative workplaces, whether virtual or in person.

One reason the ideas in this book have endured is not so much that specific consulting skills are presented in such overconfident specificity; it is more because of the attention the book gives to the emotional and personal dimensions of our workplaces. Even now, with all the rhetoric given to relationships, personal development, and even spirituality, our institutions still operate as if strategy, structure, and technology are what really matter.

Relationships continue to be treated as a necessary inconvenience—as if they have to be endured and wherever there is an opportunity to automate a transaction or communicate electronically, we take it. In 2000 most telephone conversations involved a machine on one end; now it is text messages, e-mail, and, if I want to look personal, Facebook, LinkedIn, and their successors. These are often the media of choice. Even more, we encourage people to work at home, where human interaction is minimized in the name of serenity and a more balanced life.

What is difficult about managing relationships is that something is demanded of us that technology and automated routines do not require: the need to know ourselves and be authentic. Authenticity is simply being honest with ourselves and being direct and honest with others. For whatever the reason, authenticity continues to be rare in our workplaces. Most interactions carry an element of role play, positioning, and strategy. All are reflections of our wish to control our environment and the people in it.

In some ways, this book is a long and detailed description of the landscape of authenticity. What has stood the test of time is that this rare act is not only good for the soul but also works very well. "Authentic consultant" is not an oxymoron but a compelling competitive advantage, if, unfortunately, a rare one.

What is still difficult about authenticity is that it is a high-risk strategy. It swims upstream in a culture of control, which is where most of our organizations remain. It also demands some faith in ourselves: we have to be tuned into the feeling dimension of our connection with others. Most of us have spent our days developing our brain and have left our body and its feeling parts behind, to be reclaimed after work hours. So even when we decide to risk being authentic, we might not know how.

Valuing the relationship between consultant and client, or teacher and student, or service provider and customer, and defining how to manage that relationship is where this book has found its niche. The intent of this revision is to deepen and expand that white space between strategy, structure, and technology that we label relationship.

*October 2010*                                                    Peter Block
                                                                Cincinnati, Ohio

# ACKNOWLEDGMENTS

It is a treat to have an opportunity to formally express appreciation to those who originally created the concepts expressed in this book.

Conceptually, the role of interpersonal skills in organizations and the key role that authentic behavior plays was pioneered by Chris Argyris. What I learned as a student of his in the now-famous 1960s is still powerful and relevant.

Most of us learn how to consult from watching someone who knows how to do it. I was lucky early in the game to follow around Barry Oshry, Roger Harrison, and Dick Walton. They are the best and gave support to me that was above and beyond the call of duty.

Tony Petrella, my partner in crime from the beginning, and Marv Weisbord have so deeply contributed to my understanding of consulting skills that I can't begin to separate my thoughts from theirs. I can only express appreciation for a valued partnership that has been enduring and priceless.

Neale Clapp contributed greatly in two ways. He has given unqualified support and friendship, and he recognized the value in the consulting skills workshop and theory long before I did. In conducting many of the early workshops, Neale contributed conceptually to the early sections of the book on the staff or support role and remains a close and dear friend.

The chapters on resistance were clarified by the late Jim Maselko. Through his skill and enthusiasm, Jim helped give life to the approaches to consulting that this book represents.

The first attempt at writing the original version of the book was done collaboratively with Mike Hill. Although the book eventually took a different direction, Mike was key to getting the thing started. His fingerprints remain in portions of the early part of the book.

The basic concepts on contracting are drawn from Gestalt psychology. These were crystallized in a workshop I attended run by Claire Reiker and Mike Reiker. Their ability to present them simply and powerfully was a great gift.

The drawings in the book are by Janis Nowlan. I sent her a very primitive form of the manuscript for the first edition to see whether she could enliven the copy with illustrations. I thought I had given her an impossible task. The drawings Janis sent back were incredible. Her light touch in visually expressing the concepts in many cases is much more perceptive than all the words I have put together. This is not surprising since she is a very experienced organizational development practitioner in her own right in addition to being an executive in higher education. Janis has continued to support this book with new illustrations and by updating some wording and creating a new wardrobe for the old ones. Thirty years later, her talent continues to grace the pages with new insights and creative talent.

Thanks go to Ray Bard, who was my publisher when the book was begun. Ray believed a book was possible when I thought all I had were some notes for a workshop participants workbook. Acquiring editor Matt Davis, with Jossey-Bass/Pfeiffer/Wiley, was very patient with me, and his support and encouragement directly led to this third edition.

Continuing thanks go to Phil Grosnick, Bill Brewer, and the affiliates of Designed Learning. They lead and bring to life the Flawless Consulting Skills Workshops we conduct around the world now. The bulk of this book documents the theory we have been presenting in the workshops. Most of the concepts have emerged as answers to questions from people learning about consulting. Thanks go as well to the workshop participants for their patience when the concepts were confusing and to their willingness to help us articulate the consulting process out of their own experience.

As with the original edition, Leslie Stephen helped with the editing of this revision. This is the eighth book that she has helped edit with me. She supports my voice and gives structure, simple clarity, and deep understanding to whatever she touches. Thanks as always to Maggie Rogers, who makes everything happen. She is the best. Thanks also to Beverly Miller, who copyedited this edition, Paula Goldstein, who designed the interior, and Susan Geraghty, who managed the production of this edition.

My thinking on the power of conversation was always influenced by my connection with the late Joel Henning. We ran many workshops together and I miss him. The chapters on implementation in this edition were greatly influenced by my association with the Association for Quality and Participation's School for Managing and Leading Change. The school was the laboratory where the new ideas were tested. The thoughts about designing group experiences have been influenced by watching Jill Janov do her work so well. I am especially grateful to the late Kathie Dannemiller and her associates at Dannemiller-Tyson Associates. They understood something profound about the heartbeat of large assemblies. Also Dick Axelrod and Emily Axelrod have created magic in their work with The Conference Model. Dick has written his own books on engagement, and the material in this book grew out of many conversations with him that have changed my consciousness.

All of us who consult today owe a debt of gratitude to the work of Ed Schein. He was one of the early beacons of light who gave direction and insight to those of us who contemplated working in the field of organizational change. He made understandable and explicit the process consulting path that later became a central part of how I operate, and for that I am very grateful. Finally there are two new voices in this edition, Paul Uhlig and Ward Mailliard. They are great friends and enormous innovators in health care and education, respectively. I learn so much each time we are together.

# FLAWLESS CONSULTING

# CHAPTER 1

# A CONSULTANT BY ANY OTHER NAME...

$A$NY FORM OF HUMOR or sarcasm has some truth in it. The truth in the prevailing skepticism about consultants is that the traditional consultant has tended to act solely as an agent of management: assuming the manager's role in either performing highly technical activities that a manager cannot do or performing distasteful and boring activities that a manager does not want to do. The most dramatic examples of consultants' taking the place of managers is when they identify people who will be let go or functions that will be eliminated.

When you are asked directions and you tell someone to get off the bus two stops before you do, you are acting as a consultant. Every time you give advice to someone who is faced with a choice, you are consulting. When you don't have direct control over people and yet want them to listen to you and heed your advice, you are face-to-face with the consultant's dilemma. For some of you, this may be your full-time predicament. Some of you may face it only occasionally, functioning part time as managers (having direct control) and part time as consultants (wanting to influence but lacking authority to control).

## SOME DEFINITIONS AND DISTINCTIONS

A *consultant* is a person in a position to have some influence over an individual, a group, or an organization but has no direct power to make changes or implement programs. A *manager* is someone who has direct responsibility over the action. The moment you take direct responsibility, you are acting as a manager.

Most people in staff or support roles in organizations are really consultants, even if they don't officially call themselves consultants. Support people function in any organization by planning, recommending, assisting, or advising in such matters as these:

- Human resources or personnel

- Financial analysis

- Auditing

- Systems analysis

- Market research

- Product design

- Long-range planning

- Organizational effectiveness

- Safety

- Training and development

- And many more

The recipients of all this advice are called *clients*. Sometimes the client is a single individual. Other times, the client may be a work group, a department, or a whole organization. The client is the person or persons whom the consultant wants to influence.*

In organizations, clients for the services provided by support people are called *line managers*. Line managers have to labor under the advice of support groups, whether they like it or not. But by definition, any support function has no direct authority over anything but its own time, its own internal staff, and the nature of the service it offers. This tension between the line manager (or client) who has direct control and the support person (or consultant) who does not have direct control is one of the central themes of this book.

The key to understanding the consultant role is to see the difference between a consultant and a manager.

Listen to Alfred:

> It was a great four-month project. I headed the team from administrative services that installed the new management information system. We assessed the problems, designed the system, and got Alice, the line manager, to let us install the system from top to bottom.

Alfred is clearly very satisfied—but this is the line manager's satisfaction. He wasn't really acting as a consultant; he took over a piece of the line manager's job for four months.

This distinction is important. A consultant needs to function differently from a line manager—for the consultant's own sake and for the learning goals of the client. It's okay to have direct control—and most of us want it in various forms of disguise. It is essential, though, to be aware of the difference in the roles we are assuming when we have it and when we don't.

---

* You will mainly see the terms *consultant* and *client* used throughout the rest of this book to reinforce this belief and—especially if you are in a staff or support role—assist your thinking of yourself as a consultant.

Much of the disfavor associated with the term *consultant* comes from the actions of people who call themselves consultants but act as surrogate line managers. When you act on behalf of or in the place of the manager, you are acting as a surrogate manager. When the client says, "Complete this report for me," "Hire this person for me," "Design this system for me," "Counsel this employee," or "Figure out which jobs stay and which jobs go," the manager is asking for a surrogate. The attraction of the surrogate manager role is that at least for that one moment, you assume the manager's power—but in fact you are doing the manager's job, not yours.

Your goal or end product in any consulting activity is some kind of change. Change comes in two varieties. At one level, we consult to create change in the line organization of a structural, policy, or procedural nature—for example, a new compensation package, a new reporting process, or a new safety program. The second kind of change is the end result that one person or many people in the line organization have learned something new. They may have learned what norms dominate their staff meetings, what they do to keep lower-level people in a highly dependent position in decision making, how to involve people more directly in setting goals, or how to conduct better performance evaluations.

In its most general use, *consultation* describes any action you take with a system of which you are not a part. An interview with someone asking for help is a consulting act. A survey of problems, a training program, an evaluation, a study—all are consultations for the sake of change. The consultant's objective is to engage in successful actions that result in people or organizations managing themselves differently.

I think of the terms *staff* or *support work* and *consulting work* as being interchangeable, reflecting my belief that people in a support role need consulting skills to be effective—regardless of their field of technical expertise (finance, planning, engineering, personnel, systems, law). Every time you give advice to someone who is in the position to make the choice, you are consulting. For each of these moments of consultation, there are three kinds of skills you need to do a good job: technical, interpersonal, and consulting skills.

Here are the distinctions.

## Technical Skills

Above all, we need to know what the person is talking about. We need expertise about the question. Either in college or in our first job, we were trained in a specific field or function. This might be engineering, sales, accounting, counseling, or any of the thousands of other ways people make a living. This is our basic training. It is only later, after acquiring some technical expertise, that we start consulting. If we didn't have some expertise, then people wouldn't ask for our advice. The foundation for consulting skills is some expertise—whether it is scientific, such as coke particle sizing, or nonscientific, such as management or organizational development. This book assumes you have some area of expertise.

## Interpersonal Skills

To function with people, we need to have some interpersonal skills, that is, some ability to put ideas into words, to listen, to give support, to disagree reasonably, to basically maintain a relationship. There are many books and seminars available to help people with these skills.

In fact, there is a whole industry about achieving better relationships that is devoted to improving these skills. Just like technical skills, interpersonal skills are necessary to effective consultation.

## Consulting Skills

Each consulting project, whether it lasts ten minutes or ten months, goes through five phases. The steps in each phase are sequential; if you skip one or assume it has been taken care of, you are headed for trouble. Skillful consulting is being competent in the execution of each of these steps. Successfully completing the business of each phase is the primary focus of this book.

## CONSULTING SKILLS PREVIEW

Here is an overview of what is involved in the five phases of consulting.

## Phase 1: Entry and Contracting

This phase has to do with the initial contact with a client about the project. It includes setting up the first meeting as well as exploring the problem, whether the consultant is the right person to work on this issue, what the client's expectations are, what the consultant's expectations are, and how to get started. When consultants talk about their disasters, their conclusion is usually that the project was faulty in the initial contracting stage.

## Phase 2: Discovery and Dialogue

Consultants need to come up with their own sense of both the problem and the strengths the client has. This may be the most useful thing they do. They also need skill in helping the client do the same. The questions here for the consultant are: Who is going to be involved in defining the problem or situation? What methods will be used? What kind of data should be collected? How long will it take? Should the inquiry be done by the consultant, or should it be done by the client?

## Phase 3: Analysis and the Decision to Act

The inquiry and dialogue must be organized and reported in some fashion. The consultant is always in the position of reducing large amounts of data to a manageable number of issues. There are also choices for the consultant to make on how to involve the client in the process of analyzing the information. In giving feedback to an organization, there is always some resistance to the data (if it deals with important issues). The consultant must handle this resistance before an appropriate decision can be made about how to proceed. This phase is really what many people call planning. It includes setting ultimate goals for the project and selecting the best action steps or changes.

## Phase 4: Engagement and Implementation

This involves carrying out the planning of phase 3. In many cases, the implementation may fall entirely on the line organization. For larger change efforts, the consultant may be deeply involved. Some projects start implementation with an educational event. This could be a series of meetings to introduce some change, a single meeting to get different parts of the organization together to address a problem, or a training session. In these cases, the consultant is usually involved in rather complicated design work and in running the meeting or training session.

## Phase 5: Extension, Recycle, or Termination

Phase 5 is about learning from the engagement. Following this is the decision whether to extend the process to a larger segment of the organization. Sometimes it is not until after some implementation occurs that a clear picture of the real problem emerges. In this case, the process recycles and a new contract needs to be discussed. If the implementation was either a huge success or a moderate-to-high failure, termination of further involvement on this project may be in the offing. There are many options for ending the relationship, and termination should be considered a legitimate and important part of the consultation. If done well, it can provide an important learning experience for the client and the consultant and also keep the door open for future work with the organization.

■ ■

When you look at Figure 1, you will see a preview of some of the skills and topics covered for the preliminary events leading to engagement and implementation. Consulting skills are grouped into four phases:

**Figure 1.** An Overview of Consulting Skills

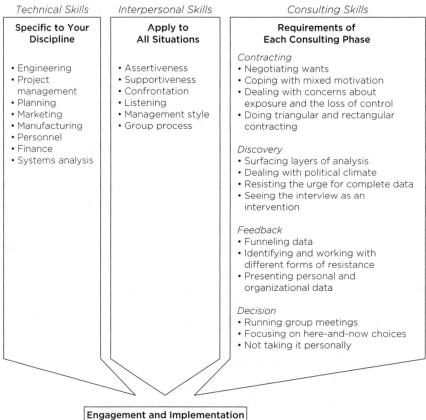

**The Preliminary Events**

| *Technical Skills* | *Interpersonal Skills* | *Consulting Skills* |
|---|---|---|
| **Specific to Your Discipline** | **Apply to All Situations** | **Requirements of Each Consulting Phase** |
| • Engineering<br>• Project management<br>• Planning<br>• Marketing<br>• Manufacturing<br>• Personnel<br>• Finance<br>• Systems analysis | • Assertiveness<br>• Supportiveness<br>• Confrontation<br>• Listening<br>• Management style<br>• Group process | *Contracting*<br>• Negotiating wants<br>• Coping with mixed motivation<br>• Dealing with concerns about exposure and the loss of control<br>• Doing triangular and rectangular contracting<br><br>*Discovery*<br>• Surfacing layers of analysis<br>• Dealing with political climate<br>• Resisting the urge for complete data<br>• Seeing the interview as an intervention<br><br>*Feedback*<br>• Funneling data<br>• Identifying and working with different forms of resistance<br>• Presenting personal and organizational data<br><br>*Decision*<br>• Running group meetings<br>• Focusing on here-and-now choices<br>• Not taking it personally |

Engagement and Implementation

contracting, discovery, feedback, and decision. They include the initial contacts, the planning meetings, the inquiry and analysis, and the feedback and decision-making meetings.

Engagement/implementation is when you finally do something with enough impact to be noticeable to many people in the organization, and they have the expectation that change, or learning, will occur because of that event. One of my beliefs is that the preliminary events are in many ways more crucial for success than the engagement. An understanding of consulting skills therefore is really an understanding of preliminary events.

## THE PROMISE OF FLAWLESS CONSULTATION

One reason consulting can be frustrating is that you are continually managing lateral relationships. As a support person or consultant, you are working with a line manager in a context in which there is no clear boss-subordinate relationship between you. Vertical relationships are easier to understand. If your boss gives you an order, you know that he or she has the right to tell you what to do. But if your client makes a demand, you don't necessarily have to obey. The power balance in lateral relationships is always open to ambiguity—and to negotiation. When we get resistance from a client, sometimes we aren't sure whether to push harder or let go. This book is about managing this ambiguity.

Taken as a whole, this book is about flawless consultation—consulting without error. It concentrates on the preliminary events because I believe competence in contracting, discovery, and feedback creates the foundation for successful outcomes in the implementation stage. I have deliberately avoided discussing and demonstrating consulting skills in an overall step-wise sequence of chapters because some concepts and competencies must be brought to bear in every stage of a consulting relationship. So I have included chapters treating consulting assumptions, goals for a consulting relationship, and consultant role choices, as well as what flawless consultation means in practice, along with the chapters that specify and illustrate the skills required for each of the preliminary events. I have also interspersed chapters on such issues as client resistance and the special considerations of the internal consultant's role to demonstrate the belief that successful consulting demands more than a methodical, step-by-step application of technical expertise.

The promise is that if you consult in the way this book describes, your consultation can be flawless and you will

- Have your expertise better used

- Have your recommendations more frequently implemented

- Work in more of a partnership role with clients

- Avoid no-win consulting situations

- Develop internal commitment in your clients

- Receive support from your clients

- Increase the leverage you have with clients

- Establish more trusting relationships with clients

My use of the term *flawless consulting* may sound presumptuous, but it is not accidental. A basic value underlying this book is that there is in each of us the possibility of perfection. There is a consulting professional inside each of us, and our task is to allow that flawless consultant to emerge. On its surface, this book is about methods and techniques. But each technique carries a consistent message more important than any method: that each act that expresses trust in ourselves and belief in the validity of our own experience is always the right path to follow. Each act that is manipulative or filled with pretense is always self-destructive.

Working in organizations means we are constantly bombarded by pressure to be clever and indirect and to ignore what we are feeling at the moment. Flawless consulting offers the possibility of letting our behavior be consistent with our beliefs and feelings and also to be successful in working with our clients. The focus in this book on techniques and skills in consulting is simply a way to identify the high self-trust choices we all have as we work in organizations. From the first day on our first job, each of us has struggled with the conflict between being ourselves and conforming to the expectations we think our employers or clients have of us. The desire to be successful can lead us into playing roles and adopting behaviors that are internally alien and represent some loss of ourselves.

Consultants are especially vulnerable to this conflict because we are supposed to be serving our clients' needs. Our projects also tend to be short term, and we work at the pleasure of the client. It is easier to terminate a consultant or support person than to terminate a subordinate. In hard times, managers end consulting projects before they reduce their own workforce. This sense of vulnerability can become a rationalization for consultants to deny their own needs and feelings and to not be authentic.

This book offers an alternative. It says that trusting ourselves is the path that serves us well with clients and increases the chances that our expertise will be used again and again.

# CHAPTER 2

# TECHNIQUES ARE NOT ENOUGH

THERE ARE DIMENSIONS to the consulting role that transcend any specific methods we might employ and contribute to our effectiveness no matter what our technical expertise. A unique and beguiling aspect of doing consulting is that your own self is involved in the process to a much greater extent than if you were applying your expertise in some other way. Your reactions to a client, your feelings during discussions, your ability to solicit feedback from the client—all are important dimensions to consultation.

In acting as a consultant, you always operate at two levels. One level is the content—the cognitive part of a discussion between yourself and the client. The client presents a certain organizational problem. Perhaps it's the need for training to improve workforce skills. Perhaps it's how the organization makes decisions. Or there may be a problem of system design or financial controls. The content level is the analytical, rational, or explicit part of the discussion, where you are working on what can be called the technical or business situation. At the same time and at another level, both you and the client are generating and sensing your feelings about each other—whether you feel acceptance or resistance, whether you feel high or low tension, whether you feel support or confrontation. So your relationship to the client during each phase is a second level of data that needs attention just as the content does.

## BEYOND CONTENT

There is much more to the client-consultant relationship than the simple content of the problem or project the consultant is working on. Feelings are the affective side of the discussion and an important source of information for the consultant—information about the client's real concerns and what the possibilities are for establishing a good relationship.

A major objective of every consultation is to encourage you to focus on and value the affective, or interpersonal, aspect of the relationship you have with the client. Most of us have a great deal of experience working at the cognitive or content level of discussion. We come to a meeting equipped with our expertise, and we feel quite comfortable talking about problems we know something about. But there should be equal balance in the attention given to the content of the problem and the feelings you are having about the interaction that is taking place as you are working with the client.

Once you value the affective side of the relationship as an important area of attention, the second step is to increase your comfort level in putting into words how you are feeling about the relationship as it's going on. The third step is to grow more skillful in putting your sense of the relationship into words so you don't increase defensiveness on the part of the client.

There are four elements to the affective side of consultant-client interaction that are always operating: responsibility, feelings, trust, and your own needs.

### Responsibility

To have a good contract with the client, responsibility for what is planned and takes place has to be balanced—50/50. In most cases, the client comes to you with the expectation that once you are told what the problem is, you provide the solution. Your goal is to act out the fact that it's a 50/50 proposition.

Here is a small example. When you start a program, communication on the program is often required—when it will take place, what the arrangements are, why you're doing it. It's important that the client take the responsibility of communicating all of this to the organization— not because it's a task that only the client can do (in fact, the consultant might be in a better position to do it) but because it's a way of visibly expressing to the organization that the client is taking at least 50 percent of the responsibility for the program.

If the client wants the consultant to do this communicating and take care of all the administrative details, the client is saying that he or she wants to take a limited amount of responsibility. As a consultant, it makes sense at times to resist taking on this responsibility. This is a substantively small issue, but it's an example of what to look for in trying to decide in your own mind whether the responsibility is balanced.

## Feelings

The second element that's always an issue is to what extent clients are able to own their own feelings. In a way, this is working on balancing responsibility. The consultant needs to constantly keep in mind how much the client is owning feelings versus talking as if he or she is just an observer of the organization. The consultant also has to keep in mind what his or her own feelings are about the client. If the consultant is feeling that the client is defensive or very controlling, or doesn't listen or doesn't take responsibility, this is important to know.

However the consultant feels working with that client, the people inside the client's organization are going to feel the same way. It is equally important for you to pay close attention to your own feelings during the consultation, particularly during the early stages, and use these as valuable information on how the organization functions and how the client manages.

## Trust

The third element is trust. When most people work with a consultant as a client, they bring with them not only the prevailing image of the consultant as the expert but also someone to watch out for. It is often useful to ask clients whether they trust your confidentiality, whether they trust you not to make them vulnerable or to take things over. You can ask them what doubts they have working with you. In this way, you're working to build trust. The more that any distrust is put into words, the more likely you are to build trust.

## Your Own Needs

The fourth element on the affective side of the consultant-client relationship is that consultants have a right to their own needs from the relationship.

It's easy to fall into a service mentality, in which you see yourself charged with solving the client's problems and serving the client's needs—and it's possible to act in such a way that you, as the consultant, appear not to have any needs. The reality is that you do have needs. You may have organizational needs to have a client, so that your own organization feels that you're doing something worthwhile. You have needs for acceptance and inclusion by the client, and you require some validation that what you have is valuable and worth offering.

On a practical level, you have needs for access to that organization—to talk to people, to ask them questions. And you also have needs for support from that manager, meeting the people in the manager's organization, and dealing with the kind of resistance that you're likely to get. You are entitled to have your needs met.

## Summing Up

The beliefs outlined here are the foundation for the rest of this book: pay close attention to your own style and your own feelings as important dimensions to the consulting relationship. Skill in consulting is not only skill in providing a program, a process, and procedures that respond to the client's needs. It's also your skill in being able to identify and put into words the issues around trust, feelings, responsibility, and your own needs.

## THE CONSULTANT'S ASSUMPTIONS

Any view of what makes for effective consultation relies heavily on the assumptions the consultant has about what makes an effective organization. These assumptions will be implicitly or explicitly a part of any recommendation the consultant makes.

Each of us doing consulting ought to be very clear about our own beliefs. Our own consulting behavior should be consistent with the style of management we advocate to our clients. If we are recommending to our clients that they tighten up controls, be more decisive, and set clear goals, we will be undermining our credibility if we ourselves operate without controls, are indecisive, and aren't quite sure where we are headed. If we think our clients should work on being more participative and collaborative, we undermine ourselves if we keep tight control of the consulting project and don't act collaboratively with the very clients we are trying to encourage to try collaboration.

Think about what your assumptions about good management might be. There are countless models to choose from. Most organizations, for example, operate from a variation of the traditional military/church model of patriarchy. Structurally there is a great emphasis on the hierarchical pyramid and the clear separation of authority and responsibility. The cornerstone of patriarchal management is "strong" leadership. This kind of leadership is seen as an individual ability to plan work, organize people to do the work, maintain control of those people and their results, and then delegate responsibility to the right people to achieve results. The products of these leader-centered assumptions are individuals with an upward-conforming and downward-controlling orientation toward their roles.

This traditional emphasis on control and leadership qualities has shifted in the past thirty years (at least in the literature) to more collaborative or participative conceptions of organizations. Participative management and empowerment is a theme that runs throughout most assumptions about effective organizations today.

Your own assumptions about organizations determine in subtle ways your own consulting style and the skills you should be working on. Here is the set of assumptions that underlie the consulting approach presented in this book.

## Problem Solving Requires Valid Data

Using valid data eliminates a major cause of confusion, uncertainty, and resulting inefficiency in problem solving. Valid data encompass two things: (1) objective data about ideas, events, or situations that everyone accepts as facts and (2) personal data. Personal data are also "facts," but they concern how individuals feel about what is happening to them and around them. If people feel they will not get a fair shake, it is a "fact" that they feel that way, and it is also a "fact" that this belief will have an effect on their behavior. To ignore this kind of "fact" is to throw away data that may be crucial to any problem-solving effort.

## Effective Decision Making Requires Free and Open Choice

Making decisions is easy. Making decisions that people will support is not so easy. Organizations seem to work better when people have an opportunity to influence decisions that have a direct impact on their work. When people feel that something is important and they have some control, they will be motivated to exert the effort to make things work. When they believe that something is important but they can exert no control, the common tendencies are to become cautious or defensive, play it safe, withhold information, protect themselves from blame.

## Effective Implementation Requires Internal Commitment

People readily commit themselves to things they believe will further their interests. If they see no link between what they are asked to do and what they want to do, the probability of getting an all-out effort from them is not likely. You can order people to do things, and ordinarily they will comply—at least while you are watching. But if you want them to apply themselves, their internal commitment is required.

## THE CONSULTANT'S GOALS

Our assumptions about what contributes to effective consultant and manager performance lead to a set of preferred goals for each consulting job. Achieving each of these goals may not always be possible, but we can always be clear about our preference.

### Goal 1: Establish a Collaborative Relationship

There are two reasons for consultants to strive for collaborative relationships with their clients. One is that a collaborative relationship promises maximum use of people's resources—both the consultant's and the client's. It also spreads the responsibility for success or failure and for implementation, and it's a nice way to work too. The second reason is that whether they know it or not, consultants are always functioning as models of how to solve problems. The message contained in the way consultants act is much more powerful than their words. To talk collaboration and behave differently is confusing and self-defeating.

### Goal 2: Solve Problems So They Stay Solved

It is possible to act in such a way that only the immediate problem gets solved. If the problem is that employees regularly come late to work, for example, actions can be taken to prevent it: station the boss at the door in the morning with a pencil and a black book, or have room checks at starting time each morning, or issue a policy statement about lateness, or have meetings with employees about the need for punctuality. These actions might reduce the problem of lateness. And if internal (or external) consultants have been involved in making these kinds of recommendations, they might have contributed to an increase in the effectiveness of the organization. But this does not mean that the managers have learned anything about how to solve similar problems and thus become more competent.

The consultant's alternative is to work with line managers at another level of analysis: the way they handle lateness problems. For example, managers may not see lateness as being a symptom of discontent, or a symptom of inexperienced supervision at the first level, or any of the other possible root problems lateness could be signaling. Also, it is possible the consultant is being asked to solve problems that line managers should be confronting themselves. Teaching managers the skills for solving a problem themselves next time requires that they understand that disturbing employee behavior is a symptom of more basic problems and that they should not ask others to address problems that belong to them.

### Goal 3: Ensure Attention Is Given to Both the Technical/Business Problem and the Relationships

Each situation has two elements: the technical/business problem that has to be resolved and the way people are interacting around that problem. In most organizations, primary attention is given to the technical/business problem. Consultants, however, are in a unique position to address the people or process issues productively. As third parties, they have no vested interest in the process issues—no power to gain or lose, no territory to expand or contract, no budget to increase or decrease. Consultants can urge attention to the process issues, and line managers will listen to them in a way in which they would not listen to each other.

## DEVELOPING CLIENT COMMITMENT—A SECONDARY GOAL OF EACH CONSULTING ACT

Because consultants or support people have no direct control over implementation, they become dependent on line managers for producing results. It is the line manager who ultimately will decide whether to take action, and this choice will be based on how internally committed he or she is to the concepts the consultant is suggesting. Therefore, the consultant needs to be conscious of building internal commitment throughout the consulting process.

Effective consulting skills are the steps and behaviors that act to create internal commitment in managers. Each of us has seen examples of consulting projects where the study or report ends up on a shelf despite its cost and relevance. When this happens, it often means that somewhere along the line, the consulting process lost the managers who had to decide to use the results of the study. In flawless consulting, you move through the steps of a consulting process designed to build commitment and reduce the chance of losing the client along the way.

Client commitment is the key to consultant leverage and impact. We can't order the client to take action. (Sometimes we decide to go to the client's boss and urge him or her to direct the client to use our recommendations, but this is a risky proposition—particularly if we want to stay in the good graces of our client.) So our impact is determined by the client's commitment to our suggestions. Building this commitment is often a process of removing obstacles that block the client from acting on our advice.

We may cling to the fantasy that if our thinking is clear and logical, our wording eloquent, and our convictions solid, the strength of our arguments will carry the day. And make no mistake: clear arguments do help. But they are not enough. The client and his or her colleagues will experience doubts and dilemmas that will block commitment.

Having leverage requires confronting the doubts at each stage of the consulting process—during contracting, discovery, analysis, and while preparing for the feedback meeting. Waiting until the implementation phase to overcome resistance is too late.

Ed Schein has identified three ways consultants work with line managers: in an expert role, a pair-of-hands role, or a collaborative role.* The choice depends on individual differences in management style, the nature of the task, and the consultant's own personal preference.

As you consult in a variety of situations, it helps to become aware of the role you typically assume and to be able to identify situations where this will help or hinder your performance. Only then can you make a conscious choice among alternatives. One discovery that people often make in such self-analysis is that they begin to identify situations where they can operate more successfully in a collaborative mode. However, the realities of most organizations are such that there will be times when the pair-of-hands or expert roles are more appropriate and other times when they cannot be avoided.

## Expert Role

One way line managers typically relate to support specialists, as well as to external consultants, is client-to-expert. The support person becomes the "expert" in the performance of a given task. For example:

An organization's new corporate benefits Web site recently was completely overhauled, and it has become clear that the site has not lived up to expectations. The overall design is okay; the problem is some-

---

*These roles were first formulated by Ed Schein in the 1960s. He was one of the first to see the limitations of the expert role for consultants and defined and opened the door to the collaborative potential in the helping process. His book *Process Consulting Revisited: Building the Helping Relationship* (Reading, Mass.: Addison-Wesley/Longman, 1998) more fully describes the power of process consultation as a vital capacity for those in a helping position. It is a book I strongly recommend.

where in the navigation and the nonintuitive way employees have to input information to the site.

At this point, the manager calls in a staff Web site design specialist, describes the difficulties, and says to the designer, "I have neither the time nor the inclination to deal with this problem. You're the expert; find out what's wrong and fix it. You have a free hand to examine the whole system and do whatever analysis and fixing is necessary. Keep me posted on your findings and what you intend to do." The Web site designer becomes, in effect, a member of the manager's staff with delegated authority to plan and implement a program of change subject to the same restrictions as other members of the manager's staff.

Here is what is happening in this kind of relationship:

- The manager has elected to play an inactive role. He or she expects to hold the consultant, that is, the Web site designer, responsible for results. The designer-as-consultant accepts the responsibility and feels free to develop and implement action plans. The manager is expected to be responsive and provide the assistance needed to solve the problem.

- Decisions on how to proceed are made by the consultant on the basis of his or her expert judgment. There is no need to involve the manager in technical details.

- The consultant gathers the information needed for problem analysis and decides what methods of data collection and analysis to use.

- Technical control rests with the consultant. Disagreement is not likely because it would be difficult for the manager to challenge "expert" reasoning. If the manager seeks to exert control over technical decisions, the consultant will see it as unjustified interference.

In this situation, collaboration is not required because the problem-solving efforts are based on specialized procedures.

Two-way communication here is limited. The consultant initiates and the client responds. The consultant expects and is expected to initiate communication in a question-and-answer mode. The consultant plans and carries out the engagement or implementation or provides detailed instructions for implementation by the manager, whose role is to judge and evaluate after the fact.

The consultant's goal in this example is to solve the immediate problem. Neither the manager nor the consultant expects the manager to develop skills to solve similar problems in the future.

### Problems

Internal consultants especially are well aware of the problems involved in operating in the role of expert. Here are two big ones.

First, consider the consultant's ability to make an accurate assessment. Given a problem of a purely technical nature, the consultant can use technical expertise to isolate the problem and develop a solution. But problems that are purely technical are rare. Most problems have a human element in them, and if the prevailing organizational climate is fear, insecurity, or mistrust, people may withhold or distort essential information on the human part of the problem. Without valid data, accurate assessment becomes impossible. Action programs based on faulty discovery have little chance for success.

Second, consider the commitment of people to take the recommended actions. Studies done by outside experts seldom carry the kind of personal ownership and commitment needed to deal with difficult management issues.

## Pair-of-Hands Role

Here the manager sees the consultant as an extra pair of hands. The manager says, in effect, "I have neither the time nor the inclination to deal with this problem. I have examined the deficiencies and have prepared an outline of what needs to be done. I want you to get it done as soon as possible." The manager retains full control. The consultant is expected to apply specialized knowledge to implement action plans toward the achievement of goals that the manager has defined.

Here are some of the clues that the consultant is acting as a pair of hands:

- *The consultant takes a passive role.* The order of the day is responding to the manager's requests, and the consultant does not question the manager's action plans.

- *The manager makes the decisions on how to proceed.* The consultant may prepare recommendations for the manager's review, but approval rests with the manager.

- *The manager selects the methods for discovery and analysis.* The consultant may do the actual data collection, but only in accordance with procedures that the manager has outlined.

- *Control rests with the manager.* The consultant is expected to make suggestions, but avoids disagreement because the manager would see this as a challenge to his or her authority.

- *Collaboration is not really necessary.* The manager feels that it is his or her responsibility to specify goals and procedures. The consultant can ask questions for clarification.

- *Two-way communication is limited.* The manager initiates, and the consultant responds. The manager initiates in a descriptive or evaluative mode.

- *The manager specifies change procedures for the consultant to implement.*

- *The manager's role is to judge and evaluate from a close distance.*

- *The consultant's goal is to make the system more effective by the application of specialized knowledge.*

### Problems

The major problem emerges in the discovery phase. In a pair-of-hands role, the consultant is dependent on the manager's ability to understand what is happening and to develop an effective action plan. If the manager's assessment is faulty, the action plan won't work, and the consultant who provided the service becomes a convenient scapegoat.

To avoid this trap, the consultant may ask for time to verify the manager's assessment. And then the consultant might face another problem: managers who have a preference for consultants who take on the pair-of-hands role may interpret such requests as questioning their experience, their authority, or both.

## Collaborative Role

The consultant who assumes a collaborative role enters the relationship with the notion that management issues can be dealt with effectively only by joining his or her specialized knowledge with the manager's knowledge of the organization. Problem solving becomes a joint undertaking, with equal attention to both the technical issues and the human interactions in dealing with the technical issues.

When consultants work through a collaborative role, they don't solve problems for the manager. They apply their special skills to help managers solve problems themselves. The distinction is significant. The key assumption underlying the collaborative role is that the manager must be actively involved in data gathering and analysis, setting goals and developing action plans, and, finally, sharing responsibility for success or failure.

Here's what happens:

- *The consultant and the manager work to become interdependent.* They share responsibility for action planning, implementation, and results.

- *Decision making is bilateral.* It is characterized by mutual exchange and respect for the responsibilities and expertise of both parties.

- *Data collection and analysis are joint efforts.* The selection of the discovery process to be used is done by both the consultant and the manager.

- *Control issues become matters for discussion and negotiation.* Disagreement is expected and seen as a source of new ideas.

- *Collaboration is considered essential.* The consultant makes a special point to reach understanding and agreement on the nature and scope of mutual expectations prior to initiating problem-solving efforts.

- *Communication is two-way.* Both the consultant and the manager take the initiative, depending on the issues. Information exchange is carried on in a problem-solving mode.

- *Implementation responsibilities are determined by discussion and agreement.* Assignments are made to maximize use of the available resources in line with the responsibilities appropriate to each party.

- *The goal is to solve problems so they stay solved.* That is, the consultant establishes a helping relationship designed to broaden the competence level of managers to develop and implement action plans that will make the system more effective. The next time a similar problem arises, the manager will have the skills to solve it.

### Problems

There are also problems in trying to work collaboratively. Consultants often have special skills (for example, in information technology or budget management) that managers see as a quick answer to their problems. Managers who prefer to work with consultants in an expert role may interpret any attempts at collaboration as indifference or foot dragging. Managers with a preference for working with consultants in a pair-of-hands role may interpret moves toward collaboration as insubordination. Plus, working collaboratively takes some time.

## COLLABORATION AND THE FEAR OF HOLDING HANDS

In a presentation on collaborative consultation, a person in the audience kept asking questions about the nature of collaboration: "Can't it be a sign of weakness? Don't you have expertise that you are denying if you operate too collaboratively? Clients want answers, not questions, don't they?" Finally, with a lot of frustration, he said, "Well, I don't want my consultants just sitting around holding hands with a client!" He was pointing to an area where there is considerable confusion about the distinction between the expert role and the collaborative role.

The core transaction of any consulting contract is the transfer of expertise from the consultant to the client. This holds whether the expertise is very tangible, such as skill in circuit design or systems design, or whether the expertise is very intangible, such as problem-solving or team-building skill. Whatever the expertise, it is the basis for the consultant's being in business.

Part of the fear of holding hands seems to be that if you get too intertwined with the client, your expertise will somehow be diluted and blurred. A collaborative approach can come across as implying that the consultant and the client have equal expertise and are partners in technical matters. This might force the consultant to unconsciously underplay his or her own expertise in order to maintain a 50/50 relationship. If this were to happen, the fear of diluting expertise would become a reality. One consultant expressed this fear and confusion by saying, "I have forgotten more about managing inventories than most of my clients will ever know. They can hardly spell the word, and I am the corporate guru! How can I be collaborative under those conditions?"

The confusion is between collaborating on the technical aspects of the problem (which I don't mean) and collaborating on how the stages of the consultation will be carried out (which I do mean). Here's an example of where you draw the line between them:

| Areas of Collaboration | Areas of Expertise |
|---|---|
| Expressing the wants of the client | Circuit design |
| Planning how to inform the organization of the study | Training design |
| Deciding who is involved in the discovery phase | Questionnaire design |
| Generating the right kind of data | Package design |
| Interpreting the results of discovery | Systems analysis |
| Deciding how to make a change | Pricing strategy |

Regardless of the area of expertise, the way the consultation process itself is managed (the left side of this list) will greatly affect the client's use of even the most technical expertise. The more the consultative process can be collaborative, the better the odds for success are after the consultant has left.

## STAGING THE CLIENT'S INVOLVEMENT, STEP BY STEP

We have been discussing in a somewhat general way the consultant role orientation and ways to make a project more collaborative. The following sequence will make this concept very concrete. The stages leading up to implementation of a change—what are called the preliminary events—can be divided into twelve specific action steps. Each step provides an opportunity to involve the client in the process without unnaturally downplaying your specific expertise.

Maximum client involvement and commitment will occur to the extent that you, the consultant, act at each stage in the following ways. These are steps you can take to make the 50/50 responsibility for the project a reality.

### Step 1: Define the Initial Problem

Ask the client to state what the problem is. If the client is thinking more of a new possibility than a problem, state this in your own words. Add to this statement what you think might be some more underlying causes of the problem or important elements of the possibility.

*Example: IT Consultant*

*IT consultant:* What do you think the problem is?

*Client:* The software you guys did for us doesn't do what it needs it to do half the time. I think the design may be faulty. I want you to check the code and make sure it works as it should.

*IT consultant:* I will check the programming code and test the software's functionality. Also, as a potential part of the problem, I think we should consider how well the users understand this application. Plus we should look into the kind of training and supervision they receive, especially on the night shift.

*Comment:* It is not just up to the client to make the initial problem statement. You should feel free to add your 50 percent, even at this early stage.

## Step 2: Decide Whether to Proceed with the Project

In deciding whether to proceed, you also have some choice. If the project is set up in a way that you think it won't succeed, you should negotiate the terms.

### Example: Financial Services Consultant

*Client:* Let's go ahead with the project to do a complete audit of the purchasing function. And let's have it done in thirty days.

*Financial services consultant:* A complete purchasing audit is a big order. To accomplish this in thirty days is almost impossible. We have a list of projects that have to be reviewed by our committee. If those expectations of yours are firm, we had better reevaluate whether we can give you what you want.

*Comment:* Clients usually feel that the decision to go ahead is strictly up to them. By questioning the decision, the consultant is acting as a 50/50 partner. The intent is not to say no to clients, but to make the decision to go ahead a joint decision.

## Step 3: Select the Dimensions to Be Studied

Given your expertise in the project, you may know best what aspect of the problem should be analyzed. The client, though, has operating experience with the problem and the people and can be asked what to look for.

### Example: IT Consultant

*IT consultant:* Next Monday I will start examining the program code and testing its functionality. I will also interview the users about how they operate the software for certain routine procedures. It would help if you and the affected department managers would make a list of the areas you would like investigated and also any questions you would like the software users to answer.

*Comment:* Although it takes only a simple question to involve the client in deciding what to look at, often the question is not asked. If a questionnaire is to be used, you can have the client select some of the questions.

## Step 4: Decide Who Will Be Involved in the Project

The client often expects the consultant to do the whole job. Creating a consultant-client team to do the job is a good way to build client commitment.

### Example: Financial Services Consultant

*Financial services consultant:* To make this project successful, I would like two people from your organization to work with me on it. I will need five days of one of your regional purchasing manager's time and eight days of one of your home office purchasing people. The three of us will be responsible for ending up with an analysis of the deficiencies and strengths of the existing purchasing system and a recommended redesign to address them. I will be in charge of the project and make the major time commitment, but two people from your group will help the project immensely.

*Comment:* Doing the job by yourself is always simpler and faster. Having people from the client organization takes more time and agony, yet this involvement directly encourages commitment and promotes eventual implementation of the work.

## Step 5: Select the Method

The client has ideas about how the data should be collected. Ask what they are.

### Example: IT Consultant

*IT consultant:* I will definitely look over the software, test its functionality, and talk to the end users. Who else should I talk to? Should we meet with people in a group or individually? What other areas of the operation should we look into, and how should we approach them?

*Comment:* Again, these are simple but important questions to ask the client. You are doing this 30 percent for the new information you might get and 70 percent to model and act out a 50/50 way of approaching this kind of project. By your behavior, you are helping the client learn how to solve problems like this for themselves.

## Step 6: Do Discovery

Have the client do the discovery with you.

### Example: IT Consultant

*IT consultant:* I would like one of your supervisors to work with me as I go through the division and talk to people. Perhaps the supervisors could interview a sample of the software users to determine what they think could be done to make it work better. Then I would like to hold a large group meeting to engage them in how we proceed.

*Comment:* There are two main risks in having the client do some of the discovery: (1) people may withhold information because they are talking to those who have some power over them, and (2) some of the data may be distorted because the line organization has a stake in making itself look competent and guilt free.

These are risks you can be willing to take. You will get your own data, and usually you have enough experience to know rather quickly what is really going on. If need be, you can go back to the people a second time, alone. The advantage of having the line people do some of the data collection is that whatever information is shared up the line, the right people are hearing it—the people who can do something about it. It does no good if the consultant hears the "truth," but the line people don't believe it. Above all, though, the process keeps beating the 50/50 drum.

## Steps 7 Through 9: Funneling the Data and Making Sense of It

Funneling a huge amount of data into a manageable amount of information, summarizing and organizing it, and making sense of it takes a lot of time. You also get a real sense of what you have by suffering through these three steps. Urge the client to be with you at certain points in this procedure. Analyzing what the data mean is fun, so involve the client in this too.

### Example: Financial Services Consultant

*Financial services consultant:* Spend three days with me organizing what we have discovered and figuring what its implications are for the purchasing system we are investigating.

*Comment:* Again, a simple, assertive request trades some of the efficient use of your own time for a client who has more invested in the outcome. On a highly technical project, the client may not have the background to meaningfully contribute to this stage of the project. In that case, you have no choice but to do it alone. Be careful, though; the client's lack of background is our favorite excuse for excluding him or her at various stages.

## Step 10: Provide the Results

Have the client share in presenting the data analysis in the feedback meeting.

### Example: Financial Services Consultant

*Financial services consultant:* For this meeting, I am going to report what we learned about the purchasing system. George, the purchasing director, will report what we learned about the purchasing agents' skills and attitudes toward purchasing procedures and controls.

*Comment:* When line managers have the experience of reporting negative findings, their defensiveness goes down, and the feedback step is less likely to become an argument.

## Step 11: Make Recommendations

More than any other stage, developing workable recommendations requires integrating your technical knowledge and the client's practical and organizational knowledge. Ask the client what he or she would do about the situation, having now heard the results of the inquiry.

### Example: IT Consultant

*IT consultant:* We know that the short formal training program for end users is a major obstacle to their operating the software properly. What can we recommend that would reduce our dependency on them to figure out how to use it on their own?

*Comment:* The action is simple once your strategy becomes clear. Even if clients cannot be creative about what to recommend, it is important that they struggle with the question.

## Step 12: Decide on Actions

Once the study is done and the recommendations made, the client may want to take over the process and dismiss the consultant from the decision-making meeting. I always resist this.

### Example: Financial Services Consultant

*Client:* Thank you very much for the new purchasing process you have developed and the structural and procedural changes needed to support it. We will think about it and let you know when we think the organization will be ready for this.

*Financial services consultant:* I would like to be a part of the meeting when you discuss this. I care a lot about the project and know I could contribute to the question of timing and implementation. I realize your usual procedure is to discuss this without the consultant present, but in this case, I wonder if you could make an exception.

*Comment:* The danger here is that the client will take 100 percent of the action and leave you out in the cold. So you have to ask to be included. In addition to your own needs for inclusion, you are also saying to the client by your action that when someone in their organization has made an important contribution to a project, the person should be included in the decision-making meeting. If the client still chooses to exclude you, there may be little you can do other than sulk and look hurt.

■ ■

Each of these twelve steps is one in a series of opportunities to engage the client, reduce resistance, and increase the probabilities of success. Taking advantage of these opportunities entails giving up some consultant prerogatives and freedom of action in the service of the longer-range goal of having a real impact.

For a downloadable copy of Checklist # 1, visit www.flawlessconsulting .com.

## CHECKLIST #1: Assessing the Balance of Responsibility

On the scales below, rate who is taking responsibility in an important project you are now engaged in. Put a check mark where it currently balances out.

|  | Client Has Major Responsibility; I Have Little | 50/50 | I Have Major Responsibility, Client Has Little |
|---|---|---|---|
| 1. Define the initial problem | \| | \| | \| |
| 2. Decide whether to proceed with the project | \| | \| | \| |
| 3. Select the dimensions to be studied | \| | \| | \| |
| 4. Decide who will be involved in the project | \| | \| | \| |
| 5. Select the method | \| | \| | \| |
| 6. Do discovery | \| | \| | \| |
| 7. Through 9. Funneling the data and making sense of it | \| | \| | \| |
| 10. Provide the results | \| | \| | \| |
| 11. Make recommendations | \| | \| |  |
| 12. Decide on actions | \| | \| | \| |

Connect the marks you made. Any place the line deviates from the center shows an opportunity for you to restructure this project or your next one to take full advantage of using client involvement to increase your chances of success—especially the chances that your project will still be active and used after you have left the scene.

# CHAPTER 3

# FLAWLESS CONSULTING

CONSULTING CAN SEEM VAGUE and overly complicated when in fact it is possible to consult without error and to do so quite simply. The way to keep it simple is to focus on only two dimensions of consulting. Ask yourself two questions whenever you are with a client:

1. Am I being authentic with this person now?

2. Am I completing the business of the consulting phase I am in?

## BEING AUTHENTIC

Authentic behavior with a client means you put into words what you are experiencing with the client as you work. This is the most powerful thing you can do to have the leverage you are looking for and to build client commitment.

There is a tendency for us to look for ways of being clever with a client. We agonize over ways of presenting our ideas, of phrasing the project so that it will appeal. Many times I have been with a client and found myself straining to figure out what will convince them that I am everything they are looking for. Projections of bottom line savings are made, solutions for sticky employee problems are suggested, confirmations that the client has been doing everything humanly possible are suggested with a nod and a smile.

It is a mistake to assume that clients make decisions to begin projects and use consultants based on purely rational reasons. More often than not, the client's primary question is: "Is this consultant someone I can trust? Is this someone I can trust not to hurt me, not to con me—someone who can both help solve the organizational or technical problems I have and, at the same time, be considerate of my position and person?" When I operate in too clever or manipulative a way, or lay it on too thick, clients pick this up. They are thinking to themselves, *Wow! This guy is really laying it on thick. He is making me look like a fool if I say no.* Line managers know when we are trying to maneuver them, and when it happens, they trust us a little less.

Lower trust leads to lower leverage and lower client commitment. Authentic behavior leads to higher trust, higher leverage, and higher client commitment. Authentic behavior also has the advantage of being incredibly simple. It is to literally put into words what you are experiencing. Here are some examples:

*Client says:* "Well, this audit shouldn't take you too long. Couple of days, and you will be done. I wish I had some time to spend with you, but there are some really important things I must attend to. My secretary can give you some assistance. Also, don't take too much time from any of my people. They are under a lot of pressure."

*Consultant experiences:* Feeling unimportant, small. My work is being treated as a trivial matter. This is how I make my living, but to this character, I am an interruption.

*Nonauthentic consultant response:* "This audit could have far-reaching implications. The home office is looking closely at these audits to assess our top divisions. They are also required by the company."

*Authentic consultant response:* "You are treating this audit as though it is unimportant and small—a trivial matter. If it is an interruption, maybe we should reassess the timing. I would like you to treat it with more importance.

*Client says:* "I want your opinion whether my people are making mistakes and what they should do to correct them. If you decide they are incompetent to operate this operating unit, I want you to report directly to me at once. With names and specifics."

*Consultant experiences:* Feeling like a judge, like I have to police the client's employees.

*Nonauthentic consultant response:* "My report will describe how the unit is being managed and why there have been so many breakdowns. It will be up to you to take corrective actions."

*Authentic consultant response:* "I feel I am being seen as a judge or police officer on this project. This is not the role I feel is most effective. I would like you to view me more as a mirror of what is happening now. You and your people can then evaluate what needs to be done and whether training is required. I am not a conscience."

*Client says:* "To really understand this problem, you have to go back thirty-five years when this operation was set up. It all started in November 1976 on a Thursday afternoon. There were three people in this operation. At the time, their only function was to fill orders and answer the phone. George was the nephew of the sales manager and had only a high school education. Our customers were mostly on the East Coast . . . [and on and on and on and on]."

*Consultant experiences:* Impatience, boredom. Spending too much time on history. Losing energy.

*Nonauthentic consultant response:* Silence to encourage the client to go on, assuming the client will get to the point or that it is therapeutically essential for the client to go through all this detail.

*Authentic consultant response:* "You are giving me a lot of detail. I am having trouble staying with your narrative. I am eager to get to the key current issues. What is the key problem now?"

*Client says:* "If you will just complete your report of findings, my management group and I will meet later to decide what to do and evaluate the results."

*Consultant experiences:* Exclusion from the real action. Postponement of dealing with the problems.

*Nonauthentic consultant response:* "There might be some information that I have not included in the report that would be relevant to your decision-making process" [or acquiescence].

*Authentic consultant response:* "You are excluding me from the decision on what to do. I would like to be included in that meeting, even if including me means some inconvenience for you and your team."

In these examples, each initial client statement acts to keep the consultant distant in some way. Each is a subtle form of resistance to the consultant's help and serves to reduce its impact. The nonauthentic consultant responses deal indirectly and impersonally with the resistance. They make it easier for the client to stay distant and treat the consultant's concerns in a procedural way. The authentic responses focus on the relationship between the consultant and the client and force the client to give importance to the consultant's role and wants for the project. Simple direct statements by the consultant about the consultant-client interaction put more balance in the relationship; they work against either total client control or total consultant control. Imbalanced control in either direction acts to reduce internal commitment to the project.

Authentic behavior by the consultant is essential to operating flawlessly. Much of the rest of this book gives detailed and specific expression to what authentic behavior looks like in the context of doing consulting.

## COMPLETING THE REQUIREMENTS OF EACH PHASE

In addition to being authentic, flawless consulting demands knowledge of the task requirements of each phase of the project. These requirements are the business of each phase and must be completed before moving on.

Here is a brief description of the requirements of each phase. They are discussed in detail in the chapters that follow.

## Contracting

1. *Negotiate wants.* Setting up a project requires the client and the consultant to exchange what they want from each other and what they have to offer each other. Too often consultants understate their wants and clients understate their offers.

2. *Cope with mixed motivation.* When clients ask for help, they always do so with some ambivalence. They want you to get involved and be helpful, but at the same time they wish they had never met you. One hand beckons you; the other says stop. A requirement of contracting is to get this mixed motivation expressed early in the project so it won't haunt you later.

3. *Surface concerns about exposure and loss of control.* Most of the real concerns clients have about pursuing a consulting project with you are expressed quite indirectly. They ask about credentials, experience, results elsewhere, cost, timing, and more. Often what they are really concerned about is (1) Are they going to be made to look or feel foolish or incompetent? and (2) Will they lose control of either themselves, their organization, or you the consultant? These concerns have to be addressed directly as part of the contracting phase.

4. *Understand triangular and rectangular contracts.* You have to know how many clients you have. Your client has a boss and you may have a boss. If your client's boss and your boss have had a heavy hand in setting up this project, they need to be part of the contract. At least, their roles need to be acknowledged between you and your client. If it is you, the client, and the client's boss, you have a triangular contract. Throw in your own boss, and the triangle becomes a rectangle. Clarifying who is involved and getting them into the contract is a requirement of the contracting phase.

## Discovery and Inquiry

1. *Layers of inquiry.* The initial problem statement in a consulting project is usually a symptom of other underlying problems. Your task as the consultant is to name the layers of the problem clearly

and simply. If the client comes to you with a possibility instead of a problem, you want to know why this matters so much and what it means to the client, in addition to exploring the nature of the possibility.

2. *Political climate.* Whether your client is a family or an organization, politics is affecting people's behavior and their ability to solve problems. Your task as consultant is to understand enough about the politics of the situation to see how it will affect your project and the implementation of your recommendations. Too often we collude with the client in pretending that organizations are not political but solely rational.

3. *Resistance to sharing information.* The client always has some reluctance to give the whole story or all the data we need to understand what's happening. This resistance, which often comes out indirectly with passive or questioning behavior during the data collection, has to be identified and expressed.

4. *The interview as a joint learning event.* Once we start collecting data, we have begun to change that organization. We are never simply neutral, objective observers. Beginning the process of our inquiry portends the implementation process, and we need to see it that way. When sticky issues come up during the discovery phase, we need to pursue them and not worry about contaminating the data or biasing the study. Too often we see our role in discovery as a passive one.

### Feedback and the Decision to Act

1. *Funneling data.* The purpose of discovery is to get some action, not to do research for its own sake. This means the data need to be reduced to a manageable number of items. Each of the final items selected for feedback to the client should be actionable—that is, they should be under the client's control.

2. *Presenting personal and organizational data.* As we inquire about equipment, or compensation, or information flow, we also pick up data on our client's management style. We learn about the politics of the situation, and about people's attitudes toward the organization. One requirement of the feedback phase is to

include this kind of information in our report. Personal and organizational data are not included to hurt anyone or to be gossipy, but as information on the context in which our recommendations might be implemented. It is also a unique kind of information that the client often cannot obtain from anyone else.

3. *Managing the meeting for action.* The feedback meeting is the moment of truth. It is the moment of highest anxiety for both client and consultant—anxiety for the consultant because of what is to be said, anxiety for the client because of what is to be heard. The consultant needs to keep control of this meeting so that the business of the meeting is covered. Presenting a clear picture to the client is only part of the agenda. The main goal is to work on the decision about what to do. The more the feedback meeting can address what to do, the better the chance is of implementation. The feedback meeting may be your last chance to influence the decision about implementation, so take advantage of the opportunity.

4. *Focusing on the here and now.* Another requirement of the feedback phase is identifying how the client is managing the feedback itself. Usually the feedback process becomes victim to the same management problems that created the need for your services in the first place. If the organization is suffering from a lack of structure or direction, for example, this will also affect how they handle your report. You need to be conscious of this and call it to your client's attention. If you are not meticulously aware of how your own project is being handled, you will simply become the latest casualty.

5. *Don't take it personally.* This is the toughest to do. The reaction of the client to your work is more a response to the process of dependency and receiving help than it is resistance to your own personal style. You do have your own peculiarities; so does everyone else. If, however, you start agonizing about them during the feedback process, even to yourself, you're in big trouble. The resistance you encounter during the process is resistance to the prospect of having to act on difficult organizational issues. Don't be seduced into taking it personally.

### Engagement and Implementation

1. *Bet on engagement over mandate and persuasion.* Although a decision has been made, the real work lies ahead. How you involve people will determine their commitment at each stage. The instinct is to focus too much on the decision and not value the importance of how people are brought together to make it work.

2. *Design more participation than presentation.* Each meeting has to be an example of the new way of working and demonstrate that employee attitude will dictate success. This demands high interaction and forms of proceeding. People will not invest in what they have been sold, even though it seems as though they just want you to be clear about what is expected from them.

3. *Encourage difficult public exchanges.* Trust is built by dealing with the difficult issues early and publicly. Create room for doubt and cynicism from the beginning. Reservations that are postponed will come back to haunt you. The way we handle the difficult conversations will determine the credibility of the project and the client's view of whether we are an agent of the top or in service of all parties.

4. *Put real choice on the table.* Bring people into the decision about change as early as possible. Commitment comes from having choice. Resist the temptation to package the whole solution early in the name of speed. Commitment may be more important than perfection. There are always several right answers to every question.

5. *Change the conversation to change the culture.* Encourage dialogue that is void of blame, history, attention to who is not in the room, and too quick to action. Structure the conversation toward personal responsibility, questions of purpose and meaning, and what will be unique and new about the proposed changes.

6. *Pay attention to place.* The structure of the way we come together has more impact on the attitude and commitment of our clients than we realize. The room itself, how everyone is seated, and the way we run the meeting carry strong messages about our intentions

and who is important to success. Most of the places where meetings are held reinforce high control and mandated strategies. When we have choice about the structure of the room, take advantage of it.

It's entirely possible to move through the phases and skip some of these task requirements. In contracting, for example, most of us are pretty good at assessing client wants. But if we fail to identify consultant wants or client offers as clearly as we assess client wants, we are in trouble. Wants skipped in the beginning are much harder to recover in later phases. An example is the consultant's desire to have the client manager support the project and tell his or her people about it. If this is not negotiated in the contracting phase, you will feel undercut later when you want to collect data from people who don't really know why you were talking to them.

Another key task of contracting is to discuss the client's motivation to proceed with the project. Sometimes your desire to begin the project may lead you to minimize this discussion. You may never ask point-blank whether the client wants to go ahead with the project and discover how much enthusiasm they have for it. If you find out later that the motivation is low, it may be too late to do anything about it.

Because of our desire to get a project going, most of us have a tendency to overlook and downplay early resistance and skepticism. We delude ourselves into thinking that once clients get into the project, they will be hooked by it and learn to trust us. This can lead to our bending over more than we wish in the beginning, hoping that we will be able to stand up straight later on. This usually doesn't work. When we bend over in the beginning, the client sees us as someone who works in a bent-over position. When we avoid issues in the beginning, the client sees us as someone who avoids issues. It is difficult to change these images and expectations of us—particularly if the client wishes us to bend over and avoid issues.

By not confronting the tasks of each phase, we are left with accumulating unfinished business that comes back to haunt us. Unfinished business always comes out somewhere, and usually indirectly. The client who felt we were coercing in the beginning of the project but never expressed that sentiment directly is the client who endlessly questions us later in the feedback meeting. Those endless questions are fueled by the early feeling of coercion, not by our faulty data. It will be much harder in the feedback meeting to rework those feelings of coercion than it would have been to discuss them in the contracting meeting when the project got started.

Finishing the business of each phase and being authentic in stating what you are experiencing to the client are all you need to consult flawlessly.

But what about getting results and what about accountability?

## RESULTS

By definition, being a consultant—and not a manager—means you have direct control and responsibility only for your own time and your own support resources. The line manager is paid to take responsibility for what the line organization implements or doesn't implement. If the client manager takes your report and chooses to do nothing about it, that is the manager's right. In the final analysis, you are not responsible for the use of your expertise and recommendations. If consultants really believe that they should be responsible for implementing their recommendations, they should immediately get jobs as line managers and stop calling themselves consultants.

This desire to take responsibility for activities that rightly belong to clients can become a major obstacle to consulting effectiveness. When we take over and act as if it is our organization (a wish we all have at times), the line manager is let off the hook. The organization may get the immediate problem solved, but managers will have learned little about how to do it for themselves. When something goes wrong with our system, as it inevitably will, we are either called back in again and again or the line organization will claim that our system was faulty to begin with. Both client overdependence and client disdain are bad for the consultant. It is essential to be clear on what you as consultant are responsible for and what the line manager is responsible for.

## ACCOUNTABILITY

Just because we are not responsible for what the client does with our efforts does not mean we don't care what happens in the end. In fact, the impact that our consulting efforts have is deeply important. We want our efforts to be used. Every time. If an engineer consultant is called in to fix a furnace in a plant, the engineer will make recommendations so the furnace will be fixed and operated to run perfectly forever. The problem is that the consultant doesn't control how that furnace is operated. If we are coaching a line manager toward greater effectiveness, that manager will decide what to listen to and act on, and that is the way it is.

This is the deepest frustration of doing consulting. You know your recommendations are sound and should be followed, but you are not responsible for how the furnace is operated and need to accept that fact. You are not responsible for whether your coaching clients keep getting in their own way. All you can do is to work with clients in a way that increases the probabilities that they will follow the advice and make the effort to learn how to operate the furnace or make the effort to deal with others in a different way.

The key to increasing the chances for success is to keep focusing on how you work with clients. All we can really control is our own way of working, our own behavior, our own strategies of involving clients and reducing their reluctance to operate the furnace differently. This is what we should be held accountable for: how we work with clients— not what clients do in managing or mismanaging their own operations.

The downside of our need to be useful is the desire to prove that our work led to good results. Needing to claim credit for the risks and efforts made by clients is a measure of our own inflation and the anxiety that underpins it. Our clients will know, even if they cannot name it easily, what contribution we made to their effort. Our need for concrete demonstration of our results is either to reassure our doubts or to serve our needs to market our services.

If I —

> know my area of expertise (a given),
>
> behave authentically with the client,
>
> tend to and complete the business of each consulting phase, and
>
> act to build capacity for the client to solve the next problem on their own,

I can legitimately say I have consulted flawlessly. Even if no action results from my efforts. Even if the project aborts in the early, contracting phase. Even if my services are terminated the day I make my recommendations. Even if all these things happen, it is possible to call it a very competent job of consultation. If these things happen, it is not a happy consultation, for we all wish for the world to transform at our touch. But it is the best we can do.

This way of viewing consulting accountability restrains us from taking over for our clients and uselessly pressuring them to do something they won't or can't do. Taking over client organizations, pressuring to be heeded, complaining about the way a manager manages: all reduce consultants' effectiveness. Focusing on our own actions and expressing our awareness of what we are experiencing with the client and how we are working all increase our effectiveness.

Our own actions, our own awareness: this is what we should be held accountable for. Fire me for not contracting well or not confronting the client's low motivation until the feedback meeting. Fire me for packaging the recommendations so completely and perfectly that the client was afraid to touch them. But reward me for contracting solidly with three managers who terminated projects when a new vice president was announced. Reward me for not beginning a project when a plant manager said it was necessary but all signs were to the contrary.

Completing the business of each phase and behaving authentically with the client: that's what flawless consultation, consultation without failure, requires. In all my years of consulting, all my failures (which I remember with distressing clarity) occurred either because I was so carried away by how I was going to solve the client's problem that I didn't pay attention to client motivation or because I wanted that client so badly that I didn't care what the contract looked like. In each case, I ignored some step in the consulting process, did not attend to the business of a particular phase, or chose not to deal authentically with my concerns about the client. Had I focused more on exactly how I was working with each client, these failures could have been avoided.

## THE RIGHT TO FAIL

Failures can be avoided, but this doesn't mean a consultant can expect to see meaningful improvement as a result of every single project. Internal consultants often ask, "You mean that if I behave authentically and take care of the business of each phase, I will win the support of a plant manager who up to now won't talk to me?" When they ask that question, they are expressing their skepticism. It is a rightful skepticism. No action by a consultant will guarantee results with a client. There are several reasons for this.

Each of us learns and uses information in different ways. It is often difficult for managers to accept help and be publicly open to suggestions. Privately they may be strongly affected by our work, and we may never know it. Pressuring clients to feel we have immediately helped them can be a tremendous obstacle to the learning we are trying to promote. If we can stay focused simply on the way we are working with clients, we will avoid compulsively pressuring the client, and the results will take care of themselves.

A second reason consultants can't judge their work just by managers' reactions is that client managers have a right to fail, whether we like it or not. Managers have a right to avoid dealing with operator problems on the furnace, to keep others at arm's length, to keep loose controls on petty cash, to have inconsistent pay policies for the field sales force. Managers have a right to suffer, and as consultants we are usually too much on the periphery of their lives to really change this.

A manager's right to fail is especially hard for internal consultants to accept. If we are in an organization we care about and see a division going down the drain, we feel obligated to the organization and ourselves to try and turn that situation around. The wish is a fine one, for it gives meaning to our work. The mistake we can make is to take on the rehabilitation of that division as a personal objective. The manager of that division, not the consultant, is responsible for its rehabilitation. Taking over the manager's rights, including the right to fail, leads to consulting errors. It can also lead to frustration and despair, for you may be taking on a task that you are not positioned to accomplish. Your own responsibility as a consultant is to present information as simply, directly, and assertively as possible and to complete the tasks of each phase of the consultation. That's all there is to do, and it's within each of us to do that perfectly.

CHAPTER 4

# CONTRACTING OVERVIEW

$A$T THE BEGINNING OF EVERY WORKSHOP we conduct on consulting skills, we ask people what they want to learn about consulting. The first wave of answers is very reasonable and task oriented:

* How do you set up a project?

* How do you measure consulting effectiveness?

* Can you act as an umpire and helper at the same time?

* What do you do to elicit client expectations?

* How do you get in the door when you are not welcome?

* How do you establish trust?

* What are consulting skills anyhow?

* When do we break for lunch?

. . . and on and on.

As we get into the workshop, it is easy to see the real desires that underlie these wishes. What do consultants want to learn about consulting? We want to learn how to have power over our clients! How do we influence them, get them to do what we want, manage in our own image? And while we are doing all of this to them, how do we keep their respect and appreciation?

The phrase "power over our clients" is a distortion of the more promising expectation to have power *with* our clients. If we want to control our clients, we put ourselves on a pedestal and our clients on the ground. This arrangement is highly unstable because clients soon realize we want to control them and they are able to topple us with ease. And why shouldn't they be able to topple us? Managers get rewarded for keeping control and have to be politically savvy or they wouldn't be managers. So the desire to have power over the client is a no-win position for consultants. The realistic alternative is to have power with clients, to have direct and constructive impact while standing on the same level.

The point of maximum leverage for consultants is probably during the contracting phase of the project. There are possibilities for impact that may be lost for the life of the project if they are not pursued in contracting. The contract sets the tone for the project, and it is much easier to negotiate a new initial contract than to renegotiate an old one. Anyone who has been married more than a year understands this.

## CONTRACTING: THE CONCEPT AND THE SKILL

A contract is simply an explicit agreement of what the consultant and client expect from each other and how they are going to work together. It is usually verbal and sometimes written down. Contracts with external consultants are more often in writing because external consultants are trusted less than internal consultants, especially when it comes to money. Some internal consultants always like to have a written document describing the project they are working on. This is probably a good idea, even if it is in the form of a letter. But essentially a contract between an internal or external consultant and a line manager is a social contract. It is designed not so much for enforcement, but for clear communication about what is going to happen on a project.

## The Word: *Contract*

"We are not lawyers," people say. "A contract is a legal document that is written in formal language, it is binding and in writing, and it is stiff and formal. Why not call it a working agreement?" The word *contract* is useful in two ways. Because we are not accustomed to thinking of social or work relationships in contractual terms, the word calls attention to the need for specific expectations in the consulting relationship. Also, some of the legal connotations of the word *contract* are applicable to consulting relationships.

Legal contracts contain two basic elements that apply to consulting relationships: mutual consent and valid consideration.

### Mutual Consent

**Key Concept:**  Both sides enter the agreement freely and by their own choosing.

The concept of mutual consent directly addresses the issue of how motivated the support person and the line manager are to engage in a project together. Many forces in organizations tend to coerce people into starting a project and working together. For example, the fact that everybody is doing it is often a pressure on managers. They don't really want to do, say, a survey of their employees, but that is the thing to do, and so it leads them into a conversation with an internal consultant about doing a survey. Internalized shoulds or the fad of the day can become powerful coercive forces. The support person also operates under many "shoulds." "A support person should never say no to a line manager" is a belief that can lead to beginning a project that the support person does not believe in. The coercion can also be very direct.

When some variation of this dialogue occurs, the client and the consultant have an agreement about work to be done, but they are not working with a solid or valid contract. The consultant is operating under coercion and has not freely entered the agreement. It is often not possible to negotiate a valid contract. That's okay. The key is that when a manager is eventually dissatisfied with the results of the new appraisal form, the problem should be defined as the imbalance of the original contract, not the elegance of the form.

### Valid Consideration

**Key Concept:** Valid consideration must be given both parties for a solid contract to exist.

For our purposes, *consideration* is the exchange of something of value between the consultant and the client. Internal consultants are especially accustomed to focusing on the consideration given to the client. The initial impetus behind a discussion between a line and support person is to discuss services to be provided to the line person. This service—or consideration—takes the form of advice, analysis, or just reflection. For a valid contract to exist, however, the support person needs to receive something of value in return. It is this side of the equation that is often undervalued, ignored, or assumed without discussion.

Support people often say that all they really need is appreciation—some knowledge that they have made a contribution. On an emotional level, that may be true, but there are some more tangible items that consultants need that should be a part of the original contract:

- *Operational partnership in the venture.* This means having influence on what happens, finding out about significant events, maintaining respect for the unique contribution you bring.

- *Access to people and information in the line organization.* Access means freedom of movement to pursue issues and data that seem relevant to you.

- *Time of people in the line organization.* The major cost to most improvement projects, even when capital investment is involved, is the time of people in the line organization to plan and incorporate changes into their operation. Many times the consultant is given an assignment with the proviso not to take up too much of the time of the line people because "they" don't want to interrupt production. This is a warning signal that the contract is inequitable and needs to be renegotiated.

- *Opportunity to be innovative.* Consultants generally want to try something different. You have a right to ask for this opportunity directly and not have to bootleg it.

In the next chapter we delve more deeply into consultant needs and wants. What's important to remember here is that you undermine your leverage if you underplay your own needs and wants at the beginning. The contract needs balanced consideration to be strong.

## Contracting Skills

To contract flawlessly is to

1. Behave authentically

2. Complete the business of the contracting phase

The business of the contracting phase is to negotiate wants, cope with mixed motivation, surface concerns about exposure and loss of control, clarify the contract for all parties, and give affirmation to the client. Before getting into the actual steps in a contracting meeting, here is a list of the consulting competencies required to complete the business of contracting. You should be able to

- Ask direct questions about who the client is and who the less visible parties to the contract are.

- Elicit the client's expectations of you.

- Clearly and simply state what you want from the client.

- Say no or postpone a project that in your judgment has less than a 50/50 chance of success.

- Probe directly for the client's underlying concerns about losing control.

- Probe directly for the client's underlying concerns about exposure and vulnerability.

- Give direct verbal support and affirmation to the client.

- When the contracting meeting is not going well, discuss directly with the client why it is not.

More detailed competencies will surface as we work through a contracting meeting in the next chapter. This list, however, contains the crucial ones, which many of us have a hard time doing. The hard time we have is not really with the action itself, but with valuing the importance of these actions. Having direct discussions with the client—about control, vulnerability, your wants, the chance of success, and how the discussion is going—makes the difference between an average contracting meeting and an excellent one. The problem is that it is possible to have a contracting meeting in which none of these subjects are discussed directly. When this happens, the consultant and client are actually colluding with each other in not bringing up certain touchy subjects. The rationalization is, "Well, I'll deal with these areas if it becomes necessary." *It is always necessary to talk about control, vulnerability, your wants, and chances of success.* If you are thinking as you read this that you always confront these areas with your clients, then you should feel good. You may already be operating more flawlessly than you think you are.

## ELEMENTS OF A CONTRACT

Up to this point we have focused on the process of developing a contract. This section offers some suggestions about what the content of the contract should include. But first, a word about form.

People always ask whether the contract should be in writing. If you have the energy and the time, the answer is yes. The reason for putting it in writing is for clarity, not enforcement. If it is in writing and the client changes his or her mind about the services wanted from you, you are going to have to renegotiate a new contract or stop the project. Having the original agreement in writing isn't going to change that. If you are investing out-of-pocket dollars or billable time in the project, then a written contract will help your claim to be paid for the money and time invested should the project be terminated. For most internal consultants, the real value of a written contract is to clarify the understanding with the line manager before the project begins. It is a good test of whether you have a solid contract. Writing down the agreement forces you to be more explicit about what you are going to do.

The form of the written document should be brief, direct, and almost conversational. The purpose is to communicate, not to protect yourself in court.

The following elements should be covered in most of your contracts, especially when the contract signals the beginning of a significant project.

## The Boundaries of Your Analysis

Begin with a statement of what problem or possibility you are going to focus on. If it was discussed in the contracting meeting, you can include a statement of what you are not going to become involved in:

**Examples**

"The study will deal with the Brogan Reactor Furnace and its peripheral supporting network. We will not get into the problems existing in Power Plant B."

"We will assess the effectiveness of the current Marketing organization structure and its interface with the Sales department."

## Objectives of the Project

This identifies the organizational improvements you expect if your consultation is successful. This is your best guess on the benefits the client can expect. Sometimes this statement is to help the client be realistic about the limitations of the project. You are not a magician and need to keep reminding the client of this.

You can expect to help the client in four general areas:

- *Solve a particular technical or business problem.* The client is willing to talk to you because there is some pain somewhere in the client's organization. The immediate goal is to reduce the pain, whether the pain is from currently unsatisfactory results or from the fact that opportunities to improve a situation are not being exploited.

- *Create a new possibility for the organization.* Sometimes the client is driven by a vision for a new future more than by the existence of a problem to be solved. The work is to give form and build support for this vision. This often entails looking at the strengths of the system and defining how to more fully expand them in pursuit of a new culture.

- *Teach the client how to solve the problem for themselves the next time it arises.* It is possible for you to develop a solution and merely hand it to the client. If there is the expectation that the client can do it alone when the problem occurs again, be clear about it. This will require a lot more involvement from the client during the life of the project if the problem-solving process you are using is going to be transferred to the client.

- *Improve how the organization manages its resources, uses its systems, and works internally.* Every business or technical problem has a component where the way the problem is being managed is part of the problem. This is sometimes called the politics of the situation. Many internal consultants are reluctant to get into this area, but the more you can include this as an objective of the project, the more long-range help you are likely to be. (The compass icon guides you to other parts of the book, in this case Chapters Ten through Twelve.)

You should be clear in the beginning about what is part of your contract—for example:

**For Business Objectives**

"The objective of the study is to decrease defects in the printed circuit board fabrication process by 4 percent."

"Our goal is to increase the responsiveness of the marketing department to shifting consumer demand. We particularly expect to develop ways to reduce the time it takes to introduce a new product by six weeks."

**For Learning Objectives**

"A second objective is to teach the plant engineering group how to perform this kind of production analysis."

"The marketing staff should become more effective in assessing their own market responsiveness and restructuring themselves in the future."

**For Organizational Development Objectives**

"This project will help the plant manager develop ways to better manage the interface between plant engineering and plant operations."

"A goal of the project is to increase cooperation between the market research group and the product directors."

"The goal is to create a culture of strong commitment and accountability and be more proactive in pursuing new market opportunities.

## The Kind of Information You Seek

Access to people and information are the key wants of the consultant. The major ambivalence of the line organization is how far to let you into the bowels of their organization. They want to tell you what is really going on and at the same time are afraid of telling you what is really going on. *Come close, but not too close.* Despite what the line manager says to you, there is always some desire for confirmation that the organization is doing the best that can be done under the circumstances. This desire at times can be stronger than the desire to solve the problem. One way to hedge against this ambivalence is to be explicit from the start about the kind of information you need. Some of the kinds of information you may want to specify in the contract are technical data, figures, and work flow; attitudes of people toward the problem; and roles and responsibilities—for example:

**For Technical Data, Figures, and Work Flow**

"To complete the project, we will require daily production figures for the etching process and the work schedules and procedures in effect now."

"We will want to see the planned and actual schedules for the last six product improvement introductions after we get into the project."

### For People's Attitudes

"We want to interview at least fifteen people to identify how they currently view the marketing function."

"We want to talk with the people in single-sided and multilayer etching and in testing and validation to uncover their perceptions of the way the supervisory group rewards good and poor performance. We also plan to ask the same questions of the supervisors."

### For Roles and Responsibilities

"The marketing organization will provide a definition of who is responsible for major decisions on new products at each stage of the process."

"We will obtain information from all supervisors on their view of their jobs and the authority they have to manage their sections of the PCB fabrication process."

## Your Role in the Project

This is the place to state how you want to work with the client. If you want a collaborative relationship, say so. Make it a statement of both intent and spirit. It doesn't pay to spell out all the ways you are going to work together. It is hard to predict at the beginning what is going to come up. You can make some statements about the desire for a 50/50 sharing of responsibility for identifying problems, interpreting the findings, and developing recommendations and action plans:

### Example

Our primary role is to give you a clear and understandable picture of how your plant is currently performing the etching and testing/validation processes in PCB fabrication. While we have expertise on equipment design and operation as well as state-of-the-art testing and validation procedures in the industry, your group has a great deal of knowledge of day-to-day operations. We would expect to present our analysis of the defects problem and then jointly develop recommendations with you on what changes should be made. A major part of our role is to help you solve this problem for yourself next time. This requires that the plant supervisors have some involvement at each step of the study. We are committed to develop specific solutions to the present concerns and to play an important educational role with you and your supervisors.

## The Product You Will Deliver

Here it is important to be specific about what you are offering. Will your feedback be an oral or written report? How long will it be—five pages or fifty? How much detail will the client receive? How far into specific recommendations will you get? Will you give some general suggestions for improvements, or will you give a list of steps that can be implemented right away? Will you present actual solutions or steps that can be taken that will eventually lead to solutions?

Of course, you can't predict all of these in the beginning, but you do know from your own experience how specific you will be. This dimension of a consulting relationship—specificity and nature of recommendations—is a major cause of client disappointment in the consulting services they have received. This doesn't mean that recommendations should always be specific or should always be general; that depends on the task the consultant is engaged in. It does mean there ought to be a clear understanding with the client on what your product will look like.

Here is a promise for specific recommendations:

> The outcome of this project will be a detailed written description of our findings running somewhere between five and fifteen pages. For each major finding, we will offer specific recommendations that you can act on.

And this is a promise for general recommendations:

> The outcome of this inquiry will be roughly a one-page outline of our major conclusions. These will identify only the critical areas to be considered. Actual recommendations will be developed jointly with you after the outline of issues has been discussed. These recommendations will be developed in the half-day feedback meeting we have scheduled at the end of the project.

In promising results to the client, remember that you will be turning the action over to the client at some point. It is the client, not you, who is going to actually deliver continuing results. You can guarantee a solution to a problem, but you can't guarantee that the solution will be followed. To take the solution totally on your shoulders may feel comfortable to you, but it can deprive clients of responsibility for the solution that is rightfully theirs.

## Support and Involvement from the Client

This section is the heart of the contract for the consultant. This is where you specify what you want from the client to make this project successful. This list is what the client is offering to you. Include here the wants that were the subject of some discussion in the verbal contracting meeting. Writing down your wants ensures clear communication and that any identified sensitive points are resolved:

**Example**

> You [the line manager] have agreed to communicate the existence and need for this project to your organization. We have also agreed to meet with the division vice president to get his view on the problem and to include him in the second feedback meeting. [Meeting with the vice president is an example of what might have been a sensitive topic of discussion.] In addition, two people from your staff will be made available to us for a maximum of seven days each to help with the data analysis and summary.

## Time Schedule

Include starting time, any intermediate mileposts, and completion date. If you want to give interim reports to the client before you tie the ribbon on the package, schedule them at the beginning. It is always easier to cancel a meeting than to set one up at the last minute:

**Example**

"We can begin this work in six weeks and plan to complete it ten weeks from when we start."

## Confidentiality

Since you are almost always dealing with a political situation as well as a technical one, who gets what report is a constant concern. It pays to be quite conservative on this and give the client control on the people they want to share the findings with. This is a luxury of being an outside consultant. If you are an inside consultant, you may not have any choice but to send a technical study or an audit report up the line. All you can do is to acknowledge to the client who you are required to give copies of your report to. This gives clients a choice about how to protect themselves, if necessary.

Here is an example of an easy case when it comes to confidentiality:

> The results of this study will be given to the director of engineering [the client]. Any further reporting will be up to the director. Should the internal consultants be required to report any results to the larger organization, the director will be informed and invited to attend any meetings held on the subject.

And here is an example of a more difficult case on confidentiality:

> The results of the audit will be reported to the management audit committee. Before the report is released, the division controller [the client] will be able to review and comment on the audit findings and recommendations. The intent (and the common practice) is that the audit report goes to the committee with the support of both the division controller and the audit team. The final report also includes the list of corrective actions that the division plans to take.

## Feedback to You Later

An optional element of the contract is to ask the client to let you know the results of your work six months after you leave. If you want to know but usually don't find out, ask for it:

**Example**

> About six months after the project is completed, the consultant will contact the client for feedback on the impact of the project. This might take the form of having people complete a questionnaire, respond over the phone, or send some recent operating data to the consultant.

For a downloadable copy of Checklist #2, visit www.flawlessconsulting.com.

## CHECKLIST #2: Analyzing One of Your Contracts

Pick a complicated contract that you have negotiated. Write up the elements of that contract using the following headings:

1. **The Boundaries of Your Analysis**

2. **Objectives of the Project**

3. **The Kind of Information You Seek**

4. **Your Role in the Project**

5. **The Product You Will Deliver**

6. **What Support and Involvement You Need from the Client**

7. **Time Schedule**

8. **Confidentiality**

9. **Feedback to You Later**

# GROUND RULES FOR CONTRACTING

A model for a contracting meeting is presented in the next chapter. Underlying the model is a set of ground rules for contracting, which have come primarily from my exposure to Gestalt psychology:*

1. The responsibility for every relationship is

*I attended a Gestalt workshop run by Claire and Mike Reiker near New Hope, Pennsylvania, too many years ago. In it they presented these ground rules in such a clear and powerful way that I have used them ever since.

50/50. There are two sides to every story. There must be symmetry or the relationship will collapse. The contract has to be 50/50.

2. The contract should be freely entered.

3. You can't get something for nothing. There must be consideration from both sides. Even in a boss-subordinate relationship.

4. All wants are legitimate. To want is a birthright. You can't say, "You shouldn't want that."

5. You can say no to what others want from you. Even clients.

6. You don't always get what you want. And you'll still keep breathing. You will still survive; you will still have more clients in the future.

7. You can contract for behavior. You can't contract for the other person to change their feelings.

8. You can't ask for something the other person doesn't have.

9. You can't promise something you don't have to deliver.

10. You can't contract with someone who's not in the room, such as clients' bosses and subordinates. You have to meet with them directly to know you have an agreement with them.

11. Write down contracts when you can. Most are broken out of neglect, not intent.

12. Social contracts are always renegotiable. If clients want to renegotiate a contract in midstream, be grateful that they are telling you and not just doing it without a word.

13. Contracts require specific time deadlines or duration.

14. Good contracts require good faith and often accidental good fortune.

# CHAPTER 5

# THE CONTRACTING MEETING

THERE IS AN OLD DAVID STEINBERG JOKE about the person showing up for his first meeting with his psychiatrist. He walks in the office and is faced with the choice of two chairs to sit in. He turns to the psychiatrist and asks, "Which chair should I sit in?" The psychiatrist says, "Either one." The person sits in one. The psychiatrist jumps up, points an accusing finger at him, and shouts, "Aha! Everything counts!"

So it is with contracting. Almost every event and action carries with it a message about what this project and what this client are going to be like.

The personal interaction between the consultant and the client during the initial contracting meetings is an accurate predictor of how the project itself will proceed. If you can accept this concept, you will pay close attention to the process of those early meetings. In fact, the critical skill in contracting is being able to identify and discuss process issues between you and the client as they occur.

The contracting meeting is usually set up by a phone call or e-mail. During this call, there are certain things to find out to help prepare for the meeting. Who requested the meeting? The answer will be the first indication of where the responsibility lies. If someone else suggested a meeting with a support person to the line manager, this is a warning flag that the manager may be feeling some pressure to proceed. Find out who will be at the meeting and what their roles will be, and how much time there is for the meeting. This gives an early indication of the importance of the project to the manager. You get a different message if you hear, "We have half an hour," than if you hear, "We have as much time as we need."

Clarify what outcome is expected from the meeting. Is it a meeting to decide how to get started or whether to do anything at all? Is a proposal going to be required? Addressing these issues before the meeting gives you more data to prepare for it. It also signals to the client that this is likely to be a 50/50 proposition—that you are a responsible actor in the process, not just a servant.

All this is easier, of course, when the client is initiating the meeting with you than when you are knocking on their door. (Later in this chapter we focus on selling to clients who don't know yet that they need your services.) When the client makes the request to meet with you, I recommend these questions, at a minimum, over the phone.

- What do you want to discuss?

- Who is the client for this project?

- Who else will be at the meeting? What are their roles?

- How much time will we have?

- Do you know that you want to begin some project, or are we going to discuss whether we do anything at all?

## WHO IS THE CLIENT?

When you meet with the client to begin contracting, the key question is: Who is the client? Most projects have multiple clients. The line manager you are talking to is one client. There are others who may

have a piece of the action too (see Chapter Seven). One of the ground rules of contracting is that you cannot contract with someone who's out of the room. If major actors are not present as you are setting up a project, you can't assume that they support the project until you actually meet with them.

In general, the clients on a project are the people who

- Attend the initial planning meeting

- Set the objectives for the project

- Approve any action to be taken

- Receive the report on the results of your work

- Are significantly impacted by the effort

This means the client can be a person, a top management team, a whole department that you work with through a representative planning group, or even your own boss. Try to have at least one meeting with each person who is part of initiating this project, even if they are at a very high level of the organization. This will allow you to get your own information on what they want from you and whether what you are planning will satisfy them.

## NAVIGATING THE CONTRACTING MEETING

Reaching agreement on how you will work with a client can follow a logical sequence. Outlined in Figure 2 is a series of steps that lead to either an agreement to work together or an agreement not to work together. Using this model will ensure that you are adequately completing the business of the contracting phase. In describing the sequence of steps below, I give you both a clear statement of each task to be accomplished and also what an authentic way of accomplishing the task would look like.

The objective we are focusing on here is to develop a stable, balanced, and workable contract between the consultant and the client.

### Step 1: Make a Personal Acknowledgment

No matter how motivated a manager is to seek your assistance, it is a difficult thing in organizations to ask for help. Even for experienced consultants, when our own organization hires a consultant to help with a problem, there is some uneasiness. So the first item on the agenda of the contracting meeting is to do something that will help to increase the personal comfort level between the consultant and the client. Some people try to do this by discussing the ball scores or the weather. My advice to people in consulting skills workshops is to make personal statements of your feelings about being in this meeting with the client today. Ask them for the same.

**Some Examples**

"This is one of the few plants I have never worked with before; I'm glad you called."

"I was surprised that you were interested in what we are doing. I hope we can work something out."

**Figure 2.** Navigating the Contracting Meeting

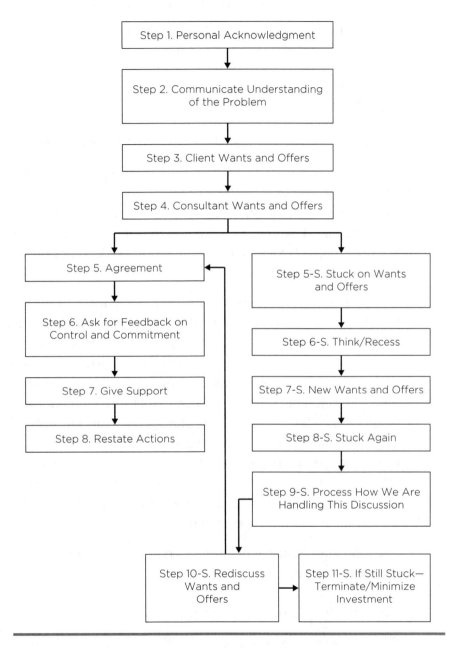

"Our history with your group has been bumpy in the past. I am concerned about that and also glad to rewrite that history."

"It looks like things are hectic for you. I hope this is a good time for us to get together."

"Any thoughts or concerns you have about working with me on this project?"

## Step 2: Communicate Understanding of the Problem

Clients are usually eager to tell you about the problem or the general situation. Behind the eagerness is often the line manager's belief that this situation is unique in some aspects and this organization is really very special. Managers can also feel that their situations are so special and unique that no one could possibly understand them without living there for a year.

The client's declaration of uniqueness, often accompanied by doubt that the consultant can understand the situation, sometimes gets expressed in very roundabout ways. Clients ask about work you are doing elsewhere in the organization or the industry, about whom you report to if they don't know, about how long you have been doing this kind of work, and whether you can be of any help anyway. Underneath all the statements and questions is the concern about whether the client can be helped and the problem can be solved. After all, before the consultant comes on the scene, clients have made their best efforts to solve the problem themselves. It is understandable that they are frustrated by the lack of a solution and somewhat skeptical about the consultant's possible contribution.

The following basic client concerns require a direct response early in the contracting meeting:

"My situation is exquisitely unique."

"The problem is complicated and defies an obvious solution."

"So how could you, a consultant, an outsider, offer significant help in a short period of time?"

The consultant needs to communicate an understanding of the problem in ways that acknowledge the unique aspects of the situation, respond to the seeming complexity of the situation, and speak to the client's fear about being beyond help. Here's how you do it.

### Acknowledge the Unique Aspects of the Situation

Because each client has different people and operates in a different environment, the line manager's claim of uniqueness has some validity. From the consultant's vantage point, we tend to be more aware of what is similar between this client and other clients we have worked with. Initially, though, it is important to put into words what is different about this project:

**Examples**

"There are two unique aspects to your situation: the pressure being placed on you from above and the desert climate of this location."

"Your situation has several unique things that make it both interesting and frustrating."

### Restate, in Your Own Words, Your Perception of the Problem

Here you express the thought that even though the problem is indeed complicated, you can already begin to understand it. This is an act of reassurance, designed to make the client feel understood and supported. At this point you don't know what the real problem is, for the real problem is often quite different from the client's opening problem statement. What you are accomplishing is letting the client know that you are listening and have enough technical expertise to grasp the situation quickly.

Most line managers have been listened to so little by experts that they are surprised by our perceptiveness. The manager says, "The design engineering and the plant engineering groups are always blaming each other for plant failures." I respond by saying, "I bet when they get together, they have trouble coming up with a single plan of action they can support." The manager says, "That's right. How did you know that? You're perceptive." It's not perceptiveness; it is just listening to and restating what the manager said.

**Examples**

"You have mentioned in great detail your concerns about expense vouchering, petty cash, and accounts payable, but what you really sound concerned about is the lack of specific controls in certain areas and people's commitment to live within them."

"I can see you are concerned about the slowdown, the wildcat strike, the suspicious explosions, the wanton destruction of property, and the fact that someone glued and soldered every moving piece of equipment over the weekend. But what I really hear you're concerned about is that people just don't seem to be happy working here."

### Reassure the Manager That There Are Solutions to This Unique and Complicated Problem and That You Can Be of Help

Your reassurance has to be genuine. You are stating that you can help find a solution, not that you know the solution right now. Your expertise is knowing the steps that have to be followed to find a solution. This is what you have to offer. The client at this stage is wondering, *Is this consultant someone I can lean on and trust to help me with this problem?* Your answer is a tentative yes—tentative at this early stage because you don't know specifically what the client wants from you or what support the client is willing to offer you. Until you know the specific wants and offers from the client, you don't know whether this is a project on which you can succeed.

**Examples**

"Despite the frustration you are feeling, I can help you with this problem. It's the kind of thing we have worked with a lot lately."

"This is the kind of situation that makes good use of my background. I think I can help."

In communicating your understanding of the problem, it helps to use short, simple sentences. Many of us have a tendency to get a little carried away, getting too deeply into an analysis of the problem at this early stage. The task here is to respond to the underlying concerns of uniqueness, complexity, and whether the client can be helped, not to analyze the nature of the problem (this comes later). Responding to the client's emotional concerns is done better with short sentences than with long sentences, short words are better than long words, and direct statements are better than inferences. Make simple statements expressing understanding and support without being overly protective or falsely reassuring. Also, don't sell. Just make a simple statement that the situation seems workable. The next step is to get into the specifics of what you and the client really expect from each other.

## Step 3. Client Wants and Offers

After saying hello and hearing an initial statement of what the line manager is concerned about, you look the manager in the eye and say, "So, what do you want from me?" The answer is the heart of the contracting process, and the question must be asked directly. It is the key qualifying question to determine whether and how you can succeed on this project.

There is a difference between what the client wants from the project and what the client wants from you. The client can be very clear about what is wanted from the project—for example, better cost control, reduced overhead charges, fewer equipment failures, better morale from the troops, more skilled first-line supervisors, an improved sales reporting system—and still not express what is expected from you, the consultant.

Some common things clients want from their consultants are

- A study of a specific business problem

- Recommendations on how to solve a problem

- A training program designed and conducted

- Personal advice and support

- An evaluation of key line personnel

- A design for a cheaper process

These are generally pretty straightforward requests for your services. It becomes more complex as you begin to understand how they would like you to work. To understand this, you ask the client whether there are any specific notions about how you should proceed or what the constraints on this project are. Asking about constraints helps you find out early that

- You have two weeks to do a four-week job.

- You shouldn't talk to any hourly people.

- Nobody else knows the real reasons for this study, and you shouldn't tell them.

- You shouldn't upset anybody or open Pandora's box.

- The project has a budget of $1.85.

- After this meeting, the client won't have any more time to spend with you.

Constraints on how you proceed are, of course, vital for you to know now. How you proceed is often the most difficult part of the contract to negotiate.

The skill in surfacing constraints is to ask clients directly for any thoughts they have on how you should work with them and what constraints exist on the way this project will be conducted. For example, the discovery method, who is involved, who hears the results, the schedule, and cost.

After hearing what the client wants from you, you next want to ask what support the client can offer you on the project. If the client is going to pay directly for your services (you are not part of the client's overhead), you want to know the budget for this project. The other two offers the client can make to you are the time of their people and access to information. Explore these areas in detail when you get around to expressing your wants.

Most people doing consulting are in fact quite good at this stage of the contracting process. Support people especially seem to be oriented to client needs and are skillful in identifying what the client wants. Internal consultants have a much harder time with the next step: identifying and expressing their own wants and needs.

## Step 4. Consultant Wants and Offers

One of the most critical skills in flawless consultation is to put directly into words what you, the consultant, want from the client to make a project successful.

When I tell internal consultants they should make clear what they want from the client, they often say, "We are in a service role, and our job is to satisfy the line manager's needs and wants. If we do this successfully, our job is done. We are not in a position to make demands on the people we serve." This pure service orientation can be self-defeating. Making clear what the consultant wants from the client is in the interest of making sure the project is successful; it is not to satisfy the consultant's own personal whims and wishes.

The consultant wants we are talking about here include such things as the need for enough time to do the job right, access to the right people and information, support from the client at difficult moments, people from the client organization to work on the project, agreements on confidentiality, follow-up to the recommendations, and uninterrupted time from the line manager. *These wants have to be expressed in the contracting phase.* The risk of not expressing your wants is that the project will not succeed, and an unsuccessful project is worse than no project at all.

Some things we want from clients are more important than others. In planning a contracting meeting, it's helpful for you to break your wants into two kinds: essential wants and desirable wants.

### Essential Wants

*Essential wants* are the things you must have as a minimum. Some people call them *must wants*. If you do not get an essential want from a client, then you would do better not to proceed with the project. Essentials vary from situation to situation; here are some examples:

- Access to the key people who have a part in the problem you are being asked to solve

- Enough time to do the job professionally

- An agreement that you will not be asked to individually evaluate the performance of people you work with on this project

- Money

- Access to certain records and documents

- The commitment of the top person in the organization to proceed with the project

- Respond to my phone calls and e-mails

Knowing what is essential comes with experience and from getting burned a few times. We never get all that we want on a project, so in the beginning, we tend to pressure ourselves to give in a little and get on with the project. If we give in on an essential—whether from hunger for a client or pressure from our boss to "get that client into the fold"—we will be sorry. Giving in on an essential means the project will be on shaky grounds, and we risk failure.

If you are in the middle of a contracting session and the suggestions from you and the client keep shifting around and suddenly you have to decide whether to agree to something or not, stop the process and give yourself a recess. You can break for coffee, go to the restroom, drop some marbles on the floor and think while you search for them, return some e-mails on your phone, or whatever else you do to give yourself space to think. During the recess, which doesn't need to be any longer than three or four minutes, ask yourself only one question: Does the suggestion on the table violate in any way what I consider essential for me on this project? If the answer is yes, then return to the meeting and say, "What you are suggesting makes great sense, but it does not give me what I consider to be essential for the success of this project." Then continue the search for agreement.

There is no better thing you can do for yourself when beginning a project than to realistically define the essentials for you on a project. If you have done this honestly—with neither greed nor self-sacrifice—then little else can happen to you during the contracting to really hurt you. A lot can happen to make you miserable, but if your essentials are met, the project can succeed. If they are not met, the project can only fail.

### Desirable Wants

*Desirable wants* are the things you would like to have from the client but you can live without them. These are not casual or capricious wants: They will help make the project more effective, but you know you can succeed without them. Here are some examples:

- Someone from the client organization to work with you on the project

- The manager to meet with all the other people involved in the project to explain it and personally seek their support

- The top management of the group to get deeply involved in your project

- An adequate time schedule

- A large group meeting of people at all levels of the organization

- Agreement that the client will spread the word to others in the organization if you do well on the project

Sometimes internal consultants are so oriented to meeting their client's needs that they have a hard time identifying what they want in return from their clients. Here is a list of what some internal consultants have said they wanted from their clients:

- Work the problem together

- Commitment to the project

- Share the blame and the glory

- No bias about the outcome

- Take care of physical needs to accomplish the job (in this case—car, driver, and translator)

- Openness to feedback during the project

- Feedback on what happened after I left

- Feedback to my boss

- Accept that certain things just can't be done

- Forgiveness

### Putting Wants into Words

Identifying what you want from the client is the first step. The next step is to act on those wants. This corresponds to the two requirements of consulting flawlessly: attending to the business of each phase and acting authentically. The business at this point is identifying what you want; acting authentically means putting those wants into words as simply and directly as possible.

Sometimes there is a tendency to complicate asking for what you want. We think we need elaborate explanations and justifications. We introduce a want with a paragraph about other experiences or the unique requirements of this organization, and we make the want rather vague and general. Sometimes we ask for what we want with a question. All this does is fog and undermine the expression.

Here is an example of a fogged expression of wants:

**The Want**

A manager of training is talking to a division director about sending her subordinate to a course on handling difficult conversations. The want is for the division director to become directly involved in the project by also attending the course.

**Fogged Expression of Wants**

*Training manager:* "We have found from prior experience that the learning in a training course tends to be retained longer if there is some visible evidence of positive reinforcement back on the job. This allows for better utilization of the newly acquired skills, and in your case, the course is introducing a totally different approach to the important and productive counseling of employees. If this positive reinforcement does not take place, then you can expect a decay of the learning, and the cost-benefit ratio of your investment is significantly diminished. Have you ever attended a course on performance appraisal?"

*Comment:* The points the training manager is making here are all true, and there are good reasons for the division director to attend the course. The problem is that the want is being buried in the justification. The question at the end may eventually lead to the suggestion that the division director take the course, but this path is indirect and unnecessary.

**Authentic Expression of Wants**

Here is an alternative—this one an authentic expression of wants:

*Training manager:* I would like for you also to attend the course on handling difficult conversations.

*Comment:* This may seem too simple a statement, but it's not. The power of the statement is that it is simple and in everyday street language. The goal of flawless consulting is to maximize your leverage and impact on the client so that your expertise gets used. Acting authentically is the most powerful thing you can do at every stage of the process.

When we identify what we want from the client, the want comes first, the justification afterward. We know that we want the manager to attend the course. Then we start to think of how we can justify it to the client. We start worrying about how to phrase it, how to explain it in bottom-line terms, to find words that the client will understand. All this effort is not only overdone, but it can act as a fog and obstacle to getting what we want.

The skill is to

1.  State the want first in simple street language

2.  Be quiet and let the client react

3.  If the client has questions, give a two-sentence answer and restate the want

4.  Be quiet and listen for a yes or no

You will not always get a yes answer. Life is like that. If you state the want simply, use silence to get the client to talk about their feelings, and offer short explanations, you have done all you can. The long paragraphs may make you feel better, but they get in your way. Making simple authentic statements gives you your best chance to get what you want and to know where you stand with the client on that issue.

**Your Chance**

Here is a useful exercise for you. Get out your laptop or a pencil and a piece of paper, and make two columns: essential wants and desirable wants. Think of a client you are concerned about, and record your list of essential and desirable wants from that client. Don't worry about whether you would ever ask for these things from a client; just write them in as uncensored a way as possible.

## Consultant Offers (Step 4 Continued)

In addition to stating wants to the client, state what you have to offer. This requires you to be realistic about the limit of what you can promise.

Most often, the consultant's promise is a clear picture of what is happening in the client organization plus recommendations on how to improve things. The consultant can promise actual improvements only if line management takes its 50 percent of the responsibility. Operating improvements must be a joint promise between consultant and client, not a unilateral consultant promise. If I offer results as a outcome of simply my own efforts as a consultant, I am presenting myself as a magician. I can't offer something that I can't control. I can't control the client's behavior or actions. If I let my enthusiasm lead me into promising specific results that are really the client's to achieve, I am colluding with the client's secret wish to sit back and watch the consultant perform miracles.

Here is an example of the choice:

*Client:* How soon can I expect results from you?

*Magical consultant offer:* We'll have the machine back onstream in three days, and you won't have any trouble with it after that.

*Realistic consultant offer:* We'll have the machine back onstream in three days. After that, it is up to you to keep it running.

For most of us doing consulting, there are two things we need to constantly work on:

1. Stating clearly, sometimes running the risk of overstatement, what we need and want from the client to make this project work

2. Being cautious, sometimes running the risk of understatement, about the results we alone will deliver on this project

## Step 5: Reach Agreement

After exchanging wants with the client, either you reach agreement or you get stuck. (I address later in this chapter what to do when you get stuck.) If, as in most cases, you can reach agreement, you should pause for a moment and just feel good about it. If you are feeling expansive, you can even say to the client, "It looks as if we agree on how to proceed. I am really happy about that." It also helps to restate what the agreement is.

Consultants often act as if the contracting meeting is over when agreement has been reached. It is not. There are still three important steps before a stable, balanced contract is assured.

## Step 6: Ask for Feedback on Control and Commitment

This is an insurance step. Most weak contracts are faulty for one of two reasons:

1. The client entered the agreement under some kind of coercion, however subtle and indirect.
2. The client agreed to the project but increasingly felt there was inadequate control over what was happening.

So at the beginning of any project, be compulsive about testing for the existence of each of these flaws.

### Testing for Client Commitment

Ask the client directly, "Is this project something that you really want to see happen? Are you satisfied with the way we have agreed to set it up?" There are many ways the line manager can feel coerced into the project. Top management may have suggested this project. It may be the latest organizational fad to begin projects like this. The manager may feel that it would be politically unwise to say no to you.

Asking the question about client commitment does not mean that you will withdraw from the project if the client is not that committed. You ask the question so that you know what you are up against from the beginning. If the client is acting out of coercion, you want to know it now. It is important to be realistic about this so that you don't overinvest or pretend that the contract is strong when it is not.

Asking clients about their commitment has one additional benefit: it forces them to take responsibility for the fact that they too are beginning a project without supporting it fully. Sometimes the act of clients' acknowledging they are acting under some coercion can actually serve to increase their commitment to a project.

Having the conversation about commitment to the project near the end of the contracting meeting is important. Do it.

### Testing for Control

After discussing client commitment to the project, ask, "Do you feel you have enough control over how this project is going to proceed?"

Line managers (as well as the rest of us) tend to value control above all else. If the client begins to feel that control of the situation is slipping away, the contract and the project will be threatened. As with your questions about commitment, you want to know now about any client uneasiness. Giving up control is a major cause of organizational uneasiness. Each time clients bring in a consultant, they give up a little bit of control, so as a consultant, you should find out the extent of the uneasiness.

When I suggest to internal consultants that they ask these questions about commitment and control, they ask in return, "Yeah, but how do we know we will get an honest answer? Will the client be truthful with us?" If you ask about control and commitment in a way that shows genuine interest in the answer, the client will give you a straight answer. If you ask the questions with a persuasive or pleading tone, honest answers are less likely. The purpose of the questions is to help managers express any reservations they are having. The questions are not indirect selling techniques.

Even if you ask the questions sincerely, sometimes you won't get a direct answer. It is still worthwhile to have asked them.

## Step 7: Give Support

Make supportive statements to the client about their willingness to begin this project with you. It takes some courage to invite or allow people into your organization to make recommendations about how you should shape up. Even if the client is seven feet tall, has scales, and breathes fire, I always assume there is a wish for support and I am happy to fulfill that wish.

You also might tell the client what they did in this meeting that was useful. If you do not say what it was, the client will never know. The support needs to be genuine and specific. Here are some examples:

"Starting a project like this takes some risk on your part, and I appreciate your willingness to take that risk with me."

"You have lived with this situation for a long time. It's terrific that you are now in a position to do something about it."

"You were very clear about your doubts and reservations."

"You told me a lot about some very personal challenges. Thank you for trusting me in that way."

"You are very perceptive about the nature of these kinds of problems. That is going to help a lot on this project."

"I know at first you were very skeptical about whether to let me in the door. I am glad we got past that."

## Step 8: Restate Actions

As a final insurance step, make sure you and the client know what each of you is going to do next. Simple statements are enough:

"You are going to send a memo to your people about the project."

"I am going to arrive on March 4 to begin interviewing people."

"Starting tomorrow, I will review the records with George. You and I will meet at 4:00 P.M. on Friday."

After agreeing on next steps, the contracting meeting is complete. No social contract will last forever; in fact, the contract usually is renegotiated often during the life of the project. If, however, you have gone through the eight steps above, you have done what you can at this stage.

## WHEN YOU GET STUCK

We have discussed what to do when you reach agreement. So what happens if agreement is difficult? In Figure 3, this is called Step 5-S (S for stuck).

## Step 5-S. Stuck on Wants and Offers

There are two phases to dealing with being stuck. First, you have to know that you are stuck. Second, you have to do something about it.

### Knowing When You Are Stuck

It is possible to feel that you are just having a reasonable discussion with the client about the pros and cons of the project and not realize that you are at an impasse. However, there are several clear operational signals of when you are stuck:

**Figure 3.** Navigating the Contracting Meeting When You Are Stuck

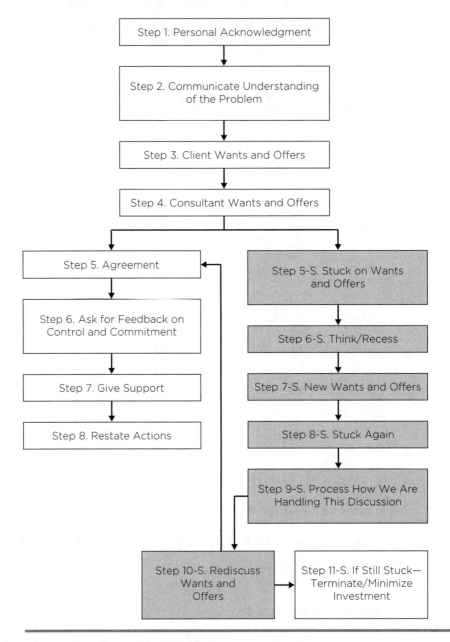

1. *You are stuck when you hear yourself reexplaining something for the third time.* The first time you explained why you want something, you might have used jargon or clumsy language. The second time you explained, you might have felt the client wasn't really listening. When you are struggling for the third time to express something in different, clearer words, you should admit to yourself that you are stuck.

Much of organizational communication is in code:

| When People Mean | They Express It by Saying |
| --- | --- |
| I don't like it. | "I don't understand it." |
| I don't want to do it. | "Let's get more data."<br>or<br>"I'll get back to you."<br>or<br>"Let me talk it over with my staff." |
| I don't understand a word you are saying. | Nothing |
| Do as I say, dammit! | "Why don't you think it over and get back to me?" |
| I wouldn't let your group even get close to my organization. | "We want to talk to some other people about alternative approaches to this problem and we'll let you know." |

You need to learn and trust this code because it is an early warning signal when you are getting stuck with the client. When you are thinking, *The client really doesn't understand what I am talking about,* the truth is that the client really does understand what you are talking about and does not agree. When this happens, don't explain for the fourth and fifth time. Instead, acknowledge that you are stuck.

2. *You are stuck when you notice the client diving into the third explanation of the same idea.* When the client thinks that you still don't understand, you will hear something like, "Let me see if I can put it another way." The reexplaining process assumes that lack of clarity is the problem. By the third try, it is not lack of clarity; it is lack of agreement. You are stuck. Acknowledge it.

3. *Your body will give you clear messages that you are getting stuck.* When you start suppressing yawns, take it as a signal that the meeting is not going your way. Boredom and fatigue are usually indirect expressions of irritation. You start to get subtly irritated with the resistance you are getting from the client. Perhaps it is the lack of enthusiasm you are getting from the client. As you get irritated, you say to yourself that you shouldn't be irritated, so you start holding back the irritation. The strain of holding back what you feel, especially if it happens unconsciously, is tiring, and your shoulders and neck start to ache. You start to yawn, but turn it into a laugh at the last minute. You start looking at your watch and think about the tennis game you played yesterday. Or you notice the client also looking very tired, turning yawns into laughs, staring out the window, or secretly napping as you talk.

All of these are signs that the conversation is stuck. If you were making progress and moving toward agreement, your energy would be increasing. If your energy is decreasing and you start feeling irritated, then it simply means that you aren't getting what you want and you are stuck.

4. *Your eyes give you the best cues that the contracting process has bogged down.* Trust what you see. Believe nonverbal messages. There is a lot written about body language—how to interpret different positions and how to posture yourself to communicate or conceal certain messages. Using body language or nonverbal behavior to either manipulate a situation or to present yourself in a certain way is a mistake. When you force your body into a position that hides how you are feeling, you look to others like someone who is forcing your body into a position to hide how you are really feeling. Noticing that you are trying to do something with your nonverbal behavior or are being psychological about others' nonverbal behavior can be a valuable source of information to you.

If you are looking for nonverbal cues during the contracting process, you will notice the client moving forward into the discussion or moving back away from the discussion. You will notice the client's hands—gestures of pushing you away, grabbing you like a fist, pointing at you like a gun, or opening wide, palms up, saying, "I am here by accident, a helpless victim of fate. What can any of us mere mortals do about this situation?"

These gestures can be accurately interpreted only at the grossest level: Are they acts of support or rejection? Does the client want into this project or out of it? Is the conversation going well or poorly?

The client's physical behavior and your own movements are only cues to help you know when you are stuck. They don't tell you why you are stuck. Resist the mind game of interpreting specific gestures. Do trust the general messages.

There is often a sharp contrast between what clients are saying and their nonverbal behavior. They are saying that they are really interested in this project, and they are also backed against the wall with their arms folded over their heads in bomb shelter fashion. If I am forced to choose between believing the words and believing the body, I believe the body. We all have sophisticated verbal defenses, but nonverbal defenses are much less sophisticated, so trust what you see. But use it only as a signal. Don't comment directly on a client's behavior and resist the temptation to say, "Each time I suggest interviewing your subordinates, you back up your chair to the wall, put your head into your arms, and hold your breath until your face turns pink. Why? Are you uncomfortable with what I am suggesting?"

The act of inferring the motives for another person's behavior is an aggressive stance and always leads to defensiveness on that person's part. Your objective is to help the client express the reservations more directly. You want to get a single message from the client so you know where things stand. When you get a double message because the body language doesn't match the words, ask an open-ended question about how the client feels about what you are discussing. "What's your reaction to what we've been discussing?" Again, the purpose of focusing on nonverbal behavior is to set up an early warning system and gather a more accurate set of cues, so you have a more realistic view of how the client is reacting to what you are saying.

Your own body is also an indication of how you are feeling about the contracting meeting. If the conversation seems to be going well on the surface and you also find yourself low on energy and slumping in the chair, you should begin to wonder whether your body is picking up some caution flags that your mind is choosing to ignore. If the conversation is going well and you are slumping in the chair, you might just be tired. And that's okay too.

What to do when you notice you're stuck?

## Step 6-S: Think/Recess

I think the most difficult part of dealing with being stuck is admitting to yourself that you have reached an impasse. When you do acknowledge to yourself that you are stuck, mentally pull back from the conversation and become an observer to the contracting meeting you are engaged in. You can continue talking and listening yet at the same time be thinking whether you can change your position in some way. Are there different wants you can ask for and still meet your objectives?

Sometimes it is wise to adjourn the meeting. Say, "We seem to be hung up on this point, and I would like some time to think about it more." This gives you an opportunity to reevaluate whether there is really an unresolvable difference between you and the client or whether the difficulty is due to some misunderstanding growing from the way the meeting itself has progressed. When you mentally or physically withdraw from the firing line, you give yourself time to identify a different way to approach the project or a different way to seal the agreement.

## Step 7-S: New Wants and Offers

If you think the differences between you and the client are negotiable, present any new ideas on what you want from the client or what you have to offer. We often get stuck in the contracting meeting over schedule. The client wants the job in thirty days, and we think we need sixty days. Both of us have good reasons, and so we get stuck.

You may decide after the thinking and recessing step that you could complete the project in thirty days if the client provides two people to work with you and agrees that your final report can be in outline form instead of elaborate prose. Here's what you say:

*Changing your offer:* "The job will be done in thirty days instead of sixty days."

*Changing your wants:* "I can get the job done in thirty days if you give me two people to work with and accept a shorter final report."

Developing different wants and offers is always worth at least one try. Sometimes it still doesn't help.

## Step 8-S: Stuck Again

If you realize that changing the wants and offers has just led to another impasse, then it is time to really shift gears. You have made two passes at reaching agreement that aren't working, so you should ask yourself whether the way you are working with the client and the relationship between you and the client might not be the real problem.

Line managers make decisions on the projects based on their feelings about the people involved. Does the manager trust you as the consultant or your department or company? Consultants also make agreements with line managers based on whether they trust the manager. When consultant and client get stuck on how or whether to proceed, a different kind of discussion is needed.

## Step 9-S: Process How We Are Handling This Discussion

When you're stuck again, the conversation needs to shift to how the meeting is going. For the moment, put aside the actual project under consideration. There are many ways of processing how a discussion is being handled, and they are covered in more detail in Chapters Eight and Nine, which address resistance and how to deal with it.

Here are a couple of ways of shifting the focus of discussion to the process of the meeting:

1. *Say, "I think we are stuck."* This simple declarative statement of fact—the meeting isn't going anywhere—is probably the most powerful thing you can do. Of course, you will use your own language and style, but the key is to put directly into words the fact that you have reached an

impasse. If the client keeps talking about the project, restate that you are stuck and encourage a discussion of why you seem to be stuck.

2. *Ask an open-ended question about how the client feels the meeting is going.* You don't have to be subtle. Say, "How do you feel we are doing in reaching agreement on how to proceed?" If you stick with the question, you will soon find out how the line manager is reacting to working with you. The manager may be worried about

- Keeping control of the project
- How stubborn you seem to be
- How misunderstood they feel
- The reputation your group has in the organization
- How vague the benefits of this project seem
- The jargon and motherhood statements you use

Most cases of stuck contracting stem from these kinds of concerns, not from the specifics of how to set up the project. The client and the consultant need to talk directly about them. When these concerns are expressed, the specifics become much easier. So just ask the question.

## Step 10-S: Rediscuss Wants and Offers

The discussion of how the meeting is going will usually unclog the impasse. You can go back to the specifics of the project and usually reach some agreement that puts you back on the original track (Step 5: Reach Agreement) and allows you to continue on to close the meeting.

Sometimes, despite all your skills, after following all these suggestions perfectly and consulting flawlessly, you remain stuck.

## Step 11-S: If Still Stuck—Terminate or Minimize Your Investment

Despite their importance to you, all projects were not meant to be. It is vital to accept this now, early in the project, and not count on later miracles to save the day.

When you are irreparably stuck with the client, you need to say, "We are having a hard time reaching agreement. Perhaps now is not a good time to do this work," or "I suggest that we not begin this project, since we can't seem to agree on how to proceed." Using your own style and own words, end the contracting process and cut your losses.

## THE PROBLEM WITH SAYING NO

Internal consultants especially feel they are taking tremendous risks if they tell line managers that they would be better off terminating a project. Despite the risk, it is in your and the client's best interests to refuse projects that do not have a reasonable chance for success. When you are stuck in contracting with a client, it is because both of you feel that if you don't get your way, the project will not succeed. If you go ahead with a project you don't believe in, you run the risk of failure. The reason to terminate projects is not because of consultant petulance, or pickiness, or the desire to engage only in exotic and professionally stimulating work. The reason to say no is to avoid failure and the waste of your resources.

Another reason to stay open to the possibility of saying no to a client is that you are trying to manage the relationship with the client in a way that you would wish the client to manage relationships with people in their organization. Saying no says that we have limits, that we have a right to declare boundaries and decide on our own what we commit to. If we cannot say no, then yes loses its meaning, and commitment also is taken off the table. We become programmed to say yes and after a while do not know when the yes is sincerely felt or simply born of institutionalized habit.

If you can't usually say no to a client, there are still some choices for you. For example, you can minimize your investment of time and hope to keep your potential losses down. The easiest way to do this is to postpone the project. Say, "I am willing to go ahead with the project as you have requested, but I suggest that we begin it in eight months." By this time, this manager may have moved on to another job, or you might have moved on to better things.

If you can't postpone the project, another choice is to minimize the scope of the job and the time it will require. Narrow the objectives of the project. Do what you can to reduce the visibility of the project, and reduce the drain on your time and energy. The key is to be honest with yourself about the limitations of the project.

So be realistic about unattractive projects. Be clear with your boss and others that the project is beginning on shaky grounds and that you would rather not proceed, but that you feel you have no choice because you can't afford to say no to this client. Then do the project in a low-key way.

The critical point to consider is whether it is really in your best interest to go ahead with a project. It may be better to live without the project, and not having "converted" that client, than to begin a project that might fail. If you pull back from one client, perhaps that client will be angry with you and feel rejected. But you lost only one client. If you proceed with a project that you think might fail and in fact it doesn't go well, you are in bigger trouble. The client is going to tell five other managers how disappointing the project was and how it failed. Now you are in the hole with six managers instead of only one.

It is just not good for business to take on low-chance-of-success projects.

## CONTRACTING CHECKPOINT

At this point, you have all the information you need to conduct a contracting meeting flawlessly.

The sequence of steps covers the business of the contracting meeting. There are three major sections to the meeting: (1) understanding the problem and exchanging wants, (2) closing the meeting by checking on client concerns and commitment, and (3) getting unstuck when agreement is difficult. Each step is essential and should never be skipped. If you cover the steps and still don't get the contract you wanted, you have done all you can and consulted flawlessly.

Use checklist 3 to help you prepare for a contracting meeting. Answer the questions before each contracting meeting and you are ready.

For a downloadable copy of Checklist # 3, visit www.flawlessconsulting .com.

## Checklist #3: Planning a Contracting Meeting

Answer these questions when you are planning a contracting meeting.

1.  **What imbalance do you expect in the responsibility for this project? Do you think the client will want to treat you as the expert and give you 80 percent of the responsibility? Or will the client treat you as a pair of hands and keep 80 percent of the responsibility?**

2.  **What do you want from the client?**
    - What are your essential wants?
    - What are your desirable wants?

3.  **What are you offering the client?**
    - Technically?
    - Personally?

4.  **What do you think the client might want? List all possibilities.**
    - Technically?
    - Personally?

5.  **Are the key clients going to be in the room?**
    - Who can make a decision on proceeding with this project?
    - Who will be strongly affected by this project?
    - Who is missing from the meeting?
    - What are their roles. For example, to get some action on the problem started or implement the outcome of your consultation or because they have the best information on the problem?

6.  **What resistance do you anticipate?**

7.  **What are the conditions under which it would be best not to proceed?**

Although some of the questions in checklist 3 may be unanswerable at this point, trying to answer them helps you focus on the essence of the meeting. If you are part of a consulting team, the checklist gives you a vehicle to get your act together. Mostly the questions keep you centered on what you need from the meeting so that you don't get swept away with overresponding to the client's view of the world.

## SELLING YOUR SERVICES: GOOD SELLING IS GOOD CONTRACTING

When the client comes to us, it's easy. We can assume there is some real need, some motivation, some respect for our abilities. Most of us, though, also have to go out and convince clients that they want to work with us. Internal consultants have their own departmental objectives to meet. They are told that a certain group ought to be using the department's services, and they are evaluated on whether they bring certain clients into the fold.

Basically the skills for selling your services are the same as those described for regular contracting. But here are a couple of additional concepts about the selling situation that might be helpful.

### Reverse the Expression of Wants

When the client calls you, you begin the discussion of wants by asking what the client wants from you. When you initiate the contact, you need to say straight out what you want from the client. Figure 4 shows the reversed sequence.

You must have a reason for choosing to talk to this client, and you explain that by defining the problem that you think the prospective client faces. Before going on to wants, stop and ask the client if the problem you have defined is indeed the problem. If it isn't, give it another try; then consider a quiet retreat.

After defining the need, state what you want from the client. Acknowledge that you are making a sales call. Support people feel successful by getting line managers to use their services. Everybody knows this,

**Figure 4.** Beginning Contracting Steps When You Are Selling

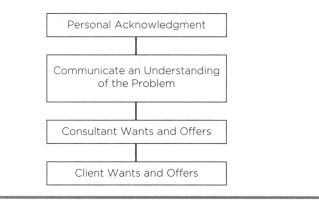

```
┌─────────────────────────────────────┐
│      Personal Acknowledgment         │
└─────────────────────────────────────┘
                  │
┌─────────────────────────────────────┐
│    Communicate an Understanding      │
│           of the Problem             │
└─────────────────────────────────────┘

┌─────────────────────────────────────┐
│      Consultant Wants and Offers     │
└─────────────────────────────────────┘
                  │
┌─────────────────────────────────────┐
│        Client Wants and Offers       │
└─────────────────────────────────────┘
```

even line managers. One thing the internal consultant wants from the meeting is to have the line manager as a client—so acknowledge it. To say you only want to be helpful is just half the story.

## Selling Is Removing Obstacles More Than Lighting Fires

We have all grown up with the image that a good salesperson is energetic, dynamic, quick with the words and phrases, and sincerely inspirational. This probably has some truth to it. But good salespeople are also people who are quiet, slow moving, struggle to find the right words, and come across as nicely average. Both kinds are successful, but there is great overemphasis on personality as the key to selling. So people who come to our consulting workshops tend to think that good consultants have to have charisma and presence.

Charisma and presence are in fact two mythical virtues that are highly overrated. I must admit that I have a vested interest in downplaying charisma and presence. I am quiet, slow moving, a struggler for words, and come across as nicely average. Workshop participants ask me if I have always been this way. I say, "What do you mean, this way?" They say, "Well, so low-keyed and half-asleep." Then they back off and think that my style is all by plan and design—that I am cooling it for the sake of their learning experience and that when I am out with clients, I release the Mack truck idling underneath the surface. Of course, this is not true. We are the way we are. Their underlying concern is that there is a certain right kind of personality to do consulting, and this concern is heightened when it comes to selling. I don't believe it, and here is why.

If I have a service that responds to a real need in the client's organization, then I assume that in some sense, the client would like to say yes to my proposition. If I have assessed the need accurately and the client is denying the need or denying that my services can help the situation, then I ask myself, *What obstacles are in the way of the client's trusting in what I offer?* For clients who are saying no, I try to understand the nature of the resistance, which usually is something like:

- They don't trust the competence or confidentiality of the department I represent.

- They feel they will lose control if they say yes.

- They feel they will become too vulnerable if they say yes.

- They don't trust or respect me as a person.

- They have had bad experiences in the past with something similar.

When I am selling a program and the client is resisting, the client's feelings give fire to the resistance. If I duck into a phone booth and step out magically equipped with my charisma and presence and really start "selling," I am just adding fuel to the fire. The client's resistance increases. My personality, high keyed or low keyed, is not the problem. The problem is that the client is not buying because negative feelings are saying not to trust me and what I am saying. The way out of the resistance is to help the client express directly, in words, the negative feelings. The more the client can express the feelings of distrust, the freer the client will be to really consider my offer on its merits. The more authentic I am, the more the client trusts me and the more quickly the resistance disappears. Here are some tips on what to do when you are selling your services:

- Don't be any different when you are selling than when the client called you in.

- Don't try to overcome the resistance with more explanations and pleas for the good of the organization.

- Do help the client express the reservations about you and your product.

- Do admit you are there to sell and want the client to buy.

- Do be authentic and follow the contracting sequence.

If you do all of this—and the reservations are expressed and there is trust in the relationship—and still get a no, then back off and reassess whether you have identified a real need and whether you are offering the right service. It is much better to lose the sale and maintain a solid relationship with the client than to keep pushing a sale that won't pan out.

## A Comment on Time and Money

Clients often refuse a contract on the grounds that they do not have the money to go ahead with the project or the organization does not have the time to invest. Both of these are indirect reasons not to do something, and I never take them at face value. These excuses are almost always a mask for the fact that the manager doesn't want to do the project.

The problem here is one of motivation, not time or money. Managers spend their own and their organization's time on things they want to do. They also spend money on things they want to do. They are managers, and they have control, and they pretty much do what they want regardless of time and money. If they wanted to do your project, they would find a way. If you agree with them that time or money is the problem, you are just colluding with them in avoiding the real reason. Don't collude. Get to the real reason, and you will have a better chance.

# THE MEETING AS A MODEL OF HOW YOU WORK

Consulting is primarily an educational process. Line managers learn something about how to manage their organization or solve a technical problem as a result of their contact with you. Even if you are brought in on a highly technical problem, the manager can learn about approaching these kinds of problems from watching you. In fact, managers probably learn more from watching consultants than from listening to them. This is why authentic behavior is an integral part of consulting flawlessly.

You can use the contracting meeting as an example of how you work with clients. In this meeting, you are collecting information on the problem, testing out some of your own theories, and giving feedback to the manager on your reaction to it. You are also jointly defining the problem and making plans. When clients ask you how you would plan to work with their organizations, you can use the contracting meeting as a mini-example of your approach, pointing out that the whole project will follow these steps in a more elaborate way.

The clearer you are about your process, the more you help reduce client fears about loss of control and vulnerability. In cases where a manager was really having a hard time understanding how I could help—even after I'd gone through the contracting meeting as an example of how I work—I have suggested that we engage in a very brief demonstration of what I do. The manager and I agree on a twenty-minute consultation right here and now, and for the next twenty minutes, I act as the manager's consultant on some problem of their choosing. At the end of twenty minutes, we stop the mini-consultation and talk about the process we just went through. This method helps me explain and demonstrate how I work, and it helps the manager decide how it would feel to work with me and whether my orientation is what they are looking for.

In a mini-consultation, the manager identifies a problem. I ask questions about the situation and react to the manager's way of looking at the problem and what the manager has done to try to solve it. I focus on the manager's own role in the problem. Near the end of the twenty minutes, I give some feedback on his or her role in the problem, along with some recommendations based on the limited data generated in this discussion. We then stop the consultation. Before we go back to contracting, I ask the manager how the twenty-minute consultation felt. This experience gives both of us some data on what proceeding together on a project would be like.

A sample consultation like this is especially useful when the project is rather broad and ambiguous and the manager is worried about losing control over it. During your brief consultation, the manager has the opportunity to experience you as someone who is responsive and collaborative, yet still has some different ways of looking at the world.

## CLOSING THE CONTRACTING MEETING

### How to Measure Success

In closing the contracting meeting, ask how you and the client will know whether you are successful. It may be an unanswerable question, but at worst, it will clarify the manager's expectations. At best, it will give good guidance on how to structure the project.

### Twenty Minutes Before the End of the Meeting

No contracting meeting should end without your asking for feedback about how the manager feels about the project, the meeting, and you. Ask, "How do you feel about the meeting? Any reservations?" and "How do you feel about what I have said and my approach to this? Any reservations, or unbridled enthusiasm?" Leave twenty minutes to discuss these questions. It may only take two minutes, but if the questions uncover new issues, it's best to discuss them now.

# AFTER THE CONTRACTING MEETING

Checklist 2 in Chapter Four gives you a way to summarize the agreements reached in a contracting meeting. Checklist 4, which follows, contains some questions you can ask after the meeting to get clear on how the interaction went with the client. The contracting meeting is a leading indicator of how the rest of the project is going to go. Examining your answers to these questions will give you an idea of what problems you are going to have to deal with on the project.

For a downloadable copy of Checklist #4, visit www.flawlessconsulting.com.

## Checklist #4:   Reviewing the Contracting Meeting

### 1.  How would you rate?

|                              | Client |  |  | Consultant |
|------------------------------|--------|-------|------------|
| • Balance of participation?  | 100% _____ | 50/50 _____ | 100% |
| • Who initiated?             | 100% _____ | 50/50 _____ | 100% |
| • Who had control?           | 100% _____ | 50/50 _____ | 100% |

### 2.  What resistance or reservations did the client express?

- Which did you explore directly, in words, with the client?

- Which did you not really explore?

### 3.  What reservations do you have about the contract?

- Which did you put into words with the client?

- Which did you express indirectly or not at all?

4. How did you give support to the client?

5. How were the client's concerns expressed:

    - Silence?

    - Compliance?

    - Attack?

    - Questions?

    - Giving answers?

    - Directly, in words?

6. What facial and body language did you observe?

7. How would you rate the client's motivation to proceed?

8. How would you rate your own motivation to proceed?

9. What didn't you express to the client?

10. Review "Navigating the Contracting Meeting." Did you skip any steps?

    - Which ones?

11. What would you do differently next time?

# CHAPTER 6

# THE AGONIES OF CONTRACTING

Some particularly rough spots in contracting are worth highlighting. The first is the difficult situation in which the client is willing to go ahead with a project, but you know the client's motivation toward the project is low. Line managers take an unnatural stance when they proceed with a project that they don't really want to do. When they agree to do a project they don't want to do, they have usually been coerced to say yes by their boss, their subordinates, or even their difficulty in saying no to you, the consultant. You also may be acting out of pressure from your boss to go ahead with the project. A recent addition to the complications of contracting is the need to operate in a virtual world. While our growing dependence on technology influences all that we do in consulting, it is in the contracting phase where it puts us most at risk.

## DEALING WITH LOW MOTIVATION

Here is some guidance on each of the steps in dealing with low motivation (see the model in Figure 5):

1. If the client has low energy for the project, the first choice is to consider just not doing it.

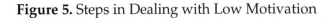

**Figure 5.** Steps in Dealing with Low Motivation

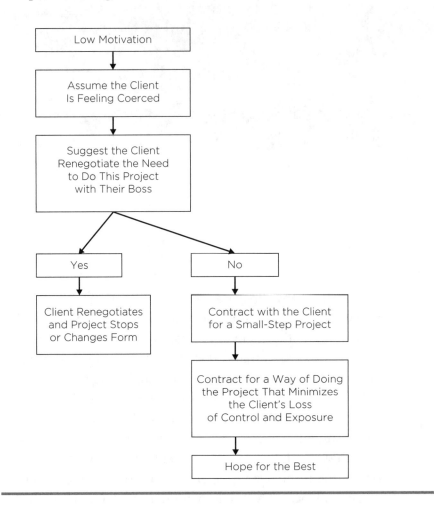

If you or the client feel you must go ahead with the project anyway:

2.  Acknowledge, at least to yourself, that the project is beginning with coercion. Ask the client if he or she is feeling at all pressured to go ahead. Usually the client will own up to any feeling of pressure.

When the client does acknowledge pressure:

3.  Suggest that the client go back to the person exerting the pressure and renegotiate whether the project has to be done. The client may either agree to stop the project or change the form it is taking

so that it feels more comfortable. If you are in an auditing or policing role and are the source of the pressure yourself, acknowledge that you realize the client has no choice but to work with you.

If you must go ahead in the face of some pressure:

4.  Contract with the client for a small-step project. Suggest that you work together on a small piece of the total project so that the client can decide whether the process is as bad as it is feared it would be. Usually if the client has a positive experience with you, concerns will go down.

Acknowledge to the client that you are proceeding despite the low motivation. Then:

5.  Ask the client whether there is some way that you could proceed that would minimize any concerns. Clients' concerns are often about losing control or being vulnerable, so ask, "Is there some way we can set this up so that you don't feel you have given up too much control over the situation? Is there some way we can set it up so that your vulnerability is protected?" You can negotiate how to proceed on the project so that you still get what you need from it and the client doesn't feel like such a victim.

Then hope for the best. These are tough contracts to manage. People in the auditing role are up against it all the time. The best thing they can do is to acknowledge the pressure and give the client support for the situation they are in by helping the client translate feelings into words. There is not much more you can do except get on with it.

## CEASELESS NEGOTIATION: THE SHIFTING TIDE OF YOUR ROLE

Consulting projects take place out in the world, in the middle of very political organizations, where the people and the pressures are constantly changing. So do some of the pieces of your consulting projects. Another thing that can change is the way the client deals with you. Because the client both wants you on the project and at the same time wants you to be more distant, your role definition with the client becomes subject to the process of ceaseless negotiation.

Sometimes a change in the project is obvious: a new manager arrives, the budget is cut, and findings in the middle of your inquiry have indicated new problems. More often, though, the changes are more subtle. Without your realizing it, the client has begun to treat you a little differently. You thought you were going to be invited to a meeting but weren't, or the scheduling the client does for one of your meetings gets fouled up. These cues are harder to read but might indicate the need for some renegotiation.

Here's an example from my work with a large drug company. A large management development conference was planned for May. About seventy-five high-level managers would attend, and the purpose was to have them do some joint problem solving on three critical new product introductions planned for the following year. It was now January, and I was working with a planning committee in preparing for the May conference. The committee was made up of two line managers, Jim and Lou; a support person, Rich; and me, an outside consultant. Jim, Lou, and Rich were vice presidents reporting to the president. I was primarily responsible for the detailed design and structuring of the meeting. The president had originally suggested having the May conference, so the committee knew we had his support. The committee had met several times, and I felt included in their process, really a part of the committee.

The scene picks up on a bleary Tuesday morning in January in a meeting with Jim, Lou, Rich, and me.

> Jim and Lou, the line executives, have been discussing how the top management group has been having a hard time getting its act together lately and that if they don't reach agreement on some things soon, they are going to look awfully foolish at the large meeting in May. Out of the discussion comes the fact that the president is part of the problem. He is very quiet, people don't know where they stand with him, and it's making everyone uncomfortable—and that discomfort is going to become obvious at the May meeting. Lou finally suggests that maybe we should postpone the May meeting until the management group is ready. Jim says maybe it would be good for the management group to stumble in the May meeting, because then

it would force them to work things out with the president. Rich, the support person, says maybe we are making too much of a thing about the management group: the problems aren't that great, and people might not notice.

Lou says to stop the May meeting, Jim says to hold the meeting, and Rich says, "What's the real problem here?" and our meeting goes around and around. I am strongly in favor of holding the meeting, but not with this cloud hanging over it. I finally suggest that we meet the next day with the president, identify the problem in a general way, and suggest he deal with the problem before the May meeting. I know that the president is quite unaware of the impact his quiet style is having on the group from other conversations I have had with him. There is a lot of discussion about my suggestion. Lou is worried he will be shot as the carrier of bad news; Jim says, "Why not meet with him?"; and Rich says, "Well, if we could phrase it right and not make it too much of a problem, maybe it would be all right." Finally, after considerable pressure from me, the group agrees to meet with the president the next afternoon at 4:00 to discuss the concern. I agree to present the idea and the others can chime in as they wish.

As we are leaving, Lou says to me, "It's easy for you to push to confront the president because you don't work for him like the rest of us do." I agree with him that it is easier for me to do it, and that's the reason I suggested it. I left the meeting tired and with the feeling that meeting now with the president was the only rational way to resolve the question and unblock the committee so it could complete its task of planning the May meeting.

On Wednesday, I arrive early for the 4:00 meeting with the president and sit down to talk with Rich. After a little small talk, he says, "By the way, the 4:00 meeting is canceled." Jim, Lou, and Rich had met first thing that morning and reconsidered the decision to meet with the president. Lou had thought it over and felt that it was too risky. Jim and Rich went along with him. So they decided to meet at 4:00 to proceed instead with the planning of the May conference.

Surprised, disappointed, and a little angry, I meet with the committee at 4:00. I ask a lot of questions about why they canceled the meeting and what we are going to do about their original concerns for the

May conference. Lou repeats his story about how risky it is to go to the president and what a vulnerable position that puts him in, reminding me once more that it was easy for me to urge a meeting with the president because I don't work there—and besides the problem isn't as big as we made it out to be. There is some truth about Lou's concern about the risk. If he feels that vulnerable, he probably has reasons.

I figure I have done what I could, and after letting them humor me for awhile, we move on to planning the May meeting. Rich makes a statement that one of these days, when the time is right, he will raise the subject of the management group's relationship with the president and see what kind of response he gets. It's a nice gesture, an offer we all know will never happen. The moment has passed.

I leave the meeting troubled about the whole thing and puzzled why I am troubled. I understand Lou's concern about the risk: I don't believe in taking blind risks. I know that the problem is not a crisis and business will go on as usual. An opportunity has been missed, but that happens every day.

After grousing around for a couple of hours, trying to pretend I'm really not upset, it starts to dawn on me what I'm really disturbed about. In the course of twenty-four hours, my role with that group has radically changed. When I left the meeting on Tuesday, I was a full-fledged member of the committee. I joined in the important decisions, and I had my share of influence (maybe more than my share). I was where the action was. When I returned the next day, all that had changed. The others had made a major strategy decision without me: not to meet with the president. And they had implemented that decision without me: they canceled the 4:00 meeting.

My role had changed in one day from a person with full status as a committee member to someone who was merely informed of a decision and had to be appeased and cooled off. They hadn't called me to see whether I could make a morning meeting, they hadn't called me to discuss what to do over the phone, and they hadn't called me to explain their change in strategy before they implemented it. I had turned from being a committee member to a specialist in charge of structuring the specifics of the May meeting. It happened right before my eyes, and I didn't even realize that my role had changed until three hours after the meeting.

After getting clear on what happened, I met with Rich a couple of days later with the intent of renegotiating my role or contract with that group. We agreed I would be treated as a full member, and it pretty much stayed that way through the rest of the project.

What is important about this incident is how quickly and subtly the consultant's contract can shift, which means that sustaining and renegotiating the agreement is a ceaseless process.

The timing of your renegotiation is important. It has to take place as soon as you sense the client is treating you differently and that something has changed. If you let it slide for awhile, it is much harder to sit down and discuss what happened, say, a month earlier. It was difficult to sit down with Rich and discuss what had happened just three days after the occurrence. His first response was to ask why I hadn't brought it up at the meeting—a question I couldn't answer. I wish I had brought it up at the meeting, because then I could have renegotiated my role with the whole committee instead of just with Rich.

When your contract appears to be starting to change or the client is changing some of the ground rules, your leverage on the situation is highest right at the moment of the change. The longer you wait to raise the issue of the client's wanting more or less from you, the more difficult it is to renegotiate your contract. Still, no matter how long the time lags, the discussion of a changed contract needs to take place. It helps a little when you know going into it that the contracting process takes place over and over through the life of the project. You are constantly recycling through different stages of the consultation, and negotiation really is ceaseless.

## SOME OTHER SPECIFIC AGONIES

The need for ceaseless negotiation is just one of the agonies of contracting. Other potential difficulties and setbacks exist at every step of the contracting phase. Here are some of them.

## The Flirtatious Client

Sometimes you find out that you are the fourth person the manager has talked to about this project. You could respond to this knowledge by selling harder. Another option is to ask the manager why a decision is so difficult. Preoccupation with the consultant selection process usually means the manager wants to start a project but does not really want anything to happen. Otherwise why control the process so meticulously?

## Credentials? With Your Experience!

Questions about your credentials will regularly come up over the course of your career: "What have you done elsewhere?" or "What are your credentials?" There are two responses to this kind of grilling. One is to have your favorite war story well rehearsed and tell it. Your best hope is that it will speak to the client's situation. The second response, after the war story, is the question: "Are you concerned about whether I can really help you?" If the manager owns up to being concerned, don't take it personally. Managers (no matter how burly or gruff) are likely to see themselves as beyond help. They need reassurance that improvement is possible, so give it to them. Don't get into a defensive recital of your degrees, clients, and successes. It is too easy to let other people's doubts about you trigger your own.

## Go-Betweens

Sometimes there is a go-between between the consultant and the manager—someone on the manager's staff or from another department. A go-between who is too active or protective can build up a screen between you and the manager, and then it will be hard for you to find out where things really stand. Try to have direct contact with the real client as early and often as possible. Urge the manager's attendance at meetings with you to discuss the project.

## Defining the Problem to Death: A Common Mistake

In conducting consulting skills workshops and watching hundreds of consultants try to deal with a resistant client, one mistake stands out clearly: we consultants spend too much time in the contracting meeting trying to define the problem.

If we have a one-hour meeting, we will spend fifty minutes understanding the problem and leave only ten minutes to conduct the real business of the meeting—negotiating wants and dealing with concerns of control and exposure. This happens because during the meeting, we can take on the confusion or obstinacy of the client. We aren't sure what to do next, so we keep asking questions about the problem. It provides a nice relief for us and the client.

Don't spend so much time figuring the problem out. You will have the whole consultation to do that. If you don't know what to do next or if the meeting is going nowhere, you have two choices:

- Look at the client and say, "Let's stop talking about the problem for a moment. Tell me what you want from me."

- Look at the client and start making statements. Anything will do; it will lead you to where you ought to be going. Say, "You seem confused about the nature of this problem"; then, "Here is what I would like from you to help us take the next step." Then move into the exchange of wants.

Keep the discussion of the problem to no more than 35 percent of the total time for the meeting. If you really don't understand what the client sees as a problem, then negotiate a small contract to find out more. If you can't get clear after twenty minutes of meeting, you aren't going to get clear in the meeting no matter how many questions you ask.

## THE VIRTUAL WORLD

Communicating with people not in the room is a growing reality. We act as if we are in a new technological age, but the invention of writing and then printing put virtual work and communicating well under way. People have been talking to people who are not in the room for a long time.

What is new is how the virtual way of being has entered every corner of our lives. We now e-mail people sitting next to us. We find love, companionship, and conversation on the Internet. We work on a regular basis with people we will never meet. We receive coaching and therapy from across the country, with no eye contact necessary. As consultants, we not only want to have influence with people over whom we have no control, we now may not even get to meet them. Plus, every minute of the day we are on call. We know that we have surrendered our privacy and solitude, our evenings and weekends in the way we sneak a look at our e-mails when no one is watching.

We are so dazzled by the speed and expanding applications of the technology that we begin to think it is an adequate substitute for what it replaces. It is sold so hard as the answer that if you question it, you are called a Luddite—a stone wall against progress. In fact, the Luddites were right in their belief that industrialization would have huge negative effect on the family, the community, and traditional values. But that is not the point here. The point is that the hard cultural sell about the magic of technology creates an exaggeration of value. Speed

is good, convenience is good, but a food processor never guaranteed a good meal and e-mailing my kids does not mean I have anything important to say to them.

Computer technology and the virtual world it creates is amazing, but it is just what it is. It is technology. It is not a substitute for relatedness, authenticity, meaning, or being of service in the world. It may not even be helpful. The big advantages of the virtual world are entertainment, speed, and cost. First, the virtual world is very entertaining. It is the answer to boredom, a distraction from all that ails me. I can fill every empty waking moment of my life with texting, e-mails, videos, podcasts, and e-books. And I control the media I turn to, so a little power is thrown in.

The big advantage for commerce is that it is fast and cheap, and these are good things. The key is to understand what aspects of work are amenable to more speed and are cost sensitive. This is where the virtual world is a mixed blessing for support functions and consulting.

Any work that is relationship based at its core is going to struggle to deliver outcomes when more speed is expected and actual time in the room with people keeps shrinking.

No matter how virtual we become, the consulting process set out in this book still applies, whether we are in the room together or on the air-waves or in cyberspace. We still need to be connected and ask how the other feels about working together. We need to exchange wants, search for doubts, listen for and surface resistance, ask the same questions in discovery. Teams still have to work together, and we have to be willing to speak to that issue. Here are some specific issues to pay attention to.

## Senses Are Obsolescent

One major limitation of virtual technology in the consulting process is that most of my senses are made obsolete. Electronic sound and sight emit a small portion of the information that being with someone produces even if the picture is life size and perfect and the sound is at its highest quality.

Working in the virtual world, I give up the ability to touch and sense and experience another human being. I see only a small portion of the surroundings that are important to understanding. There is nothing to do about this other than not pretend that electronic dialogue and relationships are equivalent to being in the room.

The effect is that all that we do electronically requires more care and attention than if we were in the room together. As a consultant, I have to double-check what the client wants from me. I have to trust my listening more diligently when I hear or see a pattern of resistance. I have to consciously create space for silence, which is more difficult long distance. The questions halfway through a meeting of "How are we doing?" or "Are you getting what you want from this?" are even more essential in the virtual world, since we know we are missing so much.

## E-mail Doesn't Count

One thing we know about e-mail is that meanings are guaranteed to get distorted. Mild sarcasm can be taken as disappointment, humor as lack of caring, and real anger gets exploded and has a longer shelf life on e-mail. Plus, if you send a message by e-mail and think that the message has reached and has been seen by the receiver simply because you sent it, you are wrong half the time. E-mail is great for the logistical side of life, but risky for the relationship side.

## Efficiency Has Hidden Costs

There has been a movement to take everything we do in person or by hand and substitute an electronic or online process for it. The online substitutes for shopping, meeting, learning, searching, and being entertained cover most of the ground.

In the realm of human development, a major concern to every consultant, there have been significant efforts to substitute online training for direct classroom experience. Online learning has been sold as learning that can occur on demand and at the convenience of the learner. All that is true. What goes unspoken is how that affects the quality of the experience and the type of learning that is possible.

The Internet is great for getting facts, to become well informed, to find out the latest news right away. It is one big encyclopedia and news service. Its possibilities are very seductive but there is a human cost is hidden in all the excitement. If our consulting is in the area of transformation and people's relationships with each other are vital to the outcome we seek, then the virtual world is a minor player.

Just as my Facebook and LinkedIn profiles have little to do with who I am, an alternative future cannot be created by a gathering of avatars. No matter how they are clothed or pictured or styled after each of us. Saccharin is not sugar, margarine is not butter. Although Skype has value—for example, I can see an electronic image of my godson Pete in Singapore—it is an electronic simulation. The technology is nice, convenient, and inexpensive, and I will take it. But it is a qualitatively poor substitute for Pete and me being in the room together.

## Make Distinctions in the Virtual World

Where this takes us as consultants is the need to decide when a virtual substitute for relatedness is useful and when coming together in person is required. Basically it is a question of depth and risk. Certain consultative questions are more difficult and emotionally require more of us than others.

Questions that the virtual world can handle are the more cognitive and nonpersonal ones—for example:

- What is the presenting problem?

- What is the history of this situation?

- Who are the players involved?

- What is the business case for our proceeding?

- How much time will this take?

- Who should be on the design team?

- What goals and outcomes are you looking for?

Make no mistake: these are important questions.

The questions that are more relational and personal and not handled well by the virtual world are:

- How do you feel about working with me?

- What is your contribution to creating the problem we are concerned with?

- How well does this group work together?

- How do you feel about the amount of control and vulnerability you have over this project?

- What doubts and reservations do you have that anything will change here?

- What have you learned about yourself in this process?

These are the questions that build intimacy. They are the questions that create the social fabric that gets us through the hard moments of a project. They are the questions where we need all our senses in order to have the influence that we seek.

You may have your own distinctions, depending on your own work, but knowing which parts of a project can be handled virtually and which demand people being in the room with one another is now a vital part of the contracting phase. We need to ask for what we think is important. This means we need to get real about the virtual world. We need to neither romanticize it nor resist it. It is a useful and entertaining tool, and it can also be a defense against engagement. Seeing the distinction is essential to the difference we are going to make.

Go to www.flawlessconsulting.com for the Bonner case, a scenario of a small consulting project that illustrates some of the essentials of the consulting skills covered so far: the phases of consulting, the steps in the contracting process and its recycling nature, plus the objective of maintaining a 50/50 balance in taking responsibility for the consulting action.

# CHAPTER 7

# THE INTERNAL CONSULTANT

**W**HEN I RUN WORKSHOPS ON CONSULTING SKILLS for internal consultants, the participants sit patiently and listen to lectures on "Saying No to a Manager," "Confront Problems with the Manager as They Happen," "Make Your Own Wants and Demands Clear," and "Deal Directly with the Politics of the Situation." Eventually someone in the back of the room raises a hand and says, "That's easy for you to say. You're an outside consultant. You don't have to live inside the organization you are consulting to. We are internal consultants. If a line manager gets mad at us, we are in trouble. You just don't understand what it's like."

I used to resist. I would say the issues are the same. They have to do the same things I do with clients, and on and on and on. The group would then lean back, I would announce a coffee break, and they would talk excitedly to each other and ignore me. I don't resist anymore. Partly it is to avoid rejection. I also have clearer ideas about how internal and external consulting are in some ways different. Some of the noticeable differences are listed in Figure 6.

**Figure 6.** Noticeable Differences Between Internal and External Consultants

|  | Internal Consultants | External Consultants |
| --- | --- | --- |
| Clothing | Blue and gray suits or skirts and jackets; occasional sport clothes depending on company | Sweaters, turtlenecks, slacks, pinpoint cotton shirts, sports coat, brown and green, occasional gold bracelet or Buddhist prayer beads obtained at global spiritual retreat |
|  | High-end country club business casual on specified days |  |
| Favorite words and phrases | Measurement | That raises an interesting issue |
|  | Long run | Fundamental and underlying |
|  | Quick | Deal |
|  | Practical | Honor your integrity |
|  | Objectives | Work through |
|  | Background | Dilemma |
|  | Cost | Model |
|  |  | Implications |
|  |  | Reassess at some point in the process |
| Personal life | Reasonably stable, responsible, and rewarding | Like Hiroshima right after the bomb: on the road so much has seen the world but can't remember it |
|  | Only one divorce, and maintaining good relations with ex-spouse and kids |  |
| Fantasy life | Wish for the freedom and variety of the external consultant | Wish for the continuity and stability of the internal consultant |
| Underlying anxiety | Being ignored, rejected, and treated as unimportant | Being ignored, rejected, and treated as unimportant |

# IMPORTANT DIFFERENCES BETWEEN INTERNAL AND EXTERNAL CONSULTANTS

As an internal consultant, you are at every moment embedded in some part of the hierarchy and the politics of the organization. You have a boss you must satisfy (at least to some extent). Your own department has certain goals it must achieve. Technical departments have a new process they want to introduce to the operating units. Financial groups want new control procedures adopted.

How does having a boss and having departmental objectives affect the way internal consultants work and contract with line managers?

- It is often not possible to respond just to the line manager's own wants and needs. You have procedures that you want the line manager to adopt that may be in conflict with what the manager's own philosophy and style are.

- You may get evaluated on how many managers adopt the support group's programs. You are often asked to sell your own department's approach, and the pressure to do this can be immense.

- You are often expected to convert an adversary. A certain line manager may have rejected your department's services for years, but it is up to you to bring him or her into the fold.

- Having one key manager angry at you can be a disaster. The potential number of clients is limited to the managers in one organization. If you blow one or two jobs, word can get around fast, and the demand for your services can disappear quickly. If this happens, you are out of a job, even if they keep you on the payroll.

- You have a status and job level that is known to most people in the organization. This can limit your access to key high-level people you should be contacting directly. An external consultant's status and level are more ambiguous, so they can bounce around from level to level more easily.

- The difficulty of being a prophet in your own land is overplayed and can be used as a defense, but there is some truth in it. Because you work for the same organization, line managers can see you as being captured by the same forces and madness that impinge on them. Thus, they may be a little slower to trust you and recognize that you have something special to offer them.

What this means is that internal consultants are often operating more by mandate than by choice. This makes internal contracting a higher-risk proposition. In the end, all the internal consultant can do is make explicit the costs of mandated change. Just because you do not have the final decision is not a reason to avoid questioning the project.

External consultants face most of these issues, but they do not have the same intensity. Being outside the organization, there is a potentially wider market for their services, and as long as their clients are happy, their own consulting organization is unlikely to complain.

The difference in intensity and setting for these issues makes the internal consultant's position more delicate and more vulnerable. This creates constraints on how internal consultants contract with clients and how much risk they feel willing to take in giving honest feedback. If the constraints lead to cautious behavior in the long run, the internal consultant can come to be used only as a pair of hands. If they ignore the constraints altogether, they may be seen as immature and disloyal and charged with "not being sensitive to how we operate around here."

The consulting approach described in this book is a way for internal consultants to operate in the realm of higher risk and higher payoff and still maintain the respect and appreciation of clients. After all, all you have to do is consult flawlessly. The rest of this chapter describes a few things to be especially careful about if you are an internal consultant.

## TRIANGLES AND RECTANGLES

The meeting with a line manager as a client is often only the beginning of the contracting process. At a minimum, the internal support person must also contract with his or her own supervisor.

Each internal consulting group—whether it is a technical engineering group, a financial auditing group, a personnel group, a corporate support group—has its own priority projects it is pushing, and it has a set of beliefs about how directive or participative they want to be with their clients. Technical organizations have certain innovative processes they want their technical consultants to sell to the operating units. Marketing groups have certain positioning and pricing strategies to be sold to their clients.

Each support group has agreed to meet some objectives that its internal consultants will have to advocate to its client line managers. Thus, often consultants must both serve the needs of the client and fulfill a contract with their own management to implement these priorities. This forces the boss into the contracting process and means internal consultants are always in at least a triangular contract (Figure 7).

**Figure 7.** A Triangular Contract

**Figure 8.** A Rectangular Contract

Sometimes the contract is a rectangle or even a pentagon (Figure 8).

The rectangular contract can begin with a general understanding between the consultant's boss and the client's boss. This means the consultant is showing up for work with the client in a situation in which neither of them has particularly chosen the consultation and yet they have a given commitment to begin. The effect of this situation is to prolong the contracting phase. It is desirable for the consultant to meet with each party of the contract to clarify expectations. Sometimes this may not be possible, but at a minimum you can know what you are up against and not treat the contracting as a simple process. Each side of the rectangle or triangle needs to be explored before the discovery process begins.

## Your Boss's Expectations

As it turns out, when you include all parties in the contracting framework, many apparent problems between internal consultants and their clients are merely symptoms of problems between internal consultants and their own bosses. The boss can have expectations of you as a consultant that you cannot fulfill. You may feel that you can never say no or that you have to convert very difficult clients.

I once asked a group of engineering consultants what messages their own organization sends about how to conduct their business. Their answers form a set of norms around internal consulting:

"No matter what, get the job done."

"If the technical issue is that important, don't worry about the sensitivities of the client."

"Don't upset or antagonize the client."

"Stay long enough to do the job, but don't stay too long."

"Convince the client to do what you recommend." "Sell the company way."

"Every problem can be solved."

"Every client can be reached."

"Be loyal to your own organization."

"Don't wash dirty linen in public."

"Don't evaluate people or bad-mouth anyone."

"Never admit a mistake to a client."

"Contracts with clients should be very, very flexible."

"Don't make any commitments for future work."

"Keep personalities out of it."

"Always stay low-key and smooth. No emotion."

"Have suitcase, will travel."

"Act with dignity, tact, confidence, and decorum."

This list of expectations, of course, represents unrealistic pressures that consultants can feel; they are not all the spoken words of any one supervisor. They do represent the quandary that an internal consultant is in when the contract with his or her boss is not clear and explicit.

## Contracts with Your Boss

Given these unfulfillable cultural norms about internal consultants, let us look at their contracts with their supervisors. The first step in contracting is to identify what you want, so we asked a group of internal consultants what they wanted from their bosses in order to deal with the pressures they were under. Here is what they said:

"A clear definition of the job before I am sent out on a project."

"Access to the boss."

"Assistance on the nontechnical and political elements of the project."

"Don't overcommit me all the time."

"Freedom to negotiate contracts based on the particulars of the situation."

"Minimum bias on how the project should turn out, what the recommendations should look like."

The same group of consultants identified what they wanted from their clients. Notice how similar the lists are:

"A clear definition of the job."

"Access to the person who really represents the client organization; also access to data."

"Work the problem together—cooperation."

"Commitment to the project."

"Share the blame and glory."

"To be wanted, to feel useful."

"No bias about the outcome."

"Take care of physical needs to accomplish the job."

"Openness and feedback."

"Feedback on what happened after I left."

The clarity of understanding and agreement with your boss greatly affects your ability to respond appropriately and flawlessly with your clients. If you are unclear about the contract with your boss, you will tend to get involved in soft contracts with clients. There will be a tendency to give in to clients too easily, to be unwilling to back away from projects that have a low chance of success. You also may find yourself pressuring for your own support organization's priorities past the point of reasonableness, and this will distance you from your clients.

**Try This Exercise**

First, list the key wants you have of your boss. Then ask your boss to make a list of the key wants they have of you. Then exchange lists  and meet together to see whether you can agree on a contract that represents a reasonable balance between what your group or department requires to meet its commitments to the overall organization and what you need to be responsive to the needs and priorities of your clients.

If the conversation does not go well, you are ready for the next two chapters—on understanding and dealing with resistance.

# CHAPTER 8

# UNDERSTANDING RESISTANCE

$\mathsf{T}$HE HARDEST PART of consulting is coping successfully with resistance from the client. As we consult, it is natural for us to feel that if we can present our ideas clearly and logically, and if we have the best interests of the client at heart, our clients will accept our expertise and follow our suggestions. We soon discover that no matter how reasonably we present data and recommendations, clients present us with resistance.

Resistance doesn't always happen, but when it does, it is puzzling and frustrating. In the face of resistance, we begin to view the client as stubborn and irrational, and we usually end up simply presenting the data and justifying the recommendations more loudly and more forcibly.

The key to understanding the nature of resistance is to realize that it is a reaction to an emotional process taking place within the client. It is not a reflection of the conversation we are having with the client on an objective, logical, rational level. Resistance is a predictable, natural reaction against the process of being helped and against the process of having to face up to difficult organizational problems.

Resistance then is not only predictable and natural; it is a necessary part of the learning process. When as consultants we wish resistance would never appear or would just go away, we are, by that attitude, posing an obstacle to the client's integrating and learning from our expertise. For a client to learn something important about how to handle a difficult problem, the feelings of resistance need to be expressed directly before the client is ready to genuinely accept and use what the consultant has to offer.

The skill in dealing with resistance is to

- Be able to identify when resistance is taking place

- View resistance as a natural process and a sign that you are on target

- Support the client in expressing the resistance directly

- Not take the expression of the resistance personally or as an attack on you or your competence

This is hard to do and is what this chapter and the next are all about.

## THE FACES OF RESISTANCE

Resistance takes many forms, some of them very subtle and elusive. In the course of a single meeting, you may encounter a variety of forms. As you begin to deal with it in one form, sometimes it will fade and reappear in a different body.

For technically oriented consultants—such as engineers, accountants, and computer and systems people—resistance can be hard to identify. Our technical backgrounds so orient us to data, facts, and logic that when we are asked to perceive an emotional or interpersonal process, it is like trying to see the picture on a badly out-of-focus photograph.

The following sections on common forms of resistance are intended to help bring the picture into focus.

### Give Me More Detail

The client keeps asking for finer and finer bits of information: "What do people who work the eleven-to-seven shift think?"

"When you put the numbers together, what worksheets did you use? And were the numbers written in red or blue ink?" The client seems to have an insatiable appetite to know everything about what is happening. No matter how much information you give the client, it is never enough. Each conversation leaves you feeling that the next time you meet, you should bring even more backup data with you. You also get the feeling that a huge amount of time is spent gathering information and too little time is spent deciding what you are going to do. Some questions from the client are reasonable; clients, after all, need to know what is going on. When you start to get impatient with the questions, even though you are able to answer them, that is the moment to start suspecting the request for detail is a form of resistance rather than a simple quest for information.

## Flooding You with Detail

A corollary to the request for detail is to be given too much detail. You ask a client how this problem got started and the response is, "Well, it all got started ten years ago on a Thursday afternoon in September. I think I was wearing a blue shirt, and the weather outside was overcast and threatening rain. I hope I am not boring you, but I think it is important for you to understand the background of the situation." The client keeps giving you more and more information, which you understand less and less. The moment you start to get bored or confused about what all this has to do with the problem at hand, you should begin to suspect that what you are getting is resistance and not just an effusive attempt to give you all the facts.

## Time

The client says she would really like to go ahead with your project but the timing is just a little off. You are kept on the string, and the client keeps impressing you with how busy things are right now. In fact, the client barely has time to meet with you. Sometimes this form of resistance gets expressed by constant interruptions during your meetings. The client starts taking phone calls or keeps glancing at their Black-Berry. Or someone pops into the office and they turn to me and say,

"Excuse me just a minute, Peter, but I have to settle this one issue with Ann." And the client starts talking to Ann while I sit there.

The message the client seems to be giving in all these examples?

- This organization is such an exciting place to work in, something is going on all the time. Aren't you impressed, and don't you wish you worked here too?

- My organization has so little time.

- I have so little time.

- I want you to think I am refusing you because of the lack of time, not because your proposal gives me feelings of great discomfort.

The whole time issue, which we all face every day, is most often resistance against the client's having to tell you how he or she really feels about your project. When you find in December that the client would really like to do the project but can't get started until the third quarter of next year, you should begin to suspect you are encountering resistance.

## Impracticality

The client keeps reminding you that this is the "Real World and we are facing Real World problems." I must have heard about the Real World a thousand times. Makes me wonder whether clients think we live in a fantasy world. This form of resistance from the client accuses us of being impractical and academic, even idealistic, the ultimate sin. As with many other forms of resistance, there may be some truth in the statement, but then there is some truth in almost any statement. It is the intensity of the emphasis on "practicality" that leads you to suspect you are up against an emotional issue.

## I'm Not Surprised

It is always amazing to me how important it is for people not to be surprised. It seems that whatever happens in the world is okay as long as they are not surprised. When you have completed a study, you can tell a manager that the building has collapsed, the workers have just walked out, the chief financial officer has just run off with the vice president of marketing, and the IRS is knocking on the door, and the manager's first response is, "I'm not surprised." It's as if being surprised is the worst thing in the world that could happen.

The manager's fear of surprise is really the desire to always be in control. When we run into it, it is kind of deflating. It can signal to us that what we have developed is really not that important or unique. It downplays our contribution. See the client's desire not to be surprised for what it is: a form of resistance rather than a reflection on our work.

## Attack

The most blatant form of resistance is when the client attacks us. Angry words, a red face, fist pounding on the desk, finger pointing in your face, punctuating the end of every sentence. It leaves the consultant feeling like a bumbling child who not only has done poor work but has somehow violated a line of morality that should never be crossed. Our response to attack is often either to withdraw or to respond in kind. Both responses mean that we are beginning to take the attack personally and not seeing it as one other form that the resistance is taking.

## Confusion

A client who comes to us for help is experiencing some legitimate confusion. This may not be resistance, but just a desire for clarity. After things become clear to you, however, and you explain it two or three times and the client keeps claiming to be confused or does not understand, start to think that confusion may be the client's difficulty in saying no to you.

## Silence

This is the toughest of all. We keep making overtures to the client and get little response in return. The client is passive. A client may present no particular reaction to what you are proposing. When you ask for a reaction, the client says, "Keep on going. I don't have any problems with what you are saying. If I do, I'll speak up." Don't you believe it. Silence never means consent. If you are dealing with something important to the organization, it is not natural for the client to have no reaction.

Silence means that the reaction is being blocked. For some people, silence or withholding reactions is really a fight style. They are saying by their actions, "I am holding on so tightly to my position and my feelings that I won't even give you words." Beware the silent client. If you think a meeting went smoothly because the manager didn't raise any objections, don't trust it. Ask yourself whether the client gave you any real support or showed any real enthusiasm or got personally involved in the action. If there were few signs of life, begin to wonder whether silence was the form the client's resistance was taking.

## Intellectualizing

When a person shifts the discussion from deciding how to proceed and starts exploring theory after theory about why things are the way they are, you are face-to-face with intellectualizing as resistance. The client says, "A fascinating hypothesis is implied by these results. I wonder if there is an inverse relationship between this situation and the last three times we went under. The crisis seems to have raised a number of questions."

Spending a lot of energy spinning theories is a way of taking the pain out of a situation. It is a defense most of us use when we get into a tight spot. This is not to knock the value of a good theory or the need to understand what is happening. It is a caution against colluding with the client in engaging in ceaseless wondering, when the question is whether you and the client are going to be able to face up to a difficult situation. The time to suspect intellectualizing is when it begins at a high-tension moment or in a high-tension meeting. When this happens, your task is to bring the discussion back to action, away from theories.

## Moralizing

Moralizing resistance makes great use of certain words and phrases: "those people" and "should" and "they need to understand." When you hear them being used, you know you are about to go on a trip into a world of how things ought to be, which is simply a moralizing defense against reality. People use the phrase "those people" about anyone who's not in the room at the time. It is a phrase of superiority used in describing people who are usually at a lower organizational level than the speaker or are unhappy about something the speaker has done and therefore "really don't understand the way things have to be."

Phrases of superiority are actually ways of putting oneself on a pedestal. Pedestal sitting is always a defense against feeling some uncomfortable feelings and taking some uncomfortable actions. The phrase, "They need to understand," actually means, "I understand; they don't. Why don't they see things clearly and with the same broad perspective that I do? Ah, the burdens of knowing are great and unceasing!" Frequently "those people" the speaker is talking about do understand. They understand perfectly. The problem for the speaker is that they don't agree. So instead of confronting the conflict in views, the speaker escapes into a moralistic position.

Moralizing can be seductive to consultants. The moralizing manager is inviting you to come into a select circle of people who know what is best for "those people" and who know what they "need to understand." This is an elite position to be in; it has the feeling of power, and it is well protected. If the rest of the organization does not appreciate what you do, this is just further indication how confused they are and how much more they need you. Resist the temptation with as much grace and persistence as possible.

## Compliance

The most difficult form of resistance to see comes from the compliant manager who totally agrees with you and eagerly wants to know what to do next. It is hard to see compliance as resistance because you are getting exactly what you want: agreement and respect. If you really trust the concept that in each manager there is some ambivalence about your help, then when you get no negative reaction at all, you know something is missing.

Each client has some reservations about a given course of action. If the reservations don't get expressed to you, they will come out somewhere else, perhaps in a more destructive way. I would rather the reservations were said directly to me; then I can deal with them. You can tell when the agreeable client is resisting by compliance. You are getting this form of resistance any time there is almost total absence of any reservations and a low energy agreement. If the agreement is made with high energy, enthusiasm, and a sincere understanding of what you and the client are facing, you might simply feel lucky and not take it as resistance, even if few reservations are expressed. But beware the client who expresses a desire to quickly get to solutions without any discussion of problems. Beware as well of the client who acts dependent on you and implies that whatever you do is fine.

## Methodology

If there has been elaborate data collection in your project, the first wave of questions will be about your methods. If you administered a questionnaire, you will be asked about how many people responded, at what level of response, and whether the findings are statistically significant at the .05 level. Next will be questions about how people in the guardhouse and on the night shift responded.

Questions about method represent legitimate needs for information for the first ten minutes, enough time for you to establish the credibility of the project if the questions are really for information. As the questions about method go past the ten-minute mark, you should cautiously begin to view them as resistance. The purpose of the meeting is not to grill you on methods; it is to understand the problem and decide what to do about it. Repeated questions about method or suggestions of alternate methods can serve to delay the discussion of problems and actions.

## Flight into Health

Undoubtedly the most subtle form of resistance occurs when, somewhere in the middle or toward the end of the project, it appears that the client no longer has the problem that you were addressing in the first place. As you get closer and closer to the time for the client to face the issue and act on the problem, you begin to hear about how much better things seem to be getting.

Here are just two variations on this theme:

- If profits were bad when you started the project, as soon as they start to pick up a little, the manager comes to you and says that people seem to be feeling better now that the profit picture has improved. Maybe the need for your services has diminished somewhat.

- You talk to the client in May and agree to start the project on June 20. When you call on June 10 to confirm the beginning of the project, the manager says, "We can still begin the project if we want to, but for some reason, it appears the problem is not so severe." Nothing can be identified that changed the way the group does business. What actually happened was that the group realized that on June 20, they were really going to have to start confronting their problems, so it seemed easier to act as if the problems weren't so important now.

I once worked as a consultant to a company where the engineering and manufacturing groups were having a difficult time working together. In the discovery phase, I learned the groups had a ten-year history of conflict at all levels, the president of the company had sided with the manufacturing group and was constantly attacking the engineering group, and responsibilities and authority between the two groups were overlapping and unclear. Just before I was to feed back the results of the study, the president called me and said that the head of engineering was changing jobs. He felt that because this one person was leaving, the problems would probably go away. He was holding on to the good feeling that this person was leaving as a way of not confronting the underlying problems facing these groups for the past ten years.

The manager's process of resisting through health is similar to what happens when a fighting couple finally makes an appointment with a marriage counselor: as the session approaches, they find they are getting along better and better. By the time they get to the marriage counselor, they look at each other and say they aren't quite sure what the problems were because they have been getting along so well lately.

Of course, there is nothing wrong with the situation improving for the client, but most surface symptoms have underlying problems that require attention. If all of a sudden the client is telling you that the symptoms are improving, I would be concerned that they are grasping for improvement too dearly and smoothing over what should be the real focus of your consultation.

### Pressing for Solutions

The last form of resistance is the client's desire for solutions, solutions, solutions: "Don't talk to me about problems; I want to hear solutions." Because the consultant is also eager to see the problems solved, some collusion can take place between consultant and client if the discussion of solutions is not held off a little.

The desire for solutions can prevent the client from learning anything important about the nature of the problem. It also keeps the client dependent on consultants to solve these problems. If the line manager hasn't the patience or stomach to stop and examine the problem, then the solutions are not going to be implemented effectively. Recognize that the rush to solutions can be a defense and a particularly seductive form of resistance for the consultant who is eager to solve problems.

## WHAT ARE CLIENTS RESISTING WHEN THEY ARE RESISTING US?

Sounds like a song title, but it's important to know.

The main thing to do in coping successfully with resistance is to not take it personally. When you encounter resistance, you are the one in the room. Clients look straight at you while they are being defensive. You are the one who has to answer the questions and weather the storm. It is natural to feel that the resistance is aimed at you. The resistance is not aimed at you. It is not you the client is defending against. Resistant clients are defending against the fact that they are going to have to make a difficult choice, take an unpopular action, confront some reality that they have emotionally been trying to avoid.

If you have been brought in to solve a problem, it means the client organization has not been able to solve it themselves. It is not that the managers aren't smart enough to solve it. Rather, they have not been able to see it clearly. They are so close to the problem and have such an emotional investment in any possible solutions that they need a third party to define the problem and possible solutions for them. In the problem or solution, then, is some difficult reality that the client has had a hard time seeing and confronting.

The difficult realities that clients are stuck on will vary—for example:

- Someone may have to be fired or told they are not performing adequately.

- People in the group may be very dissatisfied and the manager may be reluctant to surface the dissatisfaction.

- The manager may feel inadequate in some part of the job and not want to face that inadequacy.

- The political situation may be risky, and the manager doesn't want to make waves.

- The task at hand may require skills that do not exist in the organization now. This may mean getting rid of some people, which is always hard to do.

- The manager's boss may be part of the problem, and the manager may not want to confront the boss.

- The organization may be selling products or services to a declining market, and this is too discouraging to deal with.

- The manager knows he operates autocratically and doesn't want to change, yet sees the negative effects of his behavior.

- A developmental project in which a lot of money has been invested is turning up some negative results. This means bad news has to be sent up the line, and promises made earlier will be taken back.

All these difficult realities involve painful problems that seem to promise painful solutions. Most very technical or business-related problems are in some way caused or maintained by how that problem is being managed. When managers are being defensive, they are defending their own managerial adequacy—a natural thing to defend. It is even worthwhile defending. A resistant manager is much more concerned about their own esteem and competence than about our skills as consultants.

This is what resistance is about: defending against some difficult reality and how the manager has been handling it. We consultants come in and, as part of our job, start pointing to the difficult realities. It is important that we help the client face the difficulties. We shouldn't avoid them just because the client will become resistant.

When you encounter resistance, you are seeing the surface expression of more underlying anxieties. Two things are happening: the client is feeling uncomfortable, and the client is expressing the discomfort indirectly.

The reason consultants feel as if they are the victim of the resistance is that the client's discomfort is being expressed indirectly. If the client were able to be authentic and put the concern directly into words by saying—"I am concerned I am losing control of this group," or "I feel I am ill equipped to handle this particular situation," or "People expect things from me that I just can't deliver"—we consultants would not feel attacked. We would feel very supportive toward the manager.

The manager's direct expression of underlying concerns is not resistance. Resistance occurs only when the concerns about facing the difficult realities and the choice not to deal with them are expressed indirectly. They are expressed indirectly by blaming lack of detailed data, not enough time, impracticality, not enough budget, lack of understanding by "those people," and so on, as the reasons not to proceed with a project or implement some recommendations.

## UNDERLYING CONCERNS

If I am facing resistance and trying to understand what the client is really concerned about, I would wager the client was concerned about either control or vulnerability. If what you are suggesting does not generate some resistance from the client, it is probably because your proposal does not threaten the manager's control or feeling of organizational security.

## Control

Maintaining control is at the center of the value system of most organizations. There is a belief in control that goes beyond effectiveness or good organizational performance. Many managers believe in maintaining control even if keeping control results in poorer performance. Case after case demonstrates that more participative forms of management are more productive, yet the practice of participative management is not common. I have seen a division of one company where the controls on the management information system were proven to be a major obstacle to improving productivity, yet the manager chose to keep the controls at the expense of better performance.

Control is the coin of the realm in organizations. The whole reward system is geared around how much control, responsibility, and authority you have. When you perform well, you don't get a lot more money; you get more control. At some point in history, organizations realized that you can't pay people enough money to commit themselves like they do, so control is held up as the reward.

The message in all this is that control is valued very, very highly. There is nothing wrong with having control, and being out of control is a very anxious state to be in. When we get resistance, one good guess is that the manager feels he or she is going to lose control.

## Vulnerability

Concern that the manager will get hurt is the second major issue that gives rise to most of the resistance that we encounter. Organizations are competitive and political systems. It is very important to stay ahead of your peers, stay in favor with your boss, and maintain the loyalty and support of your subordinates. To do all three of these and also get your job done is difficult. As you move up in an organization and deal with people at higher and higher levels, you realize that the feeling of being judged and having to prove yourself again and again is part of every position in the organization, all the way up to the chief executive officer.

Politics is the exercise of power. Organizations operate like political systems, except there is no voting. The impact your consulting project has on the political situation and the power of your client is a very important consideration. When you get resistance, it may be that you are unintentionally disturbing whatever political equilibrium has been established.

An example comes from a research and development department where the group doing exploratory research had always reigned supreme and independent. The product development groups were much more tightly controlled and held accountable for short-term results. We were asked to help in restructuring the whole R&D department because the R&D vice president had a strong feeling that inefficiencies and overlap existed and the department was not operating as one organization. During the project, most of the resistance came from the exploratory research group. They would come late to meetings, question our methods, then be silent, and say in the end, "Whatever you think is fine with us."

So what was behind their resistance? Were our methods really faulty? Did they object to the technical basis on which our project was established? No. What they were resisting was the fact that right now, they were in a favored and powerful organizational position. They had high status, high autonomy, and a free hand at gathering resources and starting projects of their choosing. Underneath all the technical and structural questions they had, they were worried about losing status in the political system.

Their concern had some legitimacy. If an exploratory research group loses all its independence, the long-run picture for new products is dim. Yet the group's political concern—losing power in the organization—was expressed very indirectly and was therefore hard to deal with. When they finally stated their concern directly and reduced the resistance, a compromise could be worked out with the vice president and the product development group.

## SOMETIMES IT IS NOT RESISTANCE

Freud once said when he was asked whether the cigar he was smoking was also a phallic symbol, "Sometimes a cigar is just a cigar." In the same way, sometimes client objections are not resistance. The client just doesn't want to do the project.

We can all become paranoid by interpreting every line manager's objections as resistance covering some underlying anxieties. If a manager says directly, "No, I do not choose to begin this project. I don't believe in it," that is not resistance. There is nothing in that statement that blames the consultant or presses the responsibility for the difficulties on the consultant. The manager is taking responsibility for his or her own organization and has a right to choose. If we think it is the wrong choice, well, that's life.

We are getting paid to consult, not to manage. If a manager says to me, "I am in too vulnerable a position to begin this project now," I appreciate the direct expression because I know where I stand with that manager. I don't have to worry whether I should have done something differently. I also feel the manager understands the project and knows the risks, and it turned out that the risks were just too high. I may be disappointed that the project didn't go, but the process was flawless.

## THE FEAR AND THE WISH

Although sometimes consultants and clients may act like adversaries, their feelings and concerns are frequently complementary. There are some common client fears that correspond to similar consultant fears. The same is true for wishes. There are three that bring you down and three that lift you up:

| Client Fears | Consultant Fears |
| --- | --- |
| Helplessness. Futility. "I have no power to change the situation. I am a victim." | "I can have no impact. No reward for the effort." |

Alienation from the organization and people around me. "No one cares about me, and I do not care about them. I don't belong here."

Distance from the client. "We will remain strangers. We will never get close. I'll have to stay totally in role."

Confusion. "I have too much information. I can't sort it out or see clearly."

"I have too little information. They won't or can't tell me what is really happening."

Helplessness, alienation, and confusion are all underlying concerns that can cause clients to be resistant if these concerns are not expressed directly. Their indirect expression can create similar discomfort in the consultant. The way out is to help the client express them directly in words.

We can also look at the flip side of fear and resistance and identify the underlying potential for each client. Each client also has the possibility of flawlessness. As the client moves in this direction, the task of the consultant becomes easier:

**Client Potential**

Has choices and the power to act on the situation. Is an actor, not a victim.

Engages the situation. Feels a part of it. Moves toward the difficult reality and tension.

Choices are clear. Mass of information is simplified

**Consultant Potential**

High impact. Clear payoff for effort expended.

Can be authentic and intimate. No role behavior.

Is included with all information. Sees situation with clarity.

Reaching this potential is one of the objectives of any consultation. The client and consultant are taking responsibility for themselves and the situation they are in. The process of dealing with resistance helps the client move from a position of helplessness, alienation, and confusion to one of choice, engagement, and clarity. The consultant accomplishes this by internally moving from feelings of low impact, distance, and poor information to a position of high impact, authenticity, and clarity.

## Being Dependent, Asking for Help

The climates of most organizations are not conducive to managers' asking for help. Organizations tend to be quite competitive, and asking for help from internal or other consultants can be seen as a sign of weakness. Our culture also signals early, especially in men's lives, that we should be able to solve our own problems and not have to be dependent on anyone else for anything. Being a client goes against the stream of these organizational and cultural messages. Resistance comes in part from the discomforts of being dependent and asking for help.

There is a closely related feeling that also makes being a client difficult: the feeling that nothing can be done to help. Before the consultant is allowed in, the manager has tried to solve the problem with limited or no success. This can lead to the unstated belief that the problem is unsolvable; the manager or group members are so set in their ways that they think the problem must be lived with, not resolved. They feel beyond help. When you encounter resistance, this possibility should be explored. When a manager is feeling pessimistic that the prospect of being helped is remote, this stance is your immediate obstacle to solving the problem. No technical solutions will suffice if the manager has no energy to try it. The manager's feeling of being beyond help is usually not that conscious. The consultant's task is to bring it to the level of awareness. When the manager examines the feeling of futility, hope usually rises.

## Wanting Confirmation, Not Change

When we ask for help, we want both a solution to the problem and confirmation that everything we have done has been perfect.

A colleague of mine, Neale Clapp, mentioned one day that people entering therapy want confirmation, not change. On the surface, it would be ridiculous for a client to bring in a consultant for help, and then tell the consultant that no change was desired and the client did not really want to learn anything. This would not be rational. But that is the point: resistance is an emotional process, not a rational or intellectual one.

In the world of emotions, two opposite feelings often exist at the same time, and both can be genuine. Clients may sincerely want to learn and solve problems. At the same time, they also want support and to be told that they are handling that problem better than anyone else in the country. Approach—avoidance. The resistance is the avoidance. Right behind the avoidance, you will find the approach. When we help the resistance get expressed, it diminishes, and we are then working with a client who is ready and willing to learn and be influenced. Flawlessly dealing with resistance is understanding the two-headed nature of being in the client position and accepting it as okay.

When a line manager has a problem and results are suffering, at least the extent of the suffering is known. The manager has a clear idea of how bad things are and has learned to live with the difficulty. The manager may not like the difficulty but has learned to cope with it. We as consultants come along and offer an alternative way of solving the problem. With the offer is the promise that the new situation will be better than the old situation: there will be less suffering, and results will improve. But this promise carries the manager into the unknown; it requires a change.

Fear of the unknown is a major cause of resistance simply because the unknown is uncertain and unpredictable. We all see couples who have been married ten years and seem to be suffering every minute they are together. We wonder why they stay together. Perhaps it is because at least they know how bad things can get. They know what the downside looks like, and they know they can survive. There is comfort in knowing what to expect. To separate would be unpredictable. The fear of coping with unpredictability may be greater than the pain of staying together. Organizations also value predictability. The wish of systems to remain predictable (don't surprise me) is a defense that consultants have to deal with continually.

Not surprisingly, organizations that are in serious trouble tend to be the most difficult clients. They need to change the most and are least able to do it. For low-performing organizations, the tension of failure is so high that they are unable to take one more risk, and so instead they hold on to their unsatisfactory performance. In these extreme cases, there is probably not much consultants can do to surface the resistance to change. We may just have to accept it.

## OGRES AND ANGELS

In any organization, there are certain managers who are well known for their disdain for support groups and internal consultants. In workshops for people in the same organization—whether they are in human resources, auditing, or engineering—the groups can all name the one or two managers at pretty high levels who are ogres in the eyes of the support groups. The ogres are seen as stubborn, autocratic, insensitive to feelings—the Captain Ahabs of industry. When the subject of resistance comes up, the ogres are mentioned. We all seem to need at least one impossible client in our lives—the client who becomes the lightning rod of our frustrations in consulting. There is also a fatal attraction to the ogres—they embody some consultants' wish to be all powerful and successful.

Ogres don't really exist. A number of times I have heard how fire-eating and mean a certain manager is, and then actually met with the person. I approach the meeting with a lot of discomfort, not wanting to be the latest casualty. What happens is the conversation soon turns to the ogres in the ogre's life. Ogres are not really consumed with vengeance for consultants; they are worried about the people who are giving them a hard time. Behind the ogre's blustery facade are the same concerns all other managers have: losing control and becoming vulnerable. The more aggressive the client is, the more intense are the concerns and the more the client needs support.

Angels are also one-sided images. Every group I have worked with can name a manager who is willing to do anything they ask: a progressive manager, open, trusting, risk taking, secure, intelligent, good looking. But there are no angels either. Angels have a hard time saying no directly. There is a part of the most supportive manager that has reservations, avoids confronting real issues, and wants to maintain the status quo. We need to help that side get expressed. For the manager's sake and for our own sake.

## . . . AND HEROICS

The need for a heroic self-image is another myth about consulting that ought to be laid to rest. We think that we should be able to overcome all obstacles. No matter how difficult the client, or how tough the problem, or how tight the time schedule, we believe it is up to us to do the best we can. This wish to be the heroic consultant more than anything else leads to taking bad contracts. Heroics often entail a hidden bargain. If we take on this bad job now, we will be rewarded later with plums. The essence of the hidden bargain is that it is assumed and never spoken. The rewards in doing consulting need to be in the project as we are doing it now. If the doing has no reward, the project should be challenged.

This heroic impulse in the consultant is the consultant's own resistance against facing the realities of a difficult project. Resist taking unstable or unrealistic contracts. If you can't say no, say, "Later." If you can't say that, say little. Heroes have a hard life. The rewards are overrated. Most heroes, unless they are the best in the world, get paid just about what you are making right now.

# CHAPTER 9

# DEALING WITH RESISTANCE

People use the phrase "overcoming resistance" as though resistance or defensiveness were an adversary to be wrestled to the ground and subdued. "Overcoming resistance" would have you get clever and logical to win the point and convince the client. But there is no way you can talk clients out of their resistance because resistance is an emotional process. Behind the resistance are certain feelings, and you cannot talk people out of how they are feeling.

There are specific steps a consultant can take to help a client get past the resistance and get on with solving the problem. The basic strategy is to help the resistance blow itself out, like a storm, and not to fight it head-on. Feelings pass and change when they are expressed directly. The skill for the consultant is to ask clients to put directly into words what the client is experiencing— to ask the client to be authentic. The most effective way to encourage the client to be authentic is for the consultant to also behave authentically. That's all there is to it.

This way of dealing with resistance—by not fighting it head-on—has a Zen quality to it. If you fight the resistance and feel you have to conquer it, all you will do is intensify the resistance. If a client is objecting to your methodology (and has been doing it for more than ten minutes) and you keep defending the method, citing references, and

recounting other experiences, the client is going to get even more frustrated. The client is likely to become even more committed to finding holes in your method than when the discussion started. The alternative to defending your method is to ask the client more about their concerns and try to get to why your methodology is so important. Getting the client to talk more about their concerns is helping the storm to pass. Defending methodology is keeping the storm alive.

Try this exercise.

Put your palms together in front of your chest. Let your right arm be the client's resistance and your left arm be your response to that resistance. Move your right arm and palm hard to the left against your left palm. Now have the left arm and palm push at the same time, hard to the right. If you hold this position, the two hands stay stuck right in the middle, the strain increases in both your arms, and you soon get tired. That is what happens when you push back against the resistance. You get stuck, the tension goes up, and energy is drained.

Now put your palms together again in the same starting position. Move your right arm and palm to the left hard against your left hand. This time let your left hand give in, so the right hand keeps moving to the left. At some point, your right hand will stop. It will have pushed as far as it can go. If you hold that end position, you will notice that your right hand, the resistance, gets tired and drops of its own weight. The left hand, your response to the resistance, allows the right hand resistance to move to its own ends. Contacted but unopposing, the left hand can maintain its position with no tension and little loss of energy.

This is the way to deal with resistance: encourage full expression of the concerns so that they pass. Remember that resistance is the indirect expression of client reservations. The goal is to help the line manager begin stating the reservations directly and stop the subterfuge. When the client's concerns are stated directly, the consultant knows what the real issues are and can respond effectively.

# THREE STEPS FOR HANDLING RESISTANCE

There are three steps for handling resistance:

1. Identify in your own mind what form the resistance is taking. The skill is to pick up the cues from the manager and then describe to yourself what you see happening.

2. State, in a neutral, unpunishing way, the form the resistance is taking. This is called "naming the resistance." The skill is to find the neutral language.

3. Be quiet. Let the line manager respond to your statement about the resistance.

## Step 1: Pick Up the Cues

People who are technically trained in such disciplines as computer science, engineering, or accounting often find it difficult to recognize the early signs of resistance. Technical training so focuses your attention on facts, figures, data, and the rational level that you are not accustomed to closely paying attention to the interpersonal, emotional level of conversations. Developing skill in dealing with resistance requires knowing what form the resistance is taking, but the first step is simply to notice what is happening.* Here are some ways to pick up the cues.

### Trust What You See More Than What You Hear

Pay attention to the nonverbal messages from the client. Is the client

- Constantly moving away from you?

- Tied up in knots like a pretzel?

- Pointing a finger and clenching the other fist?

- Shaking his head each time you speak?

- Bent over toward you as if they are royalty?

*Gil Gordon, a friend, years ago helped me see how the step of picking up the cues from the client is separate from the step of putting the resistance into words.

Take any of these as a sign that the client is feeling uneasy about this project and is most likely being resistant.

### Listen to Yourself

Another way to know that you are encountering resistance is to use your own body as a thermometer. When you start feeling uneasy in a discussion with the client, it may be an early sign that resistance is on its way. Certainly when you are getting bored or irritated it is evidence that the client is resisting. When a discussion is confronting real issues directly, it is never boring or irritating. When you notice yourself yawning or suppressing some negative feelings, take it as a cue. These reactions of yours act as red flags, attention-getting devices. They are messages that you should begin to put words on the form of resistance you are encountering.

### Listen for Repetition and Telltale Phrases

A sure cue that you are encountering resistance is that you hear the same idea explained to you for the third time. Or you hear yourself answering the same question for the third time. Repetition of ideas and questions is resistance because expressing the idea or answering the questions the first time did not get the job done. Some underlying concern is surfacing indirectly through repetition.

You also hear certain phrases that tell you the client is not feeling understood:

"You have to understand that . . ."

"Let me explain something to you."

"I want to make sure this isn't an academic exercise."

These phrases are aggressive in a subtle way. They express some frustration and treat the consultant as if a serious mistake is about to be made, but somehow this statement from the client is supposed to save us.

There are probably certain phrases you hear a lot that signal difficulty. Take the time to make a list of them now, and update your list as you grow more skilled in picking up the cues of resistance.

## Step 2: Name the Resistance

When you become aware of resistance, the next step is to name it using neutral, everyday language. The skill is to describe the form of the resistance in a way that encourages the client to make a more direct statement of the reservation he or she is experiencing.

Here are some examples of resistance and neutral language describing the form of resistance:

| When the Resistance Takes This Form | Name It by Making This Statement |
| --- | --- |
| Client is avoiding responsibility for the problem or the solution | "You don't see yourself as part of the problem." |
| Flooding you with detail | "You are giving me more detail than I need." |
| One-word answers | "You are giving me very short answers." |
| Changing the subject | "The subject keeps shifting." |
| Compliance | "You seem willing to do anything I suggest. I can't tell what your real feelings are." |
| Silence | "You are very quiet. I don't know how to read your silence." |
| Pressing for solutions | "It's too early for solutions. I'm still trying to find out . . ." |
| Attack | "You are really questioning a lot of what I do. You seem angry about something." |

The easiest way is to look for everyday language to describe the resistance. It is easier to name the resistance if you think of what you would say to a close friend or spouse and say that to the client. The sentiment in this suggestion that is helpful is to keep the statement simple and direct.

Here are some other forms of resistance. Try naming each one in a neutral, nonaggressive way:

- Questions of methodology

- Intellectualizing and spinning great theories

- Confusion and vagueness

- Low energy, inattention

Here are some examples of naming statements you might make to these forms of resistance:

*Methodology:* "You are asking a lot of questions about my methods. Do you have any doubts about the credibility of the results?"

*Intellectualizing:* "Each time we get close to deciding what to do, you go back to developing theories to understand what is happening."

*Confusion:* "You seem very confused about what we are discussing. Are you confused about the problem or just not sure what to do about it?"

*Low energy or inattention:* "You look as if you have other things on your mind and have low energy for this project."

In a high percentage of cases, clients will respond with a more direct statement of what they are feeling about a project. Sometimes naming the resistance won't work. It may be there is nothing you can do about it.

### A Hint for Finding the Right Words

If naming the resistance isn't helping, an option is to put into words how you are feeling about the discussion. Meeting resistance is uncomfortable and frustrating. Sometimes it makes you feel stupid, irrelevant, or unimportant. Try stating this to the client with statements like these:

"I feel very frustrated by this discussion."

"It seems my comments are treated as though they are irrelevant or unimportant."

Sometimes the client will stop short and ask you why you feel that way, and this might get you to a direct discussion of the problem.

Expressing your feelings can be riskier at times than just naming the client's resistance. The client may not care how you are feeling and say, "So you are feeling uncomfortable. What has that got to do with getting this equipment working?" But stating your own feelings is being authentic and acts to encourage a like response from the client, which is what you are after.

### Step 3: Be Quiet, Let the Client Respond

After naming the resistance, we have a tendency to keep talking. For example, a consultant might say to an unmotivated client:

"You seem to have very little motivation to go ahead with this project. Let me tell you four reasons I think this project is important and you should feel differently . . ."

The first sentence is good—a neutral naming of the concern. By continuing to talk, though, the consultant is taking the client off the hook and making it easy for the client not to take responsibility for their actions.

We keep talking to reduce the tension we feel when we confront the client. Don't keep talking. Live with the tension. Make the statement about resistance and remain silent.

## DON'T TAKE IT PERSONALLY

A client's behavior is not a reflection on you. Many of us have a habit of analyzing what we did wrong. In a recent workshop, I asked a group of engineers to make a list of what they did well as consultants and what they did poorly as consultants. They were able to quickly list eight to ten things they did poorly or had problems with. The lists of positive qualities averaged two items and took twice as long to make. This passion for self-criticism is very common and gets in the way of keeping the resistance focused on the client, where it belongs.

If you must take the client's reactions personally, the rule is to do it after six o'clock in the evening—on your own time. Spend the whole

night at it, and involve your friends. But don't take resistance personally when you are with the client. If you have in fact done a poor job and the client tells you, you have to own up to it and shape up your act. This doesn't happen often—and it's not resistance from the client; it is a mistake by the consultant.

Remember that client defenses are not to be denied. In fact, they need clear expression. If suppressed, they just pop up later and more dangerously. The key is how you respond to the defenses.

A couple of points to summarize:

- Don't take it personally. Despite the words used, the resistance is not designed to discredit your competence.

- Defenses and resistance are a sign that you have touched something important and valuable. That fact is now simply coming out in a difficult form.

- Most questions are statements in disguise. Try to get behind the question to get the statement articulated. This takes the burden off you to answer a phantom question.

Dealing with resistance is harder than actually doing data collection and much harder than coming up with good ideas for implementation. The meat of the consultation is dealing with resistance.

## GOOD-FAITH RESPONSES

The majority of questions you get about methodology and the project are expressions of the discomfort and defensiveness the client is feeling. It is important, however, to respond to the substance of the questions as best you can.

One ground rule is to give two good-faith responses to every question you are asked. If you are asked about methodology and your summary or how you designed the questionnaire, answer each question twice. The third time the same question is asked, interpret it as a form of resistance and do not respond to the content of the question. Instead, realize that clients who ask the same question over and over are in effect expressing their caution about committing to the process and owning up to their own problems. So the third time the same question is asked, the only rational response is to make the statement that perhaps what the client is feeling is some reluctance to commit to the problem or the process.

After two good-faith responses, deal with the problems of commitment and taking responsibility. Don't deal with resistance as though it were merely a problem of procedure or method. Make the two good-faith responses and then treat the questions as resistance.

## CONSULTING WITH A STONE

Every once in a while you meet your match. Your consultation is flawless, yet your progress with the client is in a nosedive.

Some of our consulting workshops have the participants engage in a consulting project with a real client as part of the learning experience. One consulting team returned from their contracting meeting with the client with long faces. The client was resistant, withholding, and uncommunicative and even told the group in the contracting meeting that he thought they were doing a lousy job.

As a way of coping with our despair and frustration, we made a list of different ways of consulting with a stone:

1. Don't look for approval, emotional support, or affection.
2. Don't expect the responsibility to be shared 50/50. Stones dump it all on you.
3. Expect argument and criticism.
4. Don't ask for the client's feelings or express your own feelings.

5. Do ask the client for understanding. Don't ask for agreement.

6. Let the client have a lot of control over the procedure used in the project.

7. Minimize elaborating or explaining the data. Justification just makes it worse.

8. Give the client support.

9. Don't take the response you are getting personally.

10. Don't get hooked; avoid details.

11. Hope that the client may learn from this project later, after you are gone. You are not going to get closure from the project now.

12. Show confidence.

13. Look for comic relief.

14. Remember that the stone's anxiety is over losing control.

15. Keep moving.

16. Avoid stones whenever possible.

There aren't many real stones out there. If the surface of the client is that hard, the stuff inside must be equally soft. Often clear support to the stone will be softening. If the stone client stays a stone client, minimize your investment in the project; don't pressure yourself to be heroic. If the stone turns out to be someone you work with constantly or is your boss, either plan your escape or start putting your energy into activities outside the job. Finally, do what you can not to become a stone. That can happen if you are around them too much.

# CHAPTER 10

# FROM DIAGNOSIS TO DISCOVERY

W HEN THE CONTRACT is clear and you are ready to deal with resistance, attention turns to the discovery phase. There are two primary purposes for this phase: to develop an independent and fresh way of looking at what is going on and to create a process that leads to client commitment, ownership, and action. This means that the goal of discovery is not to be right but to be effective and powerful.

There are two quite distinct ways of thinking about this part of the work. The traditional way is to consider it a diagnosis, following the medical model of diagnosing the problem, coming up with a prognosis, and then offering a prescription. This is the expectation of most clients. They have a problem, want a solution, and want you to give it to them. As common as this expectation is, it has the limitations of being strictly problem focused, and it has the consultant doing the bulk of the discovery.

In recent years, a way of thinking different from diagnosis has emerged—one that focuses more on possibilities than problems. Instead of looking at what is wrong, at deficiencies, we look at what is working, what the strengths and gifts are, and seek to deepen and take advantage of those assets. This is variously called an *asset-based approach* or a *strength-based approach*.

The shift from problem to possibility grows out of the belief that dramatic change or transformation comes not from problem solving but from a more future-minded way of proceeding. "Are we here to solve a problem or create a new future for ourselves?" is one way to put the question.

One methodology that is future and asset based is called Positive Deviance. Developed by Jerry and Monique Sternin, this discovery strategy looks for examples in the system where something is working well. The Sternins have worked in businesses, poor villages, and hospitals where problems seemed unsolvable. Rather than showing up as experts or even researchers, they simply listen to examples of where something is working. When they discover in villages that some children are healthier than others, they ask what that family does that is unique. The act of asking this question of many people in the village alone causes an improvement in the health of children. In hospitals they achieve the same effect: disease and accidents are fewer; in businesses, sales and profits go up.

A second example is in the domain of organizational change, where there is wide support for a method called appreciative inquiry. Initiated by David Cooperrider, the whole discovery process focuses on what is working well for an organization, what traditions and rituals are worth sustaining, what dream or vision for the future is in people's minds.

Although my own practice has migrated toward the asset-based, future-based approach, enough of the world is still problem minded enough that we want to support consultation that follows both paths. Plus, when there is a specific problem, a direct analytical and technical solution is exactly what is required.

## IT IS STILL THE RELATIONSHIP THAT COUNTS

Regardless of whether you choose a problem-based discovery process or a future- and strength-based discovery, the focus on relationships that was emphasized in contracting continues to be important in the discovery phase. If we want to create ownership of what we come up with, the relationship aspect of the discovery process becomes decisive, regardless of the special expertise or worldview of the consultant.

For the content of the discovery, your particular area of consulting expertise will determine what kind of data you will collect. Systems people look at information requirements, engineers and scientists at the technical questions, financial experts at money and economics, and organization development people at asset-based or problem-solving-based change efforts.

One consistent source of tension, regardless of expertise or methodology, is that what the client may want and expect is often at odds with what is most likely to be helpful. We know that sustainable improvement comes when clients internalize what is new, make it their own, participate fully in the improvement effort, and build their own capacity. But this is not what most clients have in mind. They want an answer. Although they may agree with high engagement and capacity building in theory, it is not what they want in practice. In practice, clients want a turnkey solution.

It is similar to when we are not feeling well. We want to go to a doctor, get a prescription, swallow a pill, and get on with our life. Better living through chemistry. When the physician says we need to change our diet, reduce stress, exercise more, and make more fundamental changes, this is not what we came to hear.

When line managers decide their organization is not functioning well, they want someone to come in, take a good look with fresh eyes, and suggest a solution that will be quick, cheap, and painless. That is why the first questions from the client are, "How long will it take?" "How much will it cost?" and "Give us a solution that will cause the least disruption."

If we give clients precisely what they ask for, we run the risk of not having served them well. If, however, we tell them that the solution will take awhile, will cost more than they imagined, and more time and involvement will be required of them than they want to give, we run the risk of alienating them. Some of this will have been dealt with in the contracting phase, but this tension exists at every step of the way. What is hard for clients to realize is that long-term solutions to problems (or application of strengths) require some rethinking on their part and some rearranging of the way they work.

This relearning takes time and effort. Clients can outsource or contract to an outsider the research and technical inquiry, but implementing and sustaining a solution or new direction they always have to do themselves. This is why we serve the client best by breaking out of the medical model. We are not an organization doctor who looks them over, analyzes their symptoms, prescribes a solution, and sends them on their way. A better approach is to define our task as a process of discovery and dialogue more than as an act of diagnosis and prescription, independent of whether we are looking at problems or gifts and possibilities.

The limit to the term *diagnosis* is that it implies that a third party, a consultant, can analyze the situation, come up with an accurate picture of what is wrong, and deliver a recommendation for corrective action that will be useful. This frame of diagnosis and prescription is a comforting problem-solving model, but it is based on the belief that organizational improvement can be engineered. In many cases, especially where a shift in a complex human system is involved, this is not realistic.

For strictly technical problems, such as equipment that doesn't work or software that crashes, this might seem reasonable. It is rare, however, that problems originally defined as technical are amenable to strictly technical solutions. Often we are dealing with human systems, and human systems are not amenable to technical solutions. Human systems are complex and require more than mechanical cause-and-effect solutions. Equipment and software most often break down because people run them, people maintain them, and people ask them to do things they were not designed to do. The resolution of the problem most often requires a change in thinking and action on the part of the client, and this is the challenge.

So when we accept the term *diagnosis* as a description of this phase, we reinforce the belief that a prescriptive engineering strategy can improve a living system. This rational stance undervalues the emotional and affective requirements of real improvements.

The stance we want to take is that we can be a guide through a process of discovery, engagement, and dialogue in which our clients will find an answer to their question and launch an implementation that will be enduring and productive. This is the thinking behind the future-looking and dialogue-based methodologies. It may seem like playing with words, but it makes a difference in what we do and what we leave behind.

This chapter describes the kind of discovery, engagement, and dialogue that gives us our best shot at building client capacity and solving problems so they stay solved.

## THE CALL TO ACTION

The challenge is how to help the client to be open to the discovery process. This is much more important than for us to be correct in our analysis. This means giving more space to dealing with resistance. It also demands work on building the client's internal commitment to the process at each step of the way. To wait until a report is put together and presented in a feedback meeting is too late to worry about client acceptance of recommendations. We also must be concerned about how to handle the politics and personalities surrounding the discovery process.

Navigating through clients' management styles and organizational politics and helping them to look objectively at the data are vital tasks. The skill comes in addressing the organizational element of each challenge as rationally as we address the technical part.

This begins with understanding that there are no purely technical problems. As consultants, we always have a perspective on how the business and technology is being used or managed. Even if we hire a contractor to install an electricity generator to power our house in the event of a power outage, there are still questions of what size generator, where it should be placed, which technology is best for our lifestyle and budget, and who will run and maintain it. A good contractor will ask questions about client expectations, who in the household will be operating the generator, how much protection the household needs, how important having instant power is to the family, and, most difficult of all, whether there is agreement in the family about the answers to these questions.

These are questions about how the "problem" is being managed, what it means to the "client," what attitudes surround the seemingly simple step of purchasing some technology. A good contractor will treat these questions as being as important as the knowledge of how to purchase and install an alternative power source. Architects and contractors say that the hardest part of their job is dealing with client doubts and family dynamics. Designing and building a house they know how to do. Navigating their way through the politics of the family is where the challenge lies.

If this is true for a family, it is magnified when dealing with an organization. The politics of an organization is a reality, always present and powerful, and this is the challenge of discovery and action.

The purpose, then, of discovery is to mobilize action that will improve the organization's functioning. The purpose is not research, which is aimed at simply understanding something and treats the understanding itself as enough.

This emphasis on action and utilization has strong implications for how you approach discovery:

| Research Approach | Action Approach |
|---|---|
| Interested in all factors that have an impact on the situation at hand. | Interested in factors that are under the control of the client and affect the situation. |
| Being comprehensive and complete in the discovery phase is essential. | Completeness and comprehensiveness are not vital. They can be overwhelming at the point of deciding what to do. |
| You can do research on your own. The organization doesn't have to be involved as part of the research team. | The client's involvement in the study is important at each stage. |
| You try to eliminate bias and intuition. There is heavy emphasis on objectivity and hard data. | Consultants are getting paid for their own bias and intuition—it is called judgment. You use all the feelings and perceptions you have in addition to hard data. |
| Essentially neutral toward whether the organization approves of the outcomes of the study. | Deeply concerned about the attitude of the client toward the outcome of the study. |

These distinctions in approach may be unnaturally polarized, but the point is that our objective is action, not understanding. With that objective, we need to concentrate on four things beyond the technical considerations:

1.  Keep simplifying and narrowing the inquiry so it focuses more and more on the next steps the client can take and what is under their control.

2.  Use everyday language. The words you use should help the transfer of information, not hinder it.

3. Give a great deal of attention to your relationship with the client. Include the client at every opportunity in deciding how to proceed. Deal with resistance as it arises, even if it doesn't have an impact on your results.

4. Treat data on how the client organization is functioning as valid and relevant information. Also, assess how the group you are working with is being managed.

These four competencies affect how your expertise gets used. They take your technical skill and investigative and analytical abilities as givens. This action orientation makes the assumption that client readiness to accept your input is as important to discovery as the technical analysis of the problem to be solved or the possibilities and gifts that are in play.

Figure 9 shows the basic distinctions in the discovery phase between the technical problem and how it is being managed. You can make the same distinctions when working with possibilities and assets by imagining the possibilities in the left column.

**Figure 9.** The Discovery Model for Problem Solving

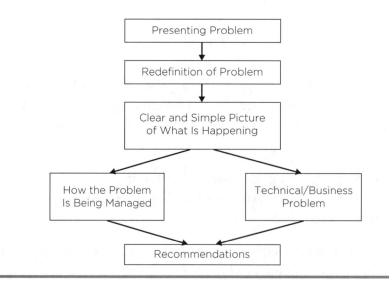

| The client gives you a . . . | Presenting problem |
|---|---|
| You begin to . . . | Redefine the problem or the cause of the problem. |
| Your goal is to develop . . . | A clear and simple picture of the situation. |
| Included in this clear and simple picture is a description of . . . | The technical or business problem the client has asked for help on. |
| And also a description of . . . | How that problem is being managed—the attitudes of people, the manager's style, the politics of the situation, the gifts' strengths, and possibilities that surround the technical or business issue. |
| This leads to . . . | Recommendations on next steps for handling the business situation and dealing with how this group manages itself. |

## THE PROBLEM IS NOT THE PROBLEM

What all this implies is that one of the consultant's most important contributions to a client is a redefinition of the problem. The line manager begins by experiencing some pain: people are restless, equipment isn't working, output is down, the invoicing process is flawed, the line extension is running way late.

Most consulting projects get started because managers feel pain. Once in a while, they get started because of a desire for further success or preventive measures, but most often there is some pain in the picture. When the organization feels the pain, managers start to describe for themselves why the pain exists. When their explanation of what is causing the pain is accurate, their attempts to solve the problem are usually successful. When consultants are called in, the line manager's attempts at solving the problem have not been that successful, or maybe the manager has no idea at all how to solve the problem. When a manager's attempts to solve the problem have not succeeded, it is probably because the manager's attempts to describe the cause of the pain have been inaccurate.

The client's initial attempt to describe to us the cause of the difficulties is called the *presenting problem*. As a consultant, I never accept the presenting problem as the real problem without doing my own discovery and analysis. The presenting problem and the real (or underlying) problem are different. Because line managers start from an incomplete definition of the problem, their attempts at solution have not entirely worked out. Therefore, an important contribution for the consultant is to redefine that initial problem statement for the client.

Here's an example of how presenting problems get redefined.

A large technical organization was having difficulty retaining new employees for more than two to three years. The people would come to work, get training, work on the job for awhile, and then leave just when they were becoming valuable employees. The managers asked the first-line supervisors why the younger people were leaving. The supervisors identified three reasons:

1. Salaries weren't high enough to match the cost of living in the area.

2. Housing was very hard to find in the most desirable areas. Apartments were scarce, and houses for sale were so expensive that an employee had to save for ten years to have enough for the down payment.

3. Young people these days want too much too soon. Their ambition and sense of entitlement are way beyond what a business can satisfy.

Top management accepted these reasons as valid. They conducted a salary survey and made some adjustments in the compensation practices for short-service employees. They also created a housing section in the personnel department to help people find apartments and work with realtors to identify moderately priced housing in the area. They held workshops about the realities of modern business careers. These solutions were a direct response to the presenting problem of poor housing, unjust compensation, and people's entitlement mind-set.

But a year and a half later, the turnover rate for the organization was not reduced, and in some sections it was even higher.

Top management brought in the training group in the company as internal consultants and asked them for help on the problem. The training people first interviewed first-line supervisors and short-service employees. From these interviews came a different explanation of why people were leaving The employees said:

1. When they were hired, they were sent to an orientation program that exposed them to the company vision, mission, and culture.

2. They didn't get a really responsible assignment until they had been there for almost a year.

3. They never got any accurate feedback from their supervisors about how they were doing. This made it hard for them to know what to work on for their own development. It also left them in limbo about their prospects with this company.

4. The first-line supervisors were under so much pressure to get the work done and to do it perfectly they just didn't have the time to spend with new hires.

The interviews revealed a very different cause of the pain the company was experiencing in losing so many people. The original presenting problem was that people were leaving, and the reasons they were leaving were low salaries, a tight housing market, and unrealistic expectations. This initial problem statement led to solutions in the form of compensation, housing aid, and workshops. The consultants developed a different explanation for the pain and essentially redefined the cause of the problem: new hires were not given enough support, attention, meaningful tasks, and feedback.

Interestingly, the shift in defining the problem was from a cause that no one had any responsibility for to one where the client was a player. This is the essence of discovery: to move from the language of innocence (salary, housing, and unrealistic expectations—not our fault) to accountability (how we bring them in and structure their experience is in our hands).

Once management had this redefinition of the problem, they could start to solve it. They began a series of programs to have supervisors and new hires contract with each other for how much time they would spend together, the tasks they would be assigned, and when they would get feedback from the supervisor. Management also supported the supervisors in devoting more time to new employees. Over the next year, the turnover rate leveled off, and in the second year it began to go down. The contribution of the consultants had been to redefine the presenting problem and present to the client a clear picture of what was causing the difficulty.

# HOW THE PROBLEM IS BEING MANAGED

How the technical or business problem is being managed is a critical area of inquiry in action-oriented discovery.

Consultants are usually aware of the client's management style and the politics of the situation, but we tend to shy away from dealing with them as part of our consultations. We feel that we have been asked to solve a business problem, not to comment on the organization. As a result, we tend to exclude organizational problems from our field of inquiry. We don't ignore the human problems entirely, though, for these are the things we talk about most with our colleagues and friends. The way the problem is being managed usually gets discussed in the restroom, between meetings, after work when we are eating or drinking, or during breaks during the day.

Sometimes the management issues are even more interesting than the technical issues. But there is a part of us (with support from the client) that does not want to get into personalities, politics, or relationships. It is a mistake to avoid these areas. The way the problem is managed has a powerful effect on the way our expertise will be used. We can't really avoid it entirely, even when the client agrees that we are only technical consultants. Technical and business problems almost always have accompanying management problems that affect how the technical or business problem gets resolved.

Figure 10 shows some examples of typical management problems that could occur along with technical or business problems in selected disciplines and functions.

**Figure 10.** Differences Between the Technical or Business Problem and How the Problem Is Being Managed

|  | Technical or Business Problems | How the Problem Is Being Managed |
|---|---|---|
| Finance systems | Inadequate control procedures and practices | Defensive cover-your-tracks environment |
|  | Too many reports | Withhold information and figures |
|  | Too few reports | Little verbal communication between groups |
| Human resources (HR) | Improve policies and practices in areas of compensation, benefits, recruiting, training | Every manager is an HR expert |
|  |  | HR function is a low-status group and is treated accordingly |
|  | Improve general organization and management development | HR specialists used as a pair of hands |
|  |  | Managers fear HR will be involved in their performance evaluation, so they are reluctant to trust and include HR |
| Marketing research, product management | Policies on pricing, promotion, and packaging | Distrust and distance between marketing and the sales force |
|  | Information on customer preferences and market characteristics | Struggle for control |
|  |  | Market research operates as a black box; the rest of the organization operates on private opinions and doesn't believe the black box |
| Management and organization development consultants | How to improve an organization's attitudes and productivity | Certain individuals and groups have a lot of power under the current system; changing the structure will change the power balance among groups |
|  | New organization structure | |
|  | New roles and responsibilities | A new structure signals who is on the way up and whose star is fading |
|  |  | A very authoritarian manager may not care how people feel |

For more examples of management and technical/business problems from other disciplines, visit www.flawlessconsulting.com.

So here is the point: each discipline or function faces both technical and organizational problems. The presenting problem is almost always about the technical or business problem. Organizational problems, or what we call *social system problems*, include how the technical or business problem is being managed. The choice is whether to address how the problem is being managed directly or indirectly.

To address the social system side is riskier for the internal consultant. You might hear clients say that they didn't invite you in to comment on their own personal style or the politics of the situation. To not address the social or organizational side is to see your technical recommendations distorted and only partially implemented because of the difficulty the organization has in communicating, trusting, and managing itself.

## FLAWLESS DISCOVERY

To consult flawlessly, you need to begin to address the organizational side of the problem as a regular part of your consultation. At a minimum, each assessment you do should have one section devoted to how the problem is being managed. This section needs only to present a clear and simple picture; it doesn't need to include specific recommendations.

The worry about confronting the client on how the client is managing the problem is a fear that resides within the consultant. Line managers usually want feedback on how they are doing, and they have a hard time getting it. Their own subordinates are reluctant to give them feedback. You, the consultant, are in a special position to provide it. The only caution is to do it in a supportive and nonpunishing manner. There is guidance on language in Chapter Fourteen.

To summarize, remember to do these things in the discovery phase:

- Ask questions about the client's personal role in causing or maintaining the presenting or target problem.

- Ask questions about what others in the organization are doing to cause or maintain the presenting or target problem.

- Involve your client in interpreting the data collected.

- Recognize the similarity between how the client manages you and how they manage their own organization.

- Condense the data into a limited number of issues.

- Use language that people outside your area of expertise will understand.

- Distinguish between the presenting problem and the underlying problem.

- Elicit and describe both the technical problem and how it is being managed.

# CHAPTER 11

# WHOLE-SYSTEM DISCOVERY

Most of the discussion on discovery so far has been written from the perspective of a third-party approach, the third party being the consultant, engineer, IT specialist, or support person who is doing the data collection, analysis, and feedback. Although this is the most typical expectation clients have when using support people, and also the way we have traditionally seen the consultant role, there is an alternative.

The option is to involve the whole client system much more directly in redefining the problem, naming a desired future, outlining alternative actions, and deciding how to proceed. This is a first-party or whole-system strategy, and the methodology has come a long way in the past two decades. Many consultants and support people have adopted the whole-system approach and redefined their role to be one of convening people to collectively develop a change strategy.

What is significant about this is that the people doing the discovery and making the recommendations are the same people who will implement the change. In other words, people from the whole system are involved early in the process and are active at every step.

The name *whole system*, though, is a little misleading because the whole system is not literally involved. You can have representatives from all parts of a system in the room but not really everyone. It means that at least a large sample of those who will be acting on the recommendations is going to play a major part in creating them. It makes the change effort more self-managing than a third-party approach.

What also is important about a whole-system approach is that it looks at the entire system, not its parts. It can involve a cross-section of people that approximates a whole system much more directly and earlier than a third-party approach. A first-party or whole-system strategy engages entire units to self-assess their current reality and plan how to improve it.

Each strategy—third party or whole system—has its advantages and limitations, and I outline them briefly. As you read, remember that your goal in each consultation is to catalyze action, not just to have an accurate assessment.

## THIRD-PARTY CONSULTING

The most traditional third-party process involves the lone consultant who studies the situation and makes recommendations for improvement. The consultant may come from inside the organization or be an outsider. Sometimes the third party is a team of people from inside the organization that is given the charge of coming up with recommendations. Often called *design teams,* these groups may number ten to fifty people, and they have six months, more or less, to work on the project, after which they are expected to return with recommended actions that management can endorse and implement.

Although the design team involves more people than the traditional lone consultant arrangement and members are taken from the organization itself, it still represents a third-party strategy: whenever some individual or group develops a solution for another, it is taking a third-party stance.

The rationale for employing a third-party approach is that consultants, and design teams, have special expertise and are positioned outside the specific system in question, even if only temporarily. This is supposed to lead to a certain objectivity and a willingness to confront difficult issues that people inside the system may be unable or unwilling to face. In addition, third parties may be aware of possibilities that people closer to the problem may miss. The idea of combining a design team with an outside consultant has the added advantage of applying local, intimate knowledge of the problem. The belief is that given adequate time for analysis and reflection, the partnership of consultant and design team, composed of organization members who know the work well, can make more practical and actionable recommendations than a consultant alone might offer.

The strength of any third-party strategy is objectivity. Third parties offer an independent point of view, an outlook that is not colored by being so much a part of a culture that they cannot see it in a new way. When we can so easily see in others those things that we are blind to in ourselves, why not use a third party to help us see ourselves? The third-party path also has the power of management sponsorship and the unique energy and impetus for improvement it may provide. We believe that if management supports the change, maybe even models it themselves, we are well down the road to making the change happen.

The limitation of third-party help comes from the separation between the discovery and the doing. Third-party recommendations have to be sold to management, and then management has to either mandate or sell the ideas to the employees. The very process of selling is based on flawed premises: it pretends that there is a right answer to the problem, that the consultant or design team knows the right answer, and that, in good engineering fashion, the line organization can (and should) be persuaded to accept the answer and act on it.

In some cases, especially when the problem is strictly technical in nature, there may be a right answer, and it may be accepted and implemented on its own merits. In most cases, however, this thinking is naive. Whenever there are questions of management or employee commitment, or issues of developing new skills or new organizational relationships, the prescriptive engineering or medical model ends in modest change at best. At worst, even if the third party's answer is right, it still may not be acted on, even with unqualified management sponsorship.

## TAKING A WHOLE-SYSTEM APPROACH

Sometimes the people who will be affected by the change can join you in the process of discovery, recommendation, decision, and implemen-

tation. This is the whole-system approach, whereby the parties to the change work through the process on their own behalf.

The essence of whole-system discovery is to get everyone in the room at the same time. This deepens an organization's sense of community and allows people to operate with the same information, a common database. All hear what is said, and you avoid the limitations of having a few people planning what is best for a large group.

The main advantage is that there is no need to sell a set of actions to anyone, especially to people at lower levels of the system. When the goal is to build internal commitment to a set of changes, selling is the worst way to do it. People will resist change that is inflicted on them, no matter how compelling the case.

The power of the whole-system approach lies not so much in management sponsorship but in the high engagement and involvement of the entire organization. The whole-system process doesn't proceed without sponsorship, for management will be in the room, but it doesn't bet on sponsorship so heavily. It is a bet on collective knowledge, collective purpose, and the commitment that grows out of deciding for oneself.

"Whole system" means you want representatives from all parts of a system in the room, but not literally everyone in the client organization. In this way, at least a large sample of those who will be acting on the recommendations is going to play a major part in creating them. It makes the change effort more self-managing than a third-party approach. But if the whole system can literally be in one room together and the work of the organization allows it, go with everybody in the room. Then you don't have to struggle with building a bridge between the sample of people in the room and those who were absent.

## YOUR CHOICE

The value of the whole-system approach is that it engages entire units to self-assess their current reality and plan how to improve it. Making a choice about a consulting strategy, then, means deciding whether to give priority to the special expertise and neutrality of the consultant, which leads to a third-party approach, or to give priority to people's commitment to implementation, which might tilt the scales toward a whole-system approach. Here are some considerations:

**Third Party**

- Neutral observer. No stake in the answer.

- Broader view. Has seen many organizations and ways to approach the problem.

- Has specialized expertise that does not reside in the unit.

- Simple decision-making process. More manager control of decision.

- Has outsider credibility.

**Whole System**

- Decision-making process creates higher commitment to implement.

- People deciding are the ones who have to make it work.

- Greater local knowledge. People are intimate with the situation.

- More realism. People know what is doable and what will work.

- The learning stays with the organization.

## PUTTING WHOLE-SYSTEM DISCOVERY TO WORK

The technique of bringing a large number of people together to assess the situation, define a future, and talk about action goes by many different names. Because it can work with several hundred people in the room, it is often called *large-group methodology*. Other proponents focus on the involvement it provides and call it a *high-interaction* approach. Because it tries to embrace all the players at once, it also can be called a *large-scale* method. The name isn't important, really, as long as it gives a sense of the intent of whole-system methods.

### Whole-System Process

The number of people is limited mostly by the size of the room. The sessions usually last for two or three consecutive days. A design team, usually guided by a consultant, typically plans the large-group event, but they focus only on the process and do not get into statements of the problem or solutions. They deal with questions of whom to invite, the right focus for the meeting(s), and how to manage the logistics and stage the activities. For specifics on how to do it, there are some good books by Kathie Dannemiller, Marvin Weisbord and Sandra Janoff, Barbara Bunker and Billie Alban, Dick Axelrod and Emily Axelrod, Harrison Owen, and Juanita Brown. They are listed in the Further Reading section at the back of this book.

What is special about whole-system discovery methods is the faith they express in people's capacity to name their own problems and find ways to address them. A whole-system process says that we do not need an outsider or a special team of insiders to tell us who we are and what we are up against. If we can create enough trust and are willing to be honest with each other, every unit has within itself the capacity to make needed changes.

## Trusting the Process

To make this approach work, consultant and client have to give up some control and start down an unpredictable path, one quite different from the way the organization usually operates and probably not destined for comfort. Here are the conditions that have to be present:

- *There has to be complete transparency.* Management has to be willing to state to the group all they know about the current reality. This includes financial information, progress on important goals, any failures occurring, and how the organization is doing in meeting its key promises to its constituents. If management is contemplating any changes in structure or functions, these need to be on the table, regardless of the anxiety it might create.

- *Management joins the proceedings as full participants.* The session is led by the design team or planners and consultant. Each manager is one among many, and management's ideas are not viewed as better than anyone else's. Although management may decide to retain some veto power, it will be hard to use without creating cries of manipulation. This is a good model when management is willing to be vulnerable to the same thing prescribed for others.

- *The groups must be a full cross section of the whole system.* This means that support people and every level of management and worker, even those from other units that have an important tie to the system, are involved.

- *Differences in status, power, title, and function disappear during the process.* There is a level playing field, and all work as equals. Each working team in the session will have several levels and functions represented. Participants must be willing to cross social and organizational barriers.

- *Employees have to be ready to speak up.* We ask that they suspend their caution and cynicism for a couple of days. They don't have to forsake caution and cynicism forever, but the meeting is not designed as a forum for complaint and response; it is a cocreated event where all have answers and all have questions.

- *If employees choose not to participate, they surrender their right to complain or be heard.* There is no claiming later that they were not part of the decision. Rights of citizenship are earned by the choice to participate.

- *There is an emphasis on the future and what the group wants to create together.* Some discussion addresses obstacles and the current reality, but the strategy is to talk more about what we want to create tomorrow than how to fix what we've got today.

- *The session ends with agreements on next steps and who is going to work on them.* Management and employees have to be willing to allow next steps to emerge out of this session. Everyone gives up some control.

- *Consultants give up the expert role.* We no longer analyze the data, make recommendations, and follow up. Our role is to conduct people through a highly participatory series of steps. We become less central, less visible, and less able to be an advocate for a certain answer.

Each of these conditions moves the organization in an egalitarian, self-governing direction. That is the power of the strategy, but also its limitation. Managers cannot start this process of sharing power and then pull back at moments of doubt and nervousness.

## THE PAYOFF

My intent in introducing the whole system and self-assessing discovery is to explain why this method is important and show how it changes the role of the consultant. But I must also admit a certain inclination toward using a whole-system strategy whenever possible. If the conditions are right, it has an advantage over a third-party stance in the way it builds the capacity of the organization to manage itself in the future. It also keeps the consultant in an educational role. It demands that we develop our ability to design learning experiences for others. It also requires that we expand our skills in how to convene and bring people together, how to encourage them to question their current reality and envision their future, and how to confront them with their freedom and responsibility through interactive activities, as opposed to confronting these issues in a more traditional face-to-face way.

# CHAPTER 12

# DISCOVERING GIFTS, CAPACITIES, AND POSSIBILITIES

IN THE SECOND EDITION of this book at the turn of the century, what was new in the discovery phase were the whole-system methodologies described in Chapter Eleven. Since then, probably the most interesting new development in discovery is the growing interest in looking at a system's gifts, capacities, and possibilities. This approach is used in addition to, or sometimes in contrast to, looking at problems—their causes and their solutions.

This approach goes under many names: asset-based community development, positive deviance, positive psychology, appreciative inquiry, future search, and more. Each of these is based on the premise that looking at what in our history we want to preserve, or what is working in a system now, or what a system longs to create in the future is a powerful way to build commitment and sustainability into any consultative or change process.

Adopting this perspective or worldview is a way of compensating for some limitations in a problem-solving focus. As soon as you call something a problem, you signal that something is wrong and needs fixing. Careful as you might be, it is difficult to avoid having others think maybe *they* are wrong and need fixing.

The problem analysis approach also has a tendency to focus on what we have been doing up to now. It asks for a history of problems, how we got into this fix, what the causes are, and what can be done to correct this. It implies that if we understand the past and the road that got us to this place, this bodes well for an alternative future. In many cases, however, this does not work so smoothly.

It is also too easy when focusing on problems to slip into trying to sell others on the need for a new future and to get into dramatizing what is often called "a burning platform" to promote the urgency of the need for change. The selling in itself can create its own resistance. Selling usually triggers as much defense as commitment.

Finally, the problem focus tends to be more rational and logic based, which is its great strength. But this emphasis on reason, which provides solid ground for us to stand on, can have trouble engaging people's hearts and spirits.

These are not arguments against a problem-solving focus; they are only a prelude to the idea that in certain situations, focusing more on possibility and capacity might make sense. That is what this chapter explores.

## WHEN ALL ELSE FAILS

The most obvious condition calling for a possibility- and strength-based approach is when the traditional model of problem solving has been tried again and again and has not worked. This is usually the case with intractable problems—for example, long-term low morale, poor market performance, or quality issues that will not go away. In a broader context, more problem solving, more programs, and more funding have had little real impact on challenges with poverty, crime, diseases, and infections.

When conditions are intractable, usually an alternative future requires a shift in a social system. Technical solutions fare poorly where improvement is dependent on a change in culture, traditional norms, or a shift in people's habits. Take education reform, an example detailed in Chapter Eighteen. We have been trying for years in public education to implement best curriculum practices, raise standards for certifying teachers, reduce class size, install better leadership practices, and implement peer review. All of these practices are reasonable; they make sense, and they have worked in some places. Yet the problem of schools where children do not learn persists and the drumbeat for reform just gets louder. Most of these change strategies for schools are deficiency or need based. They look at what is wrong and then problem-solve to make it better.

This might be an indication that dramatic new outcomes require more than simply a technical solution or better problem definition and solutions. Improvement in a school and children's learning requires a shift in the social system surrounding the child, which itself requires a changed mind-set and a search for a more fundamental shift in the ways of doing business.

I could point to other areas where problem solving might have reached its limits—for example, health care, discussed later in this chapter. Most of the discussion about health care is really about disease care, its accessibility, and its cost.

Or consider our concern for youth "at risk." This is what we call children who have dropped out of the conventional schooling trajectory of kindergarten through twelfth grade and on to college. We traditionally think of these kids as "problem children." In organizations we talk about "low performers" or "problem employees" and what programs we can implement to get them "back on board."

This language and focus on the deficiencies of people and systems may be part of why solutions are hard to find. The alternative is to focus on the gifts and capacities of a social system and the people in that system. In the case of education, for example, how do we shift our attention from the performance of the teacher to the capacity of students to learn? In health care, how do we shift the conversation on healing from the prescription and treatment emanating from the doctor, to the full participation of patients and their families, the social worker, lab people, nurses, and others who touch the patient?

With youth, how do we shift the conversation from what they are not to what do they love to do? What gifts do they have that are not being delivered? What do they do well? Suppose our goal as a community was to have all eighteen year olds simply know what they are good at?

## THE POWER OF POSITIVE DEVIANCE

One of the most powerful gift-based approaches that is gaining popularity is somewhat awkwardly named *positive deviance*. Positive deviance is a process developed by Monique Sternin and Jerry Sternin in villages in Vietnam dealing with undernourished children, ending the practice of female genital surgery in Egypt, and the curtailment of methicillin-resistant staph infections in hospitals—problems that have almost unsolvable by traditional means.*

What the Sternins, along with their associate, Richard Pascale, discovered was that focusing on the entrenched, long-term problems themselves yielded marginal results. All the education, workshops, funding, benchmarking, and intervention in the world had not touched the ingrained daily practices that sustained the poor outcomes like undernourished children in Vietnamese villages and infections in hospitals.

Here is the essence of their approach:

• They are interested in finding exceptions to conventional thinking and practice. They call this "finding observable exceptions," which they refer to as focusing "on the successful exceptions not the failing norms." They ask, "Are there any children in this village who are healthy?" Every other group had studied the malnourished children and tried to bring in best practices from other places. Their belief is that we need to focus on the premise that at least one person in a community, working with the same resources as everyone else, has already solved the problem that confounds others.

• They operate strictly through invitation. They invite as many people as possible who care about the issue to a meeting. They show the process that they have used elsewhere, take questions, and then invite those interested in the process to come to a meeting the next day. They work only with people who come the second time. No mandates allowed.

• They organize these volunteers to begin looking for people in the community who are the "positive deviants"—people who have figured something out and gone against the prevailing norms. Usually these deviants do not even know what they know, which is why they need to be observed, not interviewed.

*The approach is fully explained in their book, coauthored with Richard Pascale, *The Power of Positive Deviance: How Unlikely Innovators Solve the World's Toughest Problems* (Boston: Harvard Business School Press, 2010).

After finding examples of the positive deviants, the Sternins got really radical. They realized that this was the point where most change efforts fail: "All [failures] had occurred exactly at the moment in which we now found ourselves—the moment at which the solution (aka the 'truth') is discovered. The next, almost reflexive step was to go out and spread the word: teach people, tell them, educate them. . . . We realized that [failures] occurred because we were acting as though once people 'know' something it results in the 'doing' something." They are talking about the limitation of what we are accustomed to: the problem-solving and problem-focused approach.

Their strategy is to count on the teaching and learning capacities of regular members of the community. The community members actually decided what approach would work. They together created structures where members of the community shared, demonstrated, and helped others practice what they, the community, knew. In the case of village children, "mothers and caretakers would bring their malnourished children to a neighbor's house for a few hours every day. Together with a health volunteer, they prepared and fed a nutritious, supplemental meal to their children." This strategy counted on the wisdom and generosity of villagers. It also meant that practicing what works was more powerful than hearing or seeing what works.

Finally, they had to deal with the need to evaluate results. Most social science evaluations think a third party is necessary to provide objectivity. The Sternins instead enlisted community members themselves to measure the progress of the project. "Each health volunteer," they wrote, "carried her own growth-monitoring book with fold out pages, enabling her to record and track the weight and nutritional state of each child in her hamlet over time." After a few months, "everyone had either a child, a relative, or a neighbor's kid participating in the program."

## THE IMPLICATIONS OF POSITIVE DEVIANCE FOR CONSULTING

Many lessons from the positive deviance approach are central to our concern for the discovery process in consulting. For one, there are ways to reduce the dependence on the consultant or support person to have the answer. We can contract from the beginning that we will engage people in the system to seek solutions and treat the engagement as important as the solution. We can also agree that we want an approach that can be measured and implemented by the people in the system now.

Second, we can choose to focus on the solutions that already exist in the community, even though they are rare and not accepted as common knowledge. This honors the gifts and capacities of organization members, which are what the Sternins call "invisible in plain sight." As consultants or support people, we can decide to contract for discovering what is working and who in the client system has figured something out. It is our choice to proceed this way, even when the client or community is problem focused, which is most often the case.

Also, the gift-based strategies almost always have to work through invitation. Even with the support of senior management or leadership and their ability to mandate a process, it is better to work with a smaller group that shows interest than with strategically placed and leveraged people who are not acting so much out of interest as out of obligation.

Finally, what is appealing about the positive deviance thinking is that the Sternins have made a profound commitment to work in a true partnership with those they are intending to be of service to. They listen endlessly and carefully as a practice. They offer no solutions other than some principles of approach. They are equal learners as well as teachers at every stage and in every project.

## AN EXAMPLE OF WHAT IS WORKING

This book to this point has been about a methodology and way of thinking for making a difference when you do not have direct control. I want to take a break in outlining the methodology with an example of these ideas in action. The core message of the methodology is that influence is born of a partnership rather than parenting orientation to the world.

Partnership has three core elements:

- A capacity to contract well and being clear about our own wants and the wants of others

- A willingness to inquire and discover through listening

- A belief that answers and the decision to act ultimately reside with those who come to us with questions, regardless of how much expert knowledge we possess or they are looking for

To make these consultative elements concrete and specific, a friend and colleague, Paul Uhlig, a thoracic surgeon, has been using a partnership and consultative strategy in his work for many years. I like his

work as an example because it comes from an arena that touches us all: health care. This could be considered an unlikely place for partnership and a consultative stance to take hold.

### Health Care Reform in Action

No other profession has produced a more authoritative, knowing role than that of the physician. We may be masters of our destiny in every aspect of our lives, yet when we walk into a doctor's office, we give it all away. The very idea of diagnosis, prescription, and knowing what is best for others originates in this place. It has become sacred space where eventually our life can be at stake, and we often place it in the hands of another.

Despite its exalted status in our society, health care is churning with a desire for reform. We think it is too costly and often inequitable in who has access to it. Some feel it is too tightly managed and driven by corporate interests. Others are worried about the quality of care, the safety of patients, and the absence of proof that some procedures and prescriptions are really necessary.

What is striking is that in all the reform debate about health care—all the talk of cost, access, management, safety, and quality—the conversation is mostly about disease, needs, and deficiencies, not about what produces health. We think better health can be purchased through better control of costs, advanced chemistry, improved technology, and procedures. This amounts to trying harder at what we are now doing.

What is absent in the reform conversation is the recognition that reform grows out of transformed relationships, the primary one being the relationship between the doctor and the patient and all the other human beings who swirl around them. We take the authoritative position of the physician and the dependent position of the patient for granted. In effect, the dominant health care reform conversation is mostly within the context of the expert role orientation.

It would be easy to accept this as inevitable and in the nature of how health care must work. There are, however, places where the context is shifting and authentic reform is occurring. They give us a good example of how rethinking the contract, discovery, and feedback processes described in this book can make a big difference.

## Renegotiating the Social Contract

One person who has conceived and initiated such a shift in the basic physician-patient contract is Paul Uhlig, a cardiac surgeon now residing in Wichita, Kansas. In a letter to me, here is how Paul begins telling this story:

> Here is a paradox: a cardiac surgeon working by influence rather than authority. There are few professions we associate more with authority than being a thoracic surgeon. Yet for what we are trying to achieve, it has been essential to move beyond authority and to the challenge of working through relationships, example and influence.

Paul is interested in health care reform, but reform to him has little to do with regulations, cost control, and standardization. He is about reimagining health care by remembering its true purpose:

> The work that we are doing was given form ten years ago by a question that I and other members of my cardiac surgery team often heard from patients and families as they went about their daily work. The question was, "Don't you people talk to each other?"

> Of course we talked to each other. We worked together every day in the operating room, ICU [intensive care unit] and other patient care areas. We wrote notes to each other, paged each other and had impromptu conferences in hallways, lounges and the cafeteria. Yet despite all those conversations there was frustrating sense in patients, families and the team itself that we were often not on the same page.

"Don't you people talk to each other?" This question gave important insights into a puzzle Paul had been concerned with for years: the state of health care itself. How could it be that so many well-trained people could work so hard to offer good care and have the net effect be the runaway

costs, uneven quality, and inadequate access that left us all alienated and discouraged instead of rewarded and fulfilled? Paul and his colleagues began to see that the simple question, "Don't you people talk to each other?" was a window into these challenges.

Paul and his team decided they would change how they worked together with the goal of making the question go away. They basically decided to renegotiate their social contract with each other. They believed that if they could create new ways of working together that resulted in better-informed and better-connected caregivers, patients, and families, then costs, quality, access, and patient and caregiver satisfaction would get better too. This is the power of the contract.

One of the changes the team made was to hold weekly meetings of anyone interested in the care of cardiac surgery patients. It might seem unusual that such meetings did not already occur. But in health care, most disciplines work separately from one another, connecting only through orders in the chart. It was not common practice to sit down during the week to talk about teamwork and how it might be better. What Paul was doing was introducing a self-managed consultative process for the whole system around the patient.

## Changing the Conversation, Changing the Culture

One of the changes that emerged concerned the way the team related to patients and family members. Several respected voices, a social worker and nurse practitioner, had advocated for a new approach that actively engaged patients and family members as fully participating members of the care team. One suggested that the team make daily collaborative bedside rounds, with patients and family members actively included. They wanted to renegotiate the contract between caregivers and the patients and their families to make it a partnership.

At first many care team members laughed at this idea because of how impractical it sounded. There was no good time for everyone to meet, they said, and patients and families would not be able to understand what they were talking about. Gradually the idea was accepted, and 8:45 A.M. was chosen as the "least impossible, impossible time." And so daily collaborative bedside rounds with patients and families began.

Again in Paul's words:

> Having all of us there together with patients and families changed everything. Our work became much easier, although none of us understood that at first. At first, it was confusing and stressful. We were not used to being open about what we were thinking and doing with one another, making that accessible and asking for advice,

especially not with patients and their families. We were very concerned that we needed to be perfect in their eyes.

In reality, it turns out that just the opposite was true. The more we showed patients our unfiltered uncertainties and concerns, the more they were able to trust us and contribute. It seems paradoxical at first, but I can see now, at the far end, that it makes all the sense in the world. I think that is what is meant by *authenticity*. Our experience over time taught us the power and value of just being ourselves.

I would say that none of us, even those of us most committed to patient and family participation in rounds, was prepared for what we experienced and learned from our patients and how much those experiences changed us. We thought we understood what it meant to be patient centered. I thought I was one of the most patient-centered doctors that there could ever be. But we were wrong and I was wrong.

It was like peeling away an onion. We would make a shift—for example, one of the biggest was making a mutual commitment to use ordinary language rather than medical language for our conversations on rounds, and speaking directly to the patient and family rather than to each other—and we could see from the new perspective that much of what we thought was patient and family centered was not that at all. That eye-opening just went on and on.

We had been holding on to power. We were keeping our own expectations and our own values at the center of our interactions with our patients. We were not being truly respectful of the patient's wishes from their own unique perspectives. It was startling and humbling to experience this awakening. One thing for sure, once you understand this it changes you forever.

The goal became helping each person achieve a whole and meaningful life on his or her own terms. That is a very different goal than what I was trained to achieve. Imagine what a health care system would be like that had that as its goal—achieving life wholeness on the patient's own terms, not battling disease on my terms. It would not be recognizable. That vision is very hopeful to me.

Our patients taught that vision to us. We were just wise enough to listen and learn from them.

As Paul and his care team began working differently together and began including patients and their families, their outcomes and results improved. Recovery after surgery happened faster, deaths and complications decreased by half, and people found new meaning in the experiences of being a patient and of being a caregiver. One patient said, "For something you think would be so difficult, this was a wonderful experience." Another said, "You treated us like ordinary people, and that made all the difference."

What they had done is change the social contract with the patient and their family, going from expert to collaborator and consultant. It began with the health care professionals' recontracting with each other: they committed to be in the same room together on a regular basis. They initiated a self-managed discovery process. They got curious about each other and began to understand the problems each faced. These changes gave some early returns. As people began conversing in weekly team meetings, individuals who had worked together in the same environments, sometimes for years, got to know one another in new ways. Roles now had faces, and faces soon had names with stories.

People discovered their children attended the same schools and that they shared common interests. Interactions among members of the care team began to shift, taking on new dimensions reflecting the richer connections that were forming. Mutual understanding grew, tolerance increased, and patience expanded. People began to appreciate one another in new ways, and began relying more on others' capabilities and strengths. Work became easier and more fulfilling.

The second transformation was the contract between caregivers, including the physician, and patients and families. Paul and his team created a structure where the wants, doubts, and statement of the problem of all parties were equally relevant. They made it a consultative process, a partnership between experts and clients.

## Success Carries Its Own Set of Challenges

Paul offered a follow-up to the initial experiment that is also instructive. After some time, the team started talking about their experience. Paul and his team received the Eisenberg Patient Safety Award for their work, the highest recognition in patient safety given by the Joint Commission and National Quality Forum. You would think that would be a success story, and it is. But there is more. Again in Paul's words:

> After we received the Eisenberg Award, I was invited to many places that were excited to show me their multidisciplinary rounds. I would go with them and usually see something that looked like a target. In the center were a handful of doctors, who did most of the talking. Around them were people in other disciplines, who responded when they were pointed at and asked for their input. In the outer circle were others, often having side conversations. The patient was usually near the center of the target, being talked about, not talked with. Usually the patient's family was not present. Many people seemed bored and impatient. It looked uncomfortable for everyone. That is not the kind of collaborative rounds we had created. Theirs was multidisciplinary, but it was relationally wrong and it didn't work.
>
> When we received the Eisenberg Award we were asked to write an article about what we had done. When I look back on what we wrote, it is interesting to see that we didn't really understand what we had accomplished. In the article, we described the techniques we used in

great detail, yet we completely missed the point of what had really changed. What had changed was the nature of our working relationships, and subsequently the relationship with our patients changed and improved also. We had put in motion processes that changed how we worked together.

Most people, including us at the time, viewed this as a technical achievement rather than as a relational achievement. And consequently, when people tried to replicate our work, they were often not successful. The few programs that were successful inadvertently got the relationships right. It took many years and a lot more study before we understood that.

The story should end here, but of course it doesn't—and this is the paradoxical nature of the consultative and change-making path. After the initial success, complete with real measurable outcomes and national recognition, Paul lost his job. This had nothing to do with his work as a surgeon, but because what his team had invented so called into question the conventional status quo. The system in place refused to accept the idea that partnership made such a difference. The resistance was to value control and status over outcomes. This is not surprising; dealing with this reaction is as much a part of the work as contracting, discovery and feedback.

Just to finish the story, Paul says he lost sleep for a week, then realized that this was data about how hard it can be to change culture. Like most other true innovators, Paul kept learning and patiently found new ways to keep moving forward. He is now internationally recognized for his work in patient safety and health care teamwork. Spreading this partnership way of care is now the center of his work and is building momentum in the health care discussion despite the response of the culture within which it was invented.

## The True Nature of Health Care and Consultation

In sharing his way of working for inclusion in this book, Paul commented on the connection between the ideas in this book and his experience. He emphasized first the shift that is occurring from diagnosing problems to helping people imagine and achieve possibilities. The new world of health care that Paul imagines is about achieving possibilities. He is no longer interested in diagnosing and treating problems.

From "What's New" at the start of this book, Paul selected these phrases that he says are closest to the work that he is doing in health care:

"Relatedness based on listening, authenticity, and not knowing."

"Real reform . . . will come from changing our relationship with our service provider."

"The need for authenticity and directness about sensitive issues."

"Dialogue, interaction, doubts, and commitments move the action forward."

"It all sounds so simple, remains so rare," he says.

Paul says he would also support the summary of what is still true after all these years:

- Team and personal relationships are critical.

- Our purpose is giving structure to the emotional and personal dimensions of our workplaces.

- The need to know ourselves and remain authentic is essential.

- We must be tuned into the feeling dimension of our connection with others.

To conclude, Paul says, "As we continue the work with health care teams, our understanding of health is evolving":

> The more my colleagues and I learn about health and healing, the more we are recognizing the power and importance of community for changing the context and culture of health care. If you want to

create a better, safer health care system, bring the people involved together and ask them what works and why. Create protected time for people to meet and reflect. Their shared dedication to excellence will drive things forward from there. Creating opportunities for reflective conversations to happen—making places where people can reconsider their beliefs and expectations together—is how real reform begins.

I am coming to understand that health is more of a verb than a noun. People move together toward health and healing through engagement and co-creation, with the purpose of caring. Health and healing are fundamentally relational achievements, with science in the service of the relationships. The methods for accomplishing this are not hard. They are just different and more rewarding than what we do today.

# CHAPTER 13

# GET THE PICTURE

Now that we have navigated the discovery choices and methods, we are ready to produce a picture of what is happening to create problems for the client or to document what is a future possibility. Remember you have the choice to be problem focused or possibility and asset focused. It's up to you and the place where you are doing the work. Also in your hands is the choice to structure the discovery through the eyes of a third party (you) or make it a whole-system self-assessment effort. Again, your and the client's preferences will dictate the choice here. The possibility and whole-system choices are labeled as *Notes* within the list of steps that follow. In each of these cases, the business of this phase is

1. Collecting information at three different layers of analysis: understanding the presenting problem, what others are doing to create the problem, and what the client is doing to create the problem.

   *Note:* If this phase is about creating a new possibility rather than solving a problem, the requirement is to define the organizing question that will animate the possibility discussion.

2. Assessing the organizational and managerial climate in which action will be considered.

3. Dealing with client resistance in sharing information with you or fully engaging.

4. Choosing the right discovery process so that the structure of this phase begins to create ownership in dealing with the problem or the possibility. The discovery process itself changes an organization.

5. Reducing what is learned to a manageable number of issues.

6. Giving language, order, and meaning to what emerges in a way that leads to a change.

## THE STEPS IN GETTING THE PICTURE

No matter what kind of information you seek—whether you look at information flow, equipment design, people's attitudes, difficult long-term problems, or the social culture itself—and whatever dimensions you analyze, there are some general ways to describe the steps in discovery that might be helpful. Each time you collect information to form a picture, whether it is a six-month or six-minute project, you make these choices.

*Step 1: Redecide to Proceed.* The consultant and the client together make a decision to begin the discovery. Often this involves several people who work for the manager who can confirm that there is an incentive to initiate a new study. The motivation to proceed should be based on the desire to make improvements in the organization, not just on the desire to do research.

*Step 2: Select the Discovery Strategy.* At this point you have to decide whether you want to look at problems or possibilities, that is, to look at what is working or not working. You also have to decide if you or a third party will conduct the inquiry or whether you want a self-managed discovery process. Chapter Eleven covers these choices designing self-managed discovery in more detail.

*Step 3: Identify the Presenting Problem.* Any discovery begins with a conversation about a concern that line managers have about their organization. The manager's first description of the problem is called the *presenting problem.* It is usually about what others are doing to create the problem. The presenting problem is usually only a symptom of the real problem, and the purpose of the discovery is to elaborate and deepen the manager's initial statement. Identifying the presenting problem is the first step in discovery.

*Note:* If you are taking a positive or possibility stance, then you need to focus on what in the internal or external environment is calling for a new possibility. What is the question that, if answered, would initiate a transformation or the beginning of a new vision?

*Step 4: Decide Who Will Be Involved.* Decide what levels of the organization will be included in the discovery: the greater the diversity is, the richer will be the outcome. How many from each level? Who from which departments? Do we ask customers, suppliers, support people, others? Remember that asking people questions creates expectations that something will shift, and they will get feedback on the results.

*Step 5: Select Dimensions to Examine.* Discovery hinges on the questions to be asked. A limited number of questions need to be selected from within the discipline of the consultant or the context that gave rise to the project. A financial person will select questions about financial information and control; human resources will ask questions about compensation, attitudes, or culture.

*Note:* In the possibility approach, the questions will center around giving form to a vision or details about what is working well or who is succeeding against the odds.

In either case the dimensions and questions should be limited—fewer than twenty. Too much data from the discovery will be overwhelming.

*Step 6: Select the Methods(s) of Inquiry.* Regardless of your strategy, the information-gathering method depends on the scope and purpose of your inquiry. Select a method that fits with the time available, the motivation of management, and the intent of the effort. There are only a few ways to find out what is going on:

- *Interview.* Do it individually or use a group interview. Use either a structured or unstructured interview.

- *Survey.* Takes more time to prepare. Good for large numbers of people, but numerical results can be hard to interpret.

- *Document analysis.* Look at the numbers, results, written communication. Useful because it takes up your time only. Also gives the aura of objectivity.

- *Direct observation.* Sit in on critical events and meetings and watch what happens. Look at the equipment. It may be the only first-person data you have. This can be the best source of data if you can trust your own perceptions.

- *Your own experience.* Know that you are being managed by the client organization the same as everyone else is managed. Pay attention to how they treat you. On this project, how much information, influence, access, pressure do you have? This is valuable data on the client's management style, and it is valid data.

- *Whole system/self discovery.* Bring together those who have a stake in the problem and possibility, including those who will have to act on their commendations, to discuss the dimensions of the situation. Here you are more a facilitator than an interviewer. Again, see Chapter Eleven.

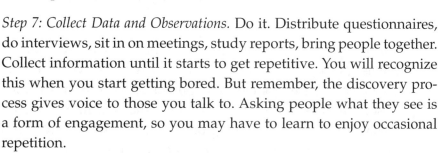

*Step 7: Collect Data and Observations.* Do it. Distribute questionnaires, do interviews, sit in on meetings, study reports, bring people together. Collect information until it starts to get repetitive. You will recognize this when you start getting bored. But remember, the discovery process gives voice to those you talk to. Asking people what they see is a form of engagement, so you may have to learn to enjoy occasional repetition.

*Step 8: Funnel the Information.* Somehow all that people have said and named, all you observed and researched needs to be reduced to manageable proportions. The purpose of the analysis is to focus energy, not describe the universe.

*Step 9: Summarize the Picture.* You need to find a format that will summarize what has been produced. Concentrate on the visual impact of the story you are creating and how easy it is to understand.

*Step 10: Construct Meaning from the Process.* What does the information mean? What is important? And why? What is the solution or alternative future the discovery points to.

*Step 11: Manage the Feedback Meeting.* Report the picture and its implications to the organization. Who should be at the feedback meeting? How are those who were involved in the study going to find out the results? Be sure you have allowed enough time in the feedback meeting to deal with the resistance you will surely get. Structure the meeting so the majority of time is for discussion, not presentation. Chapter Fifteen provides more about this meeting.

*Note:* Even with self-assessment and whole-system dialogue, the picture has to be captured and meaning extracted. All that differs from the traditional third-party process is who does it.

*Step 12: Give Recommendations.* Sometimes recommendations will come before the feedback meeting. This should be within the control of the group that requested the study. In a self-assessment strategy, recommendations come from the community.

*Step 13: Make a Decision.* The process is not complete until a decision has been made to do something.

*Step 14: Implementation.* This is the payoff, so stay around for this phase even if it's on your own time. After discovery, you have your own feel for the problems and possibilities. Your information can be useful in interpreting the hills and valleys of implementation. You also offer ways of involving people in the implementation that will increase the chances that the decision will be translated into effective change.

Most of these steps apply to all projects, regardless of our technical disciplines or particular fields of expertise or discovery strategy. You know what technical data you want, ways to get it, and what to do with it when you have it, so the rest of this chapter concentrates on discovery in dimensions you may not be used to, paying special attention to your face-to-face encounters with the client as you engage in discovery.

## A WORD ABOUT BIAS

Having an impact as a consultant is to pay attention to more than your methodology or field of expertise. Regardless of your assignment or its designated scope, the work almost always impacts the social system and touches on core issues around the management of the organization. It is important, then, to pick dimensions of how the problem is being managed that you are comfortable with and go with them in your discovery rather than worry about whether you've selected the right or wrong one.

In selecting the dimensions of your discovery, you predefine the problem, but there is no reason to feel anxiety about biasing the data. If you have contracted to look at how conflict is handled, or how much people level with each other, or how they plan, you may already have some idea of what is wrong with the organization, particularly if you are an internal consultant.

Do not treat this as bias; treat it as insight. Your predefinition of the problem is valuable and gives you good clues on how to spend your discovery time. Trust this. You do need to keep listening as you're collecting data to see whether there are other issues that you don't know about. If there are, you need to pursue them. The point is not to treat the insight of your own feeling about being part of the organization as bias but as useful information.

## ASSESSING HOW THE SITUATION IS BEING MANAGED

If you want to develop your skills in collecting information directly about the social system or how the problem is being managed, there are more than a dozen aspects of organizational life to explore. Your goal is to understand something about how this organization functions so that you will understand how it will manage the implementation of your recommendations. Paying attention to these dimensions will give you a good picture of the organization. These are also areas that people being interviewed love to talk about, so you will have fun with it.

Ask questions about these areas:

1. *Objectives.* What are the goals of the group and the person you are talking to? You want to determine how much goal clarity and goal agreement there is.

2. *Subgroups.* What is the relationship among groups that have to work together on this problem? Which groups are supportive? Which groups are in conflict? Do some groups or individuals tend to be excluded from the action? Why?

3. *Support.* How does this group express support? In many groups, support is expressed by silence: "If I like what you are doing, I will leave you alone." Who gets support, and from whom?

4. *Evaluation.* Do people know where they stand? How do they find out? What are the norms about asking where you stand and getting an answer?

5. *Positive history.* What are the stories of what made this place great? What are its strengths and assets? What do people take pride in and want to preserve?

6. *Status differences.* Which are the high-status and the low-status groups? How are the differences expressed, and what impact does this have on the problem and people's attitudes toward a particular solution or possibility?

7. *Authority and power.* Who has high and low power in this situation? How do people working with it deal with the power differences: openly or cautiously? What are people's attitudes about authority? Do they openly resist it, overly give in to it, put up with it, or not care?

8. *Decision making.* How does the group make decisions? What role does the boss play? How do people get their viewpoints considered in a decision?

9. *Norms for individual behavior.* What are the norms on taking the initiative, making demands, expressing disagreement, aggressiveness, asking for help, using questions to make statements, dealing with boredom, taking risks in expressing doubts or uncertainty, and openly confronting differences?

10. *Management information.* How are resources identified, progress monitored, movement evaluated, problems identified?

11. *Leadership style.* What are the styles of formal and informal leaders? What is their impact on this situation?

12. *Conflict.* How is conflict managed, confronted, smoothed over, compromised, forced, ignored, or suppressed?

13. *Domination.* Is the situation dominated by one or more persons? What is their impact? Are they part of the group trying to work

the problem, or are they so high up in the organization that they are unreachable?

14. *Attitudes about this project and your involvement.* To understand people's attitudes about the situation and what they think of your being involved in working on it, try asking some of these questions:

"How do you feel about my being brought in to help with this?"

"Why do you think the organization needs the help of someone like me? Do you think my help is needed?"

"What kinds of questions do you think I should ask people to get a feel for what is going on around here?"

"What ideas have been supported by people but have not gotten enough support?"

15. *Diversity.* How are differences handled? What is the mix of people from different worlds, cultures, races, and how are they valued? What positions do they hold? Is there a place to say no? Is surprise tolerated? How are strangers welcomed?

16. *Going forward.* What would people recommend if they were in your position? How hopeful are people about making real progress on this problem or possibility? What obstacles do they see to your suggestions being accepted?

Of course, you wouldn't use all of these questions. For any one situation, you can scan the dimensions, and the ones that are relevant will stand out to you. Asking any two or three of the questions will give you data on a lot of the rest. You can also assume that how the organization manages its current situation will be identical to how you and your suggestions will be managed. If you use these kinds of questions, you will know what you are getting into, and some of the answers should be part of the clear picture that you are going to report on at the feedback meeting.

Again, it is critical to use this kind of information as part of your analysis—even if the client didn't ask for it. It is one of the unique contributions you can make to the client. If you want to be of unique value to your client, then you have to take the risk of offering unique information. Accurate information about how the organization is functioning is not available to most managers. The people they work with have such a vested interest in the organization that no one is trusted to be objective. You have less of a vested interest and are in the best position to deal with sensitive issues.

## THE DISCOVERY INTERVIEW

The interview is a means of discovery that is common to all disciplines and cannot be underrated. Although there is much written about interviewing methods, the interview receives special attention here because of its interpersonal nature and the effect it has on the client organization. It is where relationship is built.

### The Interview as a Joint Learning Event

If you can take the time to talk to a wide cross section of people, it means that by the time you start making sense of what you have discovered, you have already had a large impact on the organization. The mere act of asking questions can stimulate people to rethink what they are doing. Your questions express to them without ambiguity what you think is important to focus on in solving the problem you are working on. Clients can learn a lot from your choice of what to investigate.

### Difficult Interviews

If you encounter resistance in an interview, deal with it the same way you deal with resistance at any other stage of the process: pick up the cue, name the resistance, and wait for the person to respond. If you are in an interview and it is giving you nothing, deal with it as authentically as you can. Tell the person that you are not getting what you need. If that doesn't help, at some point terminate the discussion. You will build more trust with that person if you stop the interview than if you go ahead mechanically through your questions, while both of you know that nothing productive is taking place.

## LEVELS OF ANALYSIS

Every problem facing persons or organizations has layers, like an onion. Each statement of a problem or situation is an approximation. As you go to deeper layers, you get closer to causes and actionable statements of the problem.

The initial statement of a problem, the presenting problem, is almost always made in a way that inspires futility—futility on the part of the client and the consultant. If the presenting problem did not inspire futility, it would already have been solved and you would not be talking about it. To accept the presenting problem at face value is to get stuck. The same usually goes for the client's first portrayal of gifts or possibilities. There is more than meets the eye. In discussing layers of analysis, we will stick with problem-solving language to keep things simple.

Your task is to work with the line manager—or group or organization—to shed light on the layers underneath. By position alone, you are situated advantageously to see the complexity of the layers below.

When you are working with individuals, the layers generally stack up in a pattern like this:

- *Top layer.* The presenting problem comes most often in the form of a concern expressed in organizational or business terms: "We aren't getting our product." "My group isn't going well." "The system isn't working." "This food group is not selling in certain markets."

- *Second layer.* The person's perceptions about how others are contributing to the need for change is the next level: "People are more interested in their career than in what is good for the whole." "Two members of the group do all the talking." "The people don't understand the system." "The outside world is demanding something new. "

- *Third layer.* This is a statement of how a person sees their own way of contributing to the situation. The person may be contributing by certain conscious actions or by simply not giving the situation much attention.

This statement is vital because it brings the responsibility closer to the line manager or whomever you are talking to. Instead of expressing the situation in terms of forces outside the person that are creating the problems, the focus is moved a little more internally.

The questions you ask to get information on each layer are straightforward:

**Top Layer**

- What is the technical or business problem that you are experiencing?

**Second Layer**

- What are other individuals or groups in the organization doing to either cause or maintain this problem at its current level of severity?

- What are they doing that limits the possibility?

**Third Layer**

- What is your role in sustaining all of this?

- What is there in your approach or way of managing the situation that might be contributing to the problem or getting in the way of its resolution?

- What might you be doing that gets in the way of an alternative future emerging?

  *Note on the third layer:* The person you are talking to might answer, "I don't know of anything I am doing that is a problem. That is your job to find out." If you get this response, be a little skeptical. People usually have some idea of how they are contributing to a problem; they are just reluctant to mention it.

When someone says to you, "I don't know what my role in sustaining the problem is," there is another question you can ask: "Suppose you did know what your role was. What would it be?" Sometimes this jogs them enough to answer your third-layer question.

If people really do not see themselves as part of the problem, this in itself is important. Why do they not see themselves as players? Their stance of spectators or, more precisely, as victims may be part of a pattern that speaks to the way the group is managed. Include this in your understanding of how the problem is being managed. This sense of helplessness, or being an outsider, will make a difference in the energy available to act on what you recommend.

These layers can form the basis for questions used in the discovery process. The objective of the discovery (especially with an individual) is to discover a statement of the problem that is enlightening and actionable—something someone can do something about. The objective is generally not to advance knowledge or generate wisdom about organizations—that is called research. Rather, the consultant's energy is directed toward continually uncovering issues for which people can take responsibility.

The root issue is almost always how much responsibility or ownership a person feels for the problem—how much people are in the stance of a victim versus in a position with some power to act. Uncovering deeper layers of a problem is really the search for unused resources available to solve the problem or create something new.

---

For a layers-of-analysis exercise and a discussion of issues in small group discovery, visit www.flawlessconsulting.com.

A last comment on discovery addresses your own experience. The client manages you, the consultant, in the same way the client manages other resources and people. If you want to understand the client's management style, you simply have to observe how you are treated. Are you feeling controlled, listened to, supported, treated with respect or disdain? Are decisions with the client collaborative or one way? Is the client open to options or forever on one track?

Your observations and experience about the client are valid data. Paying close attention to how you are managed by the client early in the project gives you more guidance on what to explore in determining how the technical or business problem is being managed.

For a downloadable copy of Checklist # 5, visit www.flawlessconsulting.com.

## Checklist #5: Planning a Discovery Meeting

These planning guidelines cover the business of the data collection phase and help you prepare for any resistance you might get:

1. **Asking questions is an active occasion for learning. Use the meeting as an opportunity to deal with resistance and generate interest and commitment.**

2. **The response you get provides valuable data on the ultimate implementation of your expertise. Notice how the client manages the discussion with you:**

   • How much interest and energy are there on this project?

   • On which points is the client uneasy or defensive?

   • On which points is the client open to learning and change?

   • Where is the client unrealistic in estimating the ease or difficulty of some action?

3. **What is your understanding of the presenting problem or possibility? Now, based on your experience, what do you think your layers of analysis will yield?**

   - *Layer 1:* What technical or business problems is the client likely experiencing? What client assets or possibilities exist?

   - *Layer 2:* What are others in the client's organization likely contributing to the problem? Who are the other likely actors in the problem? What are others in the client's organization likely contributing to the collection of assets and possibilities? Who are other likely contributors?

   - *Layer 3:* What is the client doing that is helping to create the problem or prevent it (unknowingly) from being solved? What is the client doing to hold back on the possibilities?

4. **What organizational folklore, history, and culture surround this project? Who are the ogres and angels in the client's setting? Acceptance of the folklore as truth is part of what blocks resolution. Identify areas of potential blind spots.**

5. **You can support and confront during the meeting:**

   - What support can you give the client at this point? Examples: make tentative recommendations, offer personal encouragement and assurance, acknowledge difficulties, describe similar situations you have known, thank the client for being candid with you?

   - How might you confront the client in this meeting? For example: are you not getting good data, is the client overanswering questions and controlling discussion too much, is the client omitting key areas to discuss or answering questions with one-word answers, are there constant interruptions in the meetings, is the client skipping around too much, does the client not believe in the project or play down the seriousness or implications of the problem, are there negative attitudes about consultants in general?

8. **What nonverbal data can you look for? What in the setting of the meeting carries a message on client commitment and involvement in your project?**

9. **What data do you want to collect about how the organization is functioning?**

For a downloadable copy of Checklist #6, visit www.flawlessconsulting .com.

## Checklist #6. Reviewing the Discovery Meeting

Your notes contain the content of the discovery meeting. Here are some questions to answer afterward about the process of the meeting. It also is a review of the discovery concepts.

1.  **How did the client manage the discussion?**

    Client Control                                              Consultant Control
    100 percent                                                 100 percent

    |———————————————————————————————————————————|

    No client energy                                            Very high
    for the project                                             client energy

    |———————————————————————————————————————————|

2.  **What is the technical problem or possibility?**

3.  **What others are contributing to it?**

4.  **What is the client doing to create the problem or prevent its resolution? Or what is the client doing to impede realization of the possibility?**

5.  **What folklore, history, ogres, and angels can you identify on this project? Are there any blind spots that the client is missing?**

6.  **What supporting statements did you make?**

7.  **What confronting statements did you make?**

8.  **What nonverbal data did you notice?**

# CHAPTER 14

# PREPARING FOR FEEDBACK

Every line manager wants to know what to do about a problem or possibility and so wants recommendations. Resist being too carried away by the struggle to develop perfect recommendations. If you have presented a clear and simple picture of why the problem or possibility exists, the client will have as many ideas for recommendations as you do. The reason the client has run out of recommendations is because of the limiting picture of the situation that they are now working with.

## A CLEAR PICTURE MAY BE ENOUGH

The consultant's primary task is to present a fresh picture of what has been discovered. This is 70 percent of the contribution you have to make. Trust it.

What you do with your discovery is to focus attention on areas that your expertise tells you are the likely causes of the problem or sources of a possibility. What to focus on is under your control regardless of the assignment. Trusting yourself to focus on what you feel is important may be the most valuable thing you have to offer the client. Treat the choice of what to examine as a highly important one and yours to influence.

## CONDENSING THE DATA

You always collect more data that you could ever use. A high anxiety point in any consulting project or ongoing relationship is what to  share. When discovery is done—when you have finished asking your questions and have all the information you are going to get—you now have to make sense of it.

You may have devised a rational, logical process to sort out and categorize the information, but the selection of what is important is essentially a judgment on your part. This is what your client is paying you for. Trust your intuition; don't treat it as bias. If you are an internal consultant, you are often familiar with the organization, the people, and how they operate. Use this information.

When I am struggling to decide what is important in a pile of data, I sometimes read through all the notes, reports, and meeting summaries once. Then I put them aside. On a blank sheet of paper, I then list what I think is important in what I know—usually about four or five items. I let that be my guide on what to report and how to organize the report.

I have faith that what I can remember is what is really important. Since a person can absorb only a limited amount of data, what stands out to me is what I want to stand out to the client. Let the information that stays in the background become part of an appendix, but don't clutter the picture with a complete list of everything you found out.

As guidelines for selecting what to highlight to the client, I prefer items that

1. The client has control over changing

2. Are clearly important to the organization

3. Have some commitment somewhere in the client organization to work on

4. Are clearly a strength or an expansion of something that is currently working or under discussion

## SOME DO'S AND DON'TS

As you get close to presenting the picture and recommendations, you start making decisions about what to include and how to say it. Here are some suggestions.

### Don't Collude

Don't give the client support for a stance that reduces the organization's ability to solve the problem or realize the possibility. If there are certain sensitive subjects that the client avoids and is uncomfortable with, don't collude with the client by also avoiding those subjects.

There are two things consultants typically do to collude with clients, thereby undermining themselves. The first is to develop explanations for problems that leave the solution outside the client's control. We blame higher management, the general economic condition, the marketplace, other groups in the organization. Each of these explanations has the benefit of reducing the immediate pain of the client's own responsibility, but carries the price of feeling helpless about improving the situation. Don't collude with the client in avoiding responsibility. You can acknowledge the role others play in the problem and at the same time keep the conversation focused on the client's role.

The second way we collude with clients is to play down the impact that difficult relationships have on the problem. The client may be having trouble with a subordinate or a boss and yet barely mention this as part of the problem. If you get wind of this kind of difficulty, mention it in your report. If the written report is slated for wide circulation, you may want to mention it only verbally. Don't avoid dealing with it. Helping the manager face up to the impact difficult relationships have on the problem may be the most important contribution you can make.

### Don't Project

Projecting is placing your own feeling onto another person. If you are feeling anxious about part of what you have discovered, you assume the client will also feel anxious. If you would not like someone to tell you that your subordinates feel you are too autocratic, you assume the client also would not like to hear that feedback. Clients have a right to all the information that you have collected. Let your clients have it.

Stay aware of your own feelings, but keep testing the limits of what the line manager can accept. If you feed back data that causes a minor uproar, stay with it. You and the client will both survive. Don't project your feelings and sensitivities onto the client. Make direct statements, and then ask how the client feels about the statements. Of course, the language you use matters, but we will discuss that later.

## Do Support the Client's Expectations

Clients (and consultants) need support. If you have parts of the picture that are confirming to the client, reinforcing the reasonableness of what the client is doing, include these in your report. If the client has a perception of the problem or possibility and you see it the same way, say so. Clients have a right to know what they are doing that is working.

I once had a client who felt that everyone in the organization was avoiding responsibility for the fact that a certain test procedure wasn't working and so poor raw material was being delivered to the customer. The customer unknowingly used the raw material in its finished product, got serious customer complaints, and eventually had to recall the product.

This became a huge crisis that returned to my client's door. He had been trying to focus attention on the problem with the test, but to no avail. When we interviewed others in the organization about the problem, it was clear that no one felt responsible for solving it, although everyone felt it should be handled by a specific research group. When we reported this to the client, he was relieved and reassured that we shared his perception of the problem. He had begun to think maybe he was crazy and everyone else knew what they were doing.

This was a confirming and valuable experience. If you have confirming data, report it. Although many clients say they want to hear only about the problem, don't you believe it. And don't you believe it when clients say they don't want to hear about the things they have already told you are working. Give support even if it is not requested.

## Do Confront

Your data will also indicate areas for improvement. You can identify what the client is doing that is self-defeating and areas in which the client is vulnerable. Report them, even if they are painful. The hardest data to report may be about the client's own personal style. Just share this information with the client in as kind and supportive a way as possible. If you avoid information that creates tension, then why does the client needs you as consultant? The client already knows how to avoid tension. Your role is to help the client move toward the tension and face the difficult reality that has been skirted. This why building a close relationship early in the process is so important: it will make the difficult conversations later in the process productive.

## LANGUAGE IN GIVING THE PICTURE

The most useful guideline for conveying the picture effectively—either written or spoken—is to behave assertively. There are many frameworks for looking at personal behavior and personal effectiveness. I think this is the clearest and most practical.

## Assertive

Every person has rights. Clients and consultants too. Assertive behavior is stating directly what you want and how you see things without putting down or infringing on the rights of others. Assertive feedback is stating to the client how you see the problem or possibility without implying that the client is a bad manager or has missed seeing the obvious.

## Aggressive

Aggressive behavior is also expressing your own wants and views, but doing it in a way that puts down or negates the other person.

Aggressive feedback is describing the situation in a way that implies the manager is incompetent, unfeeling, uncaring, or in need of fixing. The operational test for aggressive statements is whether you can add the phrase "you dummy" to the end of the sentence. If "you dummy" fits nicely at the end, the statement was aggressive.

## Nonassertive

Nonassertive behavior is when you hold back your feelings and views and don't state them at all. Nonassertive feedback, in the name of protecting the manager or yourself, occurs when you don't present the client information on how the situation is being managed, or how the management style of the manager is affecting the problem or possibility. Nonassertion also occurs when you ignore the politics of the situation or avoid sensitive issues.

## The Goal: Assertive and Authentic

Authentic behavior and assertive behavior are very close together. Aim to be authentic and assertive with a client. Aggressive behavior creates resistance unnecessarily, and nonassertive behavior does both yourself and the client a disservice.

In wording feedback, then, your goal is to describe what you have found and not to evaluate it. Your task is to present a clear and simple picture of the situation. The more the feedback is evaluative, the greater the resistance there will be. The choice is to make the narrative as descriptive as possible. For example, it is one thing to say that when the group sits down to do work, the boss does about 80 percent of the talking. That's a descriptive statement. Another way to put it would be that the boss totally dominates and overruns this group and doesn't do a good job of running meetings. This second way is the evaluative way.

The more evaluative the statement is, the more defensive people get. Words such as *weak, strong, incompetent, indecisive, dictatorial,* and *controlling* are very evaluative and should not be used. Avoid using "judging" words.

Also avoid vague stereotypes. The more specific you are about what's going on in the organization, the more useful this information is.

A general statement like, "We have a problem in decision making," is so vague that people can't really identify the problem being presented.

Long explanations and justifications should also be avoided. Most questions about method and recommendations can be answered in a paragraph or less. If the questions persist, give your two good-faith answers, and then acknowledge that it is resistance that confronts you. Deal with the resistance by naming it and waiting for a response. Resist the temptation to explain the unexplainable.

The picture you present is a statement of what is, not a statement of what ought to be. To discuss what ought to be is to moralize and sound like a judge or seer. The only time to talk about what ought to be is when your contract with the client is to predict or prescribe the future. Otherwise make neutral, descriptive statements of what is currently causing the problem or revealing the possibility. To recap:

| Use Language That Is: | Avoid Language That Is: |
| --- | --- |
| Descriptive | Judgmental |
| Focused | Global |
| Specific | Stereotyped |
| Brief | Lengthy |
| Simple | Complicated |

## PRESENTING THE PICTURE . . . AS COURTROOM DRAMA

If you can view a consulting project as a process in search of the best decision, you can view the consultant and client as taking different roles commonly found in a courtroom. Most of these roles are negative examples of what not to do. I apologize for this. But you see these roles played out so often in offices, conference rooms, and production areas that they are worth mentioning. None but the last role really serves the consultant well, though I admit some do have a certain appeal.

## Consultant as Judge

You are there to interpret the law, or interpret corporate policy, or tell the client when he is out of line. When a client makes a mistake, the consultant judge decides what the penalty should be by influencing that manager's performance appraisal next time around. Because judges sit higher than the rest of us, people fear them and don't come to see them voluntarily. The only ones really comfortable with judges are other judges (sometimes called top management).

## Consultant as Jury

Juries determine guilt and innocence. Consultant juries feel responsible for ultimately deciding on their own whether the client was wrong or right. This stance is remote and very parental.

## Consultant as Prosecutor

The prosecutor is there to present evidence to the jury. Some consultants present feedback as if they were going for a conviction. They develop irrefutable data and statistics and present them in a foolproof, totally buttoned-up package. This creates distance from the client and carries the message that success is in the hands of the consultant rather than a joint effort.

## Consultant as Defendant

Sometimes we go into a feedback meeting feeling like we are the one on trial. We have all our just-in-case files with us. We have rehearsed our presentation three times and even have an extra set of Power-Points in case of an accident. When we get questioned by the client, we overexplain and make promises to get more data, even when we know it is a waste of time.

The consultant is not a defendant. If the client is treating you as if you are a defendant, it is just resistance and the client's own anxiety about the project.

## Consultant as Witness

This is the preferred role for a consultant. The witness has no direct vested interest in the outcome of the deliberations and is there to present accurate information. Witnesses give a clear, specific picture of what they observed. Presenting what came out of discovery is designed to do just that, so view yourself as a fair witness.

It is a great luxury to be able to be just a fair witness for a client and not also to have the responsibility for guarding the corporate interest. Many internal consultants have to be part-time police officers and part-time judges. When this happens, these roles greatly interfere with developing the kind of trust with clients that we would all wish. There is no way out of this bind. The best you can do is be clear with the client when you are in uniform and when you can be just a friendly, down-home consultant. If, however, as an internal consultant you have a choice about whether to take on some policing responsibilities, think twice. The attraction is that it gives you instant access and instant power over some people in the organization. The price for that power is high, and in my opinion, it is usually not worth the distrust that you create in your potential clients by taking on the robes of judgment. Most internal consultants disagree with me on this, so there you have it.

## SUPPORT AND CONFRONT

In any conversation about what is occurring, you're doing two things: both giving support to the organization and confronting it. Viewing the dialogue process as only confrontation increases the tension and decreases the chance of getting action. It is important to express the support you feel for that organization, as well as to call attention to the problem. People need support in order to have the strength to take responsibility for problems.

Support and confrontation are not mutually exclusive. Talking about the future and possible changes is difficult for clients, even though they asked for this. They ask for the confrontation when they commission for a discovery, but they also need support. Often the more resistant the group is, the more support they need (and the harder it is to give it to them). An example is in coping with very high-control, authoritarian-style managers. On the surface, they may appear very controlling and look as if they don't care about you as a person or care about people in the organization. They may act in a way that says they don't have any problems or that their problems can be solved by mechanistic solutions.

An authoritarian style on the surface may really be an expression of the manager's own anxiety about losing control in one of two ways. One fear that managers have is to lose control of themselves or find themselves in a situation in which they would be saying things they would regret later. The second anxiety is about losing control of the organization if they really own up to problems, face them, and deal with them. Managers fear they might end up supporting a more democratic or anarchic organization than they want. To the extent that it's accurate that underneath the resistance is an anxiety about control, one good way to respond is to give support to the manager.

If people are anxious, they need support, not confrontation. Even if they are being controlling and indifferent on the surface, give them support and let them know that they will be in control of the process, that they won't be in a position of doing anything they don't want to do. They won't lose control of the organization or lose the power that they think they need to manage it.

Supporting and confronting can almost come in the same sentence. The support statement often is a simple acknowledgment that you hear what the client is saying. To give the client support does not commit you to agree. It means you have listened. The confront statement then identifies the difference between how you see a situation and how the client sees the situation. Both kinds of statements should be part of your picture to the client.

# CHAPTER 15

# MANAGING THE MEETING FOR ACTION

Anytime you present a clear and simple picture of the current situation and make your recommendations, you do it in hopes of triggering action. The action could be a decision, further discovery, or learning. It is the moment of truth and high anxiety for the client and the consultant. It is also exciting and fun. Next to that moment at the beginning of the project when the client says yes, this is the part of consulting that I enjoy most.

The excitement of the meeting for action is that it holds the promise of some movement. It holds some hope that the energy the client and I have invested in this process will pay off. This is the major agenda—the commitment to action. Even if most of the meeting is spent in understanding the problem or the possibility, the heart of the meeting is the discussion of what to do. This is the way to approach the meeting—as an opportunity to get action, not just an opportunity to present data. In this sense, the meeting is not an ending. It is the beginning of the implementation phase that will solve a problem or change the status quo. This chapter is about how to structure and manage any meeting designed to be the beginning of some action.

To flawlessly manage this meeting, you need to attend to the business of this phase:

1. *Keep the picture in focus.* Keep it simple and straightforward. Use everyday language that is accurate, specific, and nonpunishing.

2. *Present personal and organizational data.* Include in your summary information on how the situation is being managed.

3. *Manage the meeting.* Maintain control of it and structure it. Keep it moving towards what will be done about the problem or possibility.

4. *Focus on the here and now of the meeting.* To have maximum leverage and get your expertise used, you need to watch the process of the meeting and deal directly with the resistance and the movement as it occurs. If you don't deal with the resistance in the meeting, you may never get another chance. If you do not acknowledge movement, it may evaporate.

5. *Don't take it personally.* A special reminder here, because this is the phase of consulting where you are likely to get the most resistance. Remember the rule: after 6:00 P.M., you can take anything personally, but during the day, no matter how many guns are aimed at you, your task is to stay focused on the client's internal struggle to confront the reality that is being resisted.

The other half of consulting flawlessly in this phase is to behave authentically—to state to the client what you are experiencing as the meeting progresses.

## HOW TO PRESENT THE PICTURE

The picture you present should focus on a few central aspects of the problem or possibility. The mistake with most presentations is that they are too long and too intricate. When we have spent all that time analyzing data, we fall in love with all of the facts and figures. We find interesting discrepancies that defy explanation; we notice historical trends and comparisons; we discover curves and graphs with shapes, heights, and textures that are each worth an hour's discussion. Go ahead and fall in love with your data—but don't tell everyone about it. Keep your presentation short and simple. The longer and more complex you make it, the more you are open for endless questions on methodology and interpretation.

To structure the presentation, there are only four general categories of data:

- Analysis of the technical or business problem

- A picture of what is working and what the possibilities are

- Analysis of how the situation is being managed

- Recommendations

In deciding how to present data, remember:

- The purpose of discovery is to focus awareness on a manageable number of dimensions. Most feedback overloads the organization. Keep the feedback down to under ten, or even fewer, issues.

- What we want is action. We are not doing research, even if it is called research.

The report does not have to have all the answers and does not have to be complete. It is often useful to devise a format that offers a role whereby the manager or group can participate in the analysis.

The end result with a group, as with an individual, is to have it take responsibility for its own situation.

## STRUCTURING THE MEETING

The purpose of every meeting is more than the presentation of your data. You want to get the client's reaction to the data and recommendations, and you want to get the client to do something as a result of your study. Here is how to get what you want from the meeting.

First, control the flow of the meeting. You are in the best position to do this. The client is going to be busy working through resistance and is in a pretty dependent position during the course of the meeting. If you control the meeting, it serves as a model for the client to learn how to manage meetings like this.

The agenda should follow the sequence shown in Figure 11. Keep the steps in that order, and don't skip any of them.

**Figure 11.** Steps in Managing the Meeting for Action

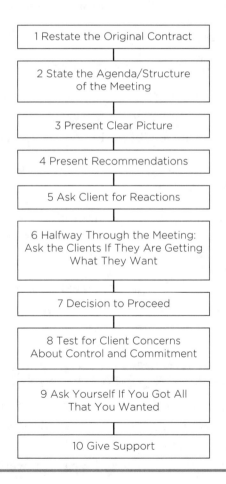

1 Restate the Original Contract

2 State the Agenda/Structure of the Meeting

3 Present Clear Picture

4 Present Recommendations

5 Ask Client for Reactions

6 Halfway Through the Meeting: Ask the Clients If They Are Getting What They Want

7 Decision to Proceed

8 Test for Client Concerns About Control and Commitment

9 Ask Yourself If You Got All That You Wanted

10 Give Support

Here is a detailed breakdown for the steps. The right-hand columns suggest how to allocate time to each sequence of steps. Beginning and ending times for each sequence in a sixty-minute meeting are shown. The percentage of meeting time that should be devoted to each step or group of steps is also listed. That way if you have planned a four-hour meeting, you know to ask the client how the meeting is going (step 6) at the end of two hours.

## Steps 1 and 2: Restate the Original Contract; State the Agenda/Structure of the Meeting

| Steps | Percent of Total Meeting | Time for a 60–Minute Meeting |
|---|---|---|
| 1. **Restate the original contract** | 5 percent | Begin: The beginning |
| 2. **State the agenda/structure of the meeting** | | End: 3rd minute |

In restating the original contract, state what the client wanted from you and what you promised to deliver—for example, "You asked us to investigate why the Brogan plant reactor broke down. We agreed to do that and come back with recommendations. We did not look into the auxiliary equipment that supports the reactor." This restates the presenting problem and reminds the client of the essentials of the contract. Sometimes consultants like to give a little history of the project. I do not. I devote only 5 percent of the meeting for steps 1 and 2.

After restating the contract, then state the purpose of the meeting and how you want the meeting structured. Remember that you want to control the flow of the meeting. You don't have to announce that you are in charge; you just have to act that way. One way to act that way is to announce right at the beginning, "Here is how I would like to structure this meeting. I would like to present the results of the discovery process and spend most of the time on what action might grow out of that. To achieve this, I would like you [the client] to react to both our picture of how things are and to our recommendations. About halfway through the meeting, I would like to stop to see if you are getting what you want from the meeting. The last 40 percent of the meeting I would like to devote to a discussion of what action you might take to deal with the problem. The meeting is planned to adjourn at . . ."

## Steps 3 and 4: Present the Picture and Present Recommendations

| Steps | Percent of Total Meeting | Time for a 60-Minute Meeting |
|---|---|---|
| **3. Present the picture** | 15 percent | Begin: 4th minute |
| **4. Present recommendations** | | End: 12th minute |

These two steps get intermingled. Some people like to start with the headlines and list recommendations after each point of the findings. Others present the whole thing and then move into recommendations. It helps to structure this part of the presentation so the client's reaction to the picture will be separate from the reaction to the recommendations because you want to protect the recommendations from any expression of resistance. If the manager is taking your feedback hard and asking you question after question, you would rather have your analysis be the victim of the barrage of resistance than sacrifice your recommendations.

If the client is eager to get to the recommendations and skip over the data, slow the process down. Say you will get to the recommendations in a minute, but first you want to get reactions to your assessment of the situation. Each organization has different norms about how to format this part of the meeting. Some are very formal; others are informal.

My preference is to avoid a lot of formality. A formal presentation, especially using PowerPoint, puts too much distance between the client and the information. When you look at a PowerPoint slide, the screen is far away, and the content looks as if it's cast in concrete, so this tool actually works against the primary objective. I know this is a blow to PowerPoint users, but the point here is not to hold the power. Presenting a perfect package at the feedback meeting is a mistake.

Remember that you have to be finished with data and recommendations after only 20 percent of the meeting is gone. In a one-hour meeting, this is the twelfth minute. Figuring it took you three minutes to introduce the meeting, you have nine minutes left. This time constraint forces you to get to the point and to the recommendations quickly.

The major mistake people make is to use the whole meeting for reporting data. When you are presenting the results of discovery, you are discussing a subject of great fascination to both you and the client. If you let yourselves get carried away with this fascination, the meeting will slip by, and neither you nor the client will know what is going to happen after they leave. This leaves you—and the client—hanging.

You also need enough time to deal with the client's resistance. In fact, *how the client reacts to the data is more important to implementation than the data itself.* If the analysis is brilliant but the client is indifferent to it, nothing is going to happen. If the analysis is noticeably mediocre and the client is really turned on by it (despite its mediocrity), some action is going to take place. So keep the presentation time down; give the major portion of the meeting to the client's reactions.

## Step 5: Ask for Client Reactions

| Step | Percent of Total Meeting | Time for a 60-Minute Meeting |
|---|---|---|
| **5. Ask for client reactions** | 30 percent | Begin: 13th minute<br>End: 30th minute |

This is the heart of the meeting. The client's reaction will determine the amount of organizational commitment that exists when you leave and whether your expertise gets used.

This is the point at which you want the client's reservations expressed. If the manager holds back reservations about the data or the methodology in the middle of the meeting, those reservations will come out later, at a much less desirable time—either at the moment of decision or after you have left the scene.

Sometimes you need to ask direct, specific questions to get the client's reactions. Clients often give their reactions with no prompting at all. If you get a silent or very quiet response, you need to ask the client, "What is your reaction to the information I am reporting?" or "What concerns do you have about the data or the analysis?" There may be a portion of the data that you know touches a very sensitive issue. I would ask about this directly: "Part of our report is on how you have been managing the problem and your boss's role in this problem. How do you feel about the way we have summarized the situation?" The goal here is to move toward any tension in the situation and elicit any unexpressed concerns.

A certain amount of tension is useful in any meeting. If there is no tension, then it is likely that the issues and recommendations are ones that nobody really cares about, which means there also won't be any energy to implement. If the tension is too high, the client and the consultant can be so threatened as to be unable to take responsibility and plan for any realistic, useful next steps. What you want is a moderate level of tension.

You have 30 percent of the meeting to devote to client reactions. This is the time you want the client to express his or her feelings, so don't get defensive when you hear them. The client's reactions are not against you; they are against having to face the pain in acting on and confronting the data you present.

If you find yourself being defensive, you are in danger of being captured by part of the same anxiety that has infected the client. Be aware of when you are getting defensive and stop it.

It is also important to stick to your assessment of the situation and your belief in your recommendations. There must have been a good reason that it made sense to you. Don't cave in when you meet resistance. You trust what you are suggesting, and although you don't need to defend it, don't give it up too easily.

## Step 6: Halfway Through the Meeting, Ask the Client, "Are You Getting What You Want?"

| Step | Percent of Total Meeting | Time for a 60-Minute Meeting |
|---|---|---|
| 6. Halfway through the meeting, ask the client, "Are you getting what you want?" | 10 percent | Begin: 31st minute<br>End: 36th minute |

The most powerful thing you can do is to ask clients, at the halfway point in meetings, whether they are getting what they want from the meeting. This is an insurance question. I used to ask the manager about the meeting just before the meeting was about to end, say with about five to ten minutes left. This was too late. A few times when the manager was in fact disappointed by the meeting, I had no time to recover. If the manager wanted more specific recommendations, or had concerns that he or she was feeling but not expressing, there was no time left to respond. If half the meeting is left, there is a good chance you can come up with what the manager might want or can help the manager surface the reservations fully enough to get past them.

Despite the emphasis we give to this step in training other consultants, they rarely are able to ask for feedback halfway through the meeting. The consultant and the client are so immersed in the task that the time slips by. The consultant can also be reluctant to ask how the meeting is going for fear there will be no way to respond to the client's disappointment. It is better to at least make the recovery attempt than to find out after the meeting what went wrong. (What to do when the meeting is not going well are covered later in this chapter.)

### Step 7: Decision to Proceed

| Step | Percent of Total Meeting | Time for a 60-Minute Meeting |
| --- | --- | --- |
| 7. **Decision to proceed** | 30 percent | Begin: 37th minute<br>End: 54th minute |

The purpose of the meeting is to see some action take place. The question of what to do next should be asked early enough in the meeting so you can participate in the decision.

If you wait until near the end of the meeting, the real discussion of how to proceed might take place at a time and place that will exclude you. If the client makes a decision when you are not present, the chances are somewhat less that the decision will really deal with the difficult realities your study has surfaced. This is particularly true if your discovery has at all focused on the way the problem is being managed and the client's management style. It is hard for clients to see their own roles in maintaining or creating a problem, and your presence makes it easier.

When you participate in the discussion of what to do, there are some key tasks to concentrate on:

1. Keep the discussion centered on things that are under the client's control.

2. Keep raising the parts of the situation or recommendations that you think are essential to addressing the immediate and the longer-term problem or possibility. The essentials are often the more sensitive parts of the situation: a difficult relationship, a poor performer, or some political consideration. As a consultant, you can focus on the sensitive issues without vested interest and perform a service by doing this.

3. Keep balance in the discussion by surfacing the viewpoints of everyone in the room. You usually have a clear picture of how different people in the organization see a situation. As the client is considering what to do, you can make sure the different viewpoints are considered in the decision and that each person's voice is heard.

4. Support the right of the responsible manager to make the choice with minimal coercion from others, including the consultant.

At times, the client will want to exclude the consultant from the decision-making discussion. I always ask to be present. To be present at the decision-making point is something to ask for in your initial contract. The reason the client might want to exclude you from the decision is to maintain control. It is really another form of resistance.

## Steps 8, 9, 10: Test for Client Concerns About Control and Commitment, Ask Yourself if You Got What You Wanted, Give Support

| Steps | Percent of Total Meeting | Time for a 60-Minute Meeting |
|---|---|---|
| 8. Test for client concerns of control and commitment | 10 percent | Begin: 55th minute |
| 9. Ask yourself if you got what you wanted | | |
| 10. Give support | | End: 60th minute |

Closing the meeting is similar to closing the contracting meeting. You want to ensure that the decisions made have the commitment of the client. You can also view the meeting as the entry stage of the next contract you might have with this client. The closing should be as direct and complete as possible.

Here are the steps.

Ask the client, "How do you feel about the control you will have if we go ahead with the solution?" If the client is uneasy, you may want to discuss ways the uneasiness can be managed.

Ask the client, "Is the solution we discussed something that really makes sense to you?" If the client's commitment seems low, you may want to pursue it further in the meeting or raise the matter at a later time.

You may want some continuing involvement. You may want feedback later on the effect of your consultation. You may want feedback now from the client on whether you were helpful on this project and how you might have been more effective. You may want the client to informally tell your boss that you did good work. You may want another contract with the client, either to implement this project or to begin a different one. If there are things you want, now is the time to ask for them.

Finally, give support. Implementation is a time when the heaviest burden is on the client. Give support for this responsibility, and tell the client what they did right in this meeting. This is what completes the process.

## A RECAP

Figure 12 gives a recap of the steps in managing the meeting for action.

Following this meeting structure ensures that you have attended to the business of the feedback phase. This is half the way to consulting flawlessly. The other half is behaving authentically at each stage of the meeting. The greatest strain in doing this is dealing with the resistance that is sure to arise in the meeting. Here are some reminders to help overcome these hurdles.

**Figure 12.** Summary: Managing the Meeting for Action

| Steps | Percentage of Total Meeting | Time for a 60-Minute Meeting | |
|---|---|---|---|
| | | Begin | End |
| 1. Restate the original contract | 5 percent | The beginning | |
| 2. State the structure of the meeting | | | 3rd minute |
| 3. Present the picture | 15 percent | 4th minute | |
| 4. Present recommendations | | | 12th minute |
| 5. Ask for client reactions | 30 percent | 13th minute | 30th minute |
| 6. Halfway through the meeting, ask the client, "Are you getting what you want?" | 10 percent | 31st minute | 36th minute |
| 7. Decision to proceed | 30 percent | 37th minute | 54th minute |
| 8. Test for client concerns about control and commitment | | 55th minute | |
| 9. Ask yourself if you got what you wanted | 10 percent | | |
| 10. Give support | | | 60th minute |

Every meeting is part of the client's discovery and learning process. The crucial skill in conducting any meeting is to stay focused on the here-and-now process. This is more important than even the content of the findings being discussed. Many of the issues explored in the discovery phase that deal with dysfunctional ways of operating will be acted out in this meeting. Being conscious of this will help you resist getting stuck, which can take many forms:

- Having to rigorously defend the data against people who are supposed to learn from it

- Finding yourself providing the energy for the next steps for an organization or group that you are not really a member of

- Being expected to have all the answers

- Being in the position of providing solutions to highly complex problems in less than three minutes

The way out of most stuck places is to put what is happening into words as it is happening: "I find myself having to defend data against people who are supposed to be learning from it," or "I keep hearing myself come up with next steps for your organization, and I am not even going to be around!" or "One of the norms I mentioned is that people express support with silence. Is that happening right now?"

The resistance you get to suggestions for next steps is valuable because it means you are on target. You shouldn't view it as a rejection or disinterest on the part of the client. It means that you're dealing with something that's important to the client, so you should move toward the resistance rather than away from it.

The response that you get in any meeting will reenact all the problems that the organization has in solving other issues and managing its other business. The response to difficult issues may be a retreat into detail, a postponement of a decision to act, or a denial of problems. Whatever the response, you can interpret it as being the characteristic way the organization handles its decisions. It is important to interpret the response in this fashion and give support to an organization in seeing what it is doing.

Also, as in all the other phases of consulting, you have to trust your own feelings in talking about implementation or planning. If you are feeling uneasy about something—confused, frustrated, or not listened to—or if you are feeling excited and positive and supportive, you should put your feelings into words as part of the model and methodology you offer the client.

As in contracting, every meeting involves an affective dimension—feelings about the interaction itself. There's a process going on between you, the consultant giving the recommendations, and the client who is hearing a statement of their situation. For example, suppose you are feeling confused and uncertain and don't know where to go next. There are two ways to deal with this. One is to try to speak with more certainty, more clarity. The second way is to simply say, "You know, as we're talking here, I feel confused and uncertain where to go next." You're much more likely to get to the heart of the problems around responsibility and commitment and owning up to problems if you react and present your own feelings as the discussion is going on.

For a downloadable copy of Checklist # 7, visit www.flawlessconsulting .com.

## Checklist #7: Planning a Meeting for Action

Here are some guidelines you can use to help you prepare for the meeting:

1. What do you want from the meeting? Understanding? Agreement? Action? Further work?

2. Structure the meeting so you have at least as much time for discussion as for presentation of results.

3. Review the wording of the "picture" to make it as nonevaluative and descriptive as possible.

4.  Think of where you are likely to get resistance in the meeting. What questions might you ask to get the underlying concerns expressed directly?

5.  Think about who might be missing from the meeting who has a high stake in the outcome.

6.  How can you ask for feedback on how this consultation is going?

## WHEN GROUP MEMBERS ARE AT ODDS AMONG THEMSELVES

When you are reporting your findings and recommendations to a group of people, your task takes on an added dimension. If the group is not used to working together or works together poorly, they might take out their difficulties with each other on the consultant. You become an easy target when they cannot confront each other directly. The skill is not to let the meeting be set up as client versus consultant.

There are some ways you can counter that:

- *Treat the group as a collection of individuals.* Don't assume that everyone is in agreement, that they all support each other, and that they feel or think alike. One by one, ask each person what they want from the meeting. This question will surface differences and force the group to take responsibility for some of the difficulties that may arise. If they are not listening to each other, ask them, by name, to react to what another is saying. This takes some of the focus off you and puts it on the group, where it belongs. Give support at all times. When people are under stress and things are not going well for them, they need support, not more confrontation.

- *There is always going to be some segment of the group that is going to feel tremendous anxiety and resist.* They will express this in the form of aggressive questions about the change or your data or the program. The ground rule is not to overinvest in the resistant people. Again, the questions deserve two good-faith responses, but you have to have some political sensitivity about where the power really is in the group and whose opinion is going to sway the group. Invest your energy in those people rather than in the most verbal or vocal people who are raising questions. You might say at some point, "Well, we've heard several questions from Bob and John. I don't know how the rest of you are feeling. Jean [if Jean is the boss], what do you feel about this?"

- *If your client gives quick compliance to a suggestion, beware.* Many people and teams handle conflict in either a passive or compliant way, and I would be very suspicious of that.

---

For a downloadable copy of Checklist #8, visit www.flawlessconsulting .com.

## Checklist #8: Reviewing the Meeting

Here are some questions to ask yourself after a meeting for action. Answering them should help you to assess your own learning from each meeting and prepare for the next one.

1. What was the outcome?

2. What was the final understanding of the choices or possibilities? How did this shift as a result of the meeting?

3. What form did the resistance take?

4. How did you respond to the resistance?

   • Take it personally?

   • Give more explanation and data?

   • Seek underlying concerns about control and vulnerability?

5. Did you get stuck at any point?

6. What nonverbal messages did you notice?

7. What connections can you make between the way the meeting was managed and the way the technical or business problem is being managed?

8. What effect on your relationship with the client did this meeting have?

## MODELING THE MEETING

These are the important competencies for managing a meeting for action:

• Confronting the client with all relevant data collected, even if it wasn't part of your original assignment

• Naming the possibility as well as the problem

• Giving descriptive rather than evaluative feedback

• Feeding data back to the client about personal behavior in handling the target problem

• Understanding that the client criticism and resistance are not directed at you personally

• Being present at the meeting where the action steps are determined

• Structuring and controlling the feedback meeting to elicit client reaction and choice of next steps

In your work with managers, you need to model the same kind of authentic behavior that you're suggesting they engage in when dealing with their subordinates. You're always acting as a model for a style of working problems or acting on possibilities. In fact, the most meaningful vehicle for managers' learning is to have them experience how you handle these situations. That may mean much more than anything you say verbally or any kind of process you would have them engage in with their subordinates.

# CHAPTER 16

# IMPLEMENTATION

W HEN I WROTE the first edition of this book, I devoted exactly two pages to implementation. I can't remember whether I was just rushing to finish the book or had little to say about it. Over the years, though, I have become increasingly aware of how many consulting efforts have been aimed at doing the right thing but have resulted in little change. It is frustrating, to say the least, to contract well, develop an accurate picture of the current reality, give feedback, and make a good decision and yet see few concrete results from the effort.

Implementation is, in theory, the point of the consultation, the fruit of our labor. Unfortunately, knowing what to do (the product of the discovery phase) and finding the right way to do it (the focus of implementation) are two different worlds. Consultants have traditionally given too much attention to analysis and recommendations and too little attention to the complexity of translating those answers into action.

Our mistake is treating implementation as a fundamentally rational process. We believe that logical, step-by-step problem solving can bring the fulfillment of our plans. Our love of lists, milestones, and electronic calendar living is an example of this. If we can keep a list of what we need to do in one place, these things will get done. Although it is hard to argue against being organized, we tend to oversimplify what it takes to act on what we know to be true. At a personal level, it is the gap between having a vision and living it out. The more serious we are about being true to a vision, the more we realize it is our life work.

## CHOOSING ENGAGEMENT OVER INSTALLATION

For an organization, shifting a way of thinking and a way of operating is even more difficult. Part of what makes implementation difficult is that we often treat change as if it can be installed, managed, and engineered. Installation plans rely heavily on having clear goals, a defined set of steps, and carefully specified objectives and measures—as if a blueprint can be developed for others to follow. This is the engineering mind at work, which works well for solving mechanical problems but is incomplete in trying to have an impact on living systems. Change cannot be installed and engineered, and so it always takes longer and is more difficult than we ever imagined. The positive deviance people mentioned earlier understand this, and it is why they have been so successful. The same is true with whole-system approaches, betting on communal gatherings and insights to make a difference.

The engineer in us needs to be complemented with the thinking of the social architect and the skills of a community organizer. Any imple-

mentation requires not only a shift in what is tangible, such as methods or structure, but also a shift in what is intangible, such as relationships and personal faith and commitment. This chapter and the next two are about ways to approach the intangibles. They focus on an essential aspect of implementation: bringing people together to create and plan how to make something work.

The art of bringing people together is termed *engagement.* The ideas here are really about the means of engagement as an alternative or enhancement to strategies of installation. The steps offered are the elements of engagement. What I am proposing is that we become engaged. If you can find a better offer, take it.

There are two aspects of implementation for consultants. One is the technical work using the expertise you have spent years developing. If you are a financial analyst, you begin introducing a system of controls. If you are an IT specialist, you redesign the software. If you are a training manager, you start the training program.

The second aspect of implementation is how to build support for the business or technical change you are planning. This is no easy task. Implementation does not actually begin until the people who do the work decide whether they are going to make real changes or simply go through the motions. Real changes require real commitment, and part of your role is to help fire that spark. To get serious about building internal commitment among those who have to live in the system where you are simply a guest requires dispelling some conventional beliefs that actually get in the way.

## DECIDING DOESN'T GET IT DONE

Too many consulting projects result in cosmetic change: the thinking and rhetoric about the change are perfect, but the experience of people does not match the promise. Much of the cynicism about consultants is that we collude with strategies that begin with great fanfare and end with a world where the promises of change have made no difference to people's day-to-day work lives. Much of our collusion with cosmetic change is our belief that new behavior can be defined, modeled, induced, driven, purchased, and measured into existence. Many of the ways consultants try to change institutions actually serve as a defense against change.

One of the obstacles to change (I use *change* and *implementation* to mean essentially the same thing) is rooted in our belief in executive decisiveness. In our adoration of leaders and stubborn belief in individualism, we think that when the boss's mind is made up, action will follow. This is rarely the case. No single person runs a business, no one person makes or delivers a product, and no one general ever fought a war.

It is interesting that managers understand their limitations better than consultants do. Managers know that the fact that they have made up their minds does not mean that decisions will be acted on. Every day they face the reality that many of their best intentions have little impact on the way work gets done. It is consultants who have a hard time accepting this. Any gathering of consultants will at some point complain that managers lack the courage, will, or persistence to follow through on their decisions and make sure that our recommendations are implemented.

We hold on to the magical belief that leadership and decisiveness are the point and what we need is more of both. Change in human systems, even in a monarchy, has much more to do with the consent of the governed than the will and ability of those who govern. Even in a monarchy.

## THE LIMITS OF INSTALLATION

The blueprint for traditional installation-style implementation is to

- Articulate a vision

- Set standards for what is expected

- Define measures for the change

Kept in perspective, all of these are legitimate elements of day-to-day life in every workplace. What interferes with implementation is that

we misuse these tools. When we do, they become subtle forms of coercion rather than neutral ways of managing and defining a future. We think we have to sell and induce support for a new way of operating. When consultants and managers apply centrally created vision, standards, and measures as primary tools to maintain control and make the world predictable, they interfere with the implementation effort.

What could be an opportunity for people to choose accountability by designing their own answers to these questions is lost. Instead of confronting people with their freedom, we invite their compliance. It is the mandated institutionalization of useful practices that takes the life out of most implementation efforts. Here are some major ways that efforts at implementation stumble over themselves.

## Leadership by Lamination

We interfere with real change and service when we think that progress grows out of the vision of the leader, regardless of whether the leader is "us," as consultant or trainer, or "them," as managers. The myth is that if we can just make the message sufficiently clear and compelling, if we can describe the burning platform with enough urgency and a bright tomorrow with enough zeal, change will occur. This leads to a great emphasis on communicating the vision and the business case for change.

I contributed to the problem when I wrote a chapter on vision in my book *The Empowered Manager.* It was about the power of vision and how transformation begins with imagining a different future. This became the most popular chapter in the book. I received hundreds of vision statements in the mail and in my travels. Most were compelling, and most were laminated in wallet-sized versions so we could carry them with us. Many vision statements hung on office walls and reception rooms, many signed by the management team. All had a common theme: building a lasting organization required the top to have a vision.

The problem here was twofold. First, we affirmed, at the moment of lamination, that top management's vision was the one that counted. We all wanted to know what top management was seeking. Once we knew this, we could all align ourselves and proceed to live it out. This gave rise to a cottage industry in vision articulation. We consultants began each project helping the top define and express their vision. This could take days or months. Most often it was actually a support person or consultant who wrote the vision and brought it back to management for approval. But the product reflected management's thoughts, and they gave it their stamp. This was fine for the managers who created the vision—fine, that is, if they had created it primarily for themselves and sought guidance for their own actions through it.

Unfortunately, the visions were usually designed for others. We believed that the top should decide the culture that the middle and bottom would live by. This is the mind-set that takes the power out of vision, even though the middle and the bottom want to hear what the top has in mind. The fact that everyone wants to know the vision of the top does not make it meaningful.

Most frequently, when the organization hears the vision of the top, they are vaguely disappointed. The large meeting designed to mobilize energy actually drains it. It became clear to me after I started to read the four hundred or so vision statements I received: they all read the same. Every organization cares about customers, values teamwork, exists for shareholders or the community, believes in excellence in all they do. If we all threw our vision statements in a hat and then drew one out, we would think it was ours regardless of where it came from. I finally realized that it was the act of creating a vision that matters, not so much the content of what it was.

The second consequence of lamination was that management's vision could now withstand the ravages of wind, and rain, and dark of night. That is why we laminated it: so it would last forever. That management's vision should be permanent and enduring is the fallacy. Management vision is not only not the point, but it is not immortal. Everyone needs to struggle with the question of what kind of future we want to create, and that vision is something that is alive and open to change. Vision is more a dialogue than a declaration. It is an important conversation, a significant stretch of the imagination, and it needs to emerge as a collective work-in-progress from each unit. Once a vision is laminated, it loses its life.

In practical terms, if a group needs a clearer vision for themselves, by all means help them create one. But don't make any videos of leaders calling for transformation. Don't hold some large meeting for the purpose of clarifying the vision of top management. If implementation requires that people know the state of the union and where we are headed, don't have those in charge declare it. Bring people together to define the state of their own union and pool their knowledge of what the future might bring. But we are getting ahead of the story.

## We Need Higher Standards, and This Time We Mean Business

There is a widespread belief that we have not set the standards high enough. This is most visible in education, where every state legislature thinks that it can improve public education by being tougher on performance standards, students, and teachers. They have been doing this for years, continue to be disappointed with its results, and keep on doing it.

Of course, the belief that low standards are the problem is not confined to education. It invades all of our institutions. It is born of the belief that people will not set high standards for themselves—that they need an outside agency to motivate and inspire them. At heart it is a fear-based strategy, where those who set the standards are the subject and those who must meet them are the object.

There is some validity to the idea that standards and performance are related. We do know that people will be responsive to the expectations others have for them. If a boss expects the team to perform well, it is more likely to happen. If a boss expects failure, that may happen also. There is a difference, though, between expectations between boss and subordinate or teacher and student, and standard setting.

To have high expectations of others is to have faith in them. It is an expression of optimism and hope in the capacities of another. It is an expression of the connection between people and is experienced as support. Standard setting, as it is most commonly used to trigger change, is born not of support but of disappointment and demand.

To judge others to be performing poorly because of low standards is to hold them in contempt. It is a belief that they need our standard-setting intervention to wake them up and motivate them. It is an institutional act that depends on coercion. If we don't raise the bar, they will not jump higher. There is little care or connection in the strategy, and it therefore builds as much resistance as it was designed to overcome.

The myth is that setting standards will increase accountability. What it most often creates is compliance. People may be forced to find a way to meet those standards, but the institution suffers in other, less measurable ways. Instead of a more accountable culture, we find more bureaucracy, more people working to rule, more caution, and less flexibility.

Bosses, of course, have a legitimate role in defining a playing field and what outcomes the organization requires of each unit. But defining outcomes is different from standard setting as a tactic in initiating change or implementing some recommendation. What corrupts the process is the belief that one group knows what is best for another. And that is why these engineering and installation strategies fall short. The focus on standards is also very seductive for the consultant. After we have been through a contracting and discovery effort with a client manager, we want to be on their side and too easily align with that person's traditional ways of making things happen.

## People Need Fixing

We need to avoid planning something in a huddle with our client manager that is supposed to change the behavior of others outside our circle. We are not here to fix people. Our task is to stay focused on the gifts and capacities of people in the room and what they can do about their own actions. If managers believe in higher standards, let them set them for themselves and live according to them for a while.

This keeps legitimacy in the consulting effort and in our relationship with the client manager. When we join with bosses to plan for the changes in their subordinates, we have been co-opted into the belief that the employees need to change and the managers are just fine. We then miss the opportunity to shift in a more fundamental way the beliefs about how change happens and accountability is created. Change and accountability occur when we live them, not preach them. The common instinct to begin implementation with clearer and higher standards is most often a trap.

## If We Can't Measure It, It Doesn't Matter

One more way we interfere with implementation is through our attitude about measurement. We have turned it into a god. The question here is similar to the questions above. No argument with the need for measurement; it's the question of how central it should become and who should provide it. When we impose measurements systemwide, we have to be very careful that we really need and can make use of the measures that are collected.

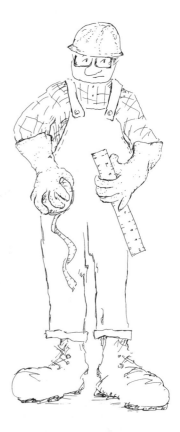

Measuring the quantitative elements of work has definite value. The simplest example of the legitimate need for common measures is common accounting practices. The economics of each unit in the organization need to be folded together to meet regulatory requirements, and so we know our economic viability. There is the need for common measures of product quality and customer service, and for many more measures that assess the success of the institution. We move on to soft ground, though, when we invite the economist in to develop common measures for how we are working together, what processes will create quality, and, in general, anything in the realm of how human systems operate. Every measurement of the human or qualitative dimension of work leaves more untested than it covers.

The belief that if we cannot measure something, it does not exist treats the human system as if it were a mechanical one. The belief that people will do only what they are measured against is a cynical view of the human condition, and while it may be true of certain sales situations or certain classroom dynamics, we have taken the value of measurement to places it does not belong. When we attribute to measurement the capacity to create the behavior we want, we have moved into a simple cause-and-effect relationship and hold on to the belief that implementation and change can be engineered. With a human system, that is more fancy than fact.

Each of us wants feedback on how we are doing. But the feedback does not create the doing. Imposed measures on the qualitative aspect of work may actually get in the way of the doing.

We particularly dilute the value of measurement when we separate the people who evaluate from the people who do the work. Quality control used to be separated from those who did the work. It was a judging function and created alienation between the doing and the quality assessment. This has changed in the past ten years, for the betterment of both the quality of the product and the quality of the relationships that surround the workplace.

We can learn from the quality movement that while there are useful tools for measuring, they need to be under the control of those doing the work and need to be kept in perspective as simply one part of making change. Much of what matters cannot be measured, and our consulting needs to reflect that.

## BETTING ON ENGAGEMENT

None of this is an argument against vision, standards, or measurement. They are important elements of organizing people's efforts. It is just that we have abused them when we make them coercive instruments of control. And then we compound the error. When they do not result in genuine change, we try harder to make them work instead of betting on other strategies. Trying harder, pressuring, and persuading have limited impact on changing a social system. And when they do help, they soon develop their own immune system.

A social system is a living system and not that amenable to linear or mechanical beliefs about organizations.

Whenever management or consultants bet on definitions, inducements, measures, and standards, they unintentionally reinforce the bureaucratic mind-set that we are trying to reduce. They are the tools of engineers and economists. Engineering and economic strategies do not build commitment and accountability, despite their appealing face value.

What we have undervalued is the power of engagement and dialogue. The movements toward the learning organization, total quality, and teamwork are in the direction of engagement, but with a few exceptions, they are rarely given the importance that they deserve. The next two chapters explore engagement in the implementation process and offer some concrete examples for involving people in a way that increases the likelihood of real, lasting change.

# CHAPTER 17

# THE ELEMENTS OF ENGAGEMENT

Oൠ POWERFUL SERVICE OF THE CONSULTANT may be to raise clients' consciousness about the value of engagement in the implementation process. Engagement has power independent of the content of the recommendations. The most technical content or important business decision will not be acted on without a different interaction within the client system. If the quality of the interaction does not change, no standards, measurement, and rewards will have an impact. Consultants can help leaders engage others in implementing decisions by following the same principles for building commitment that we explored in the process of contracting and discovery. To review briefly:

The contracting phase was based on

- A deep understanding of the problem

- The clear expression of wants

- An exploration of concerns about control and vulnerability

- Giving support

The discovery phase emphasized

- Treating each interaction as a learning event

- Persistently asking what the client was doing to contribute to the problem

- Seeking language that gave clarity to reality without judging it

Sustaining that same spirit when you are dealing with the client during implementation and action requires

- Designing each gathering to strengthen engagement

- Balancing between presentation and participation

- Supporting full disclosure and the public expression of doubt

- Placing real choice on the table

- Initiating new conversations

- Choosing a physical structure of the room that supports community

## THE MEETING IS THE MESSAGE

Implementation of any change boils down to whether people at several levels are going to take responsibility for the success of the change and the institution. This is it. Period.

We can broadcast our intent to give people at the bottom more choice and involvement, but if the meeting that broadcasts this intent is not itself an example of the content of the broadcast, the promise has little legitimacy. The nature, tone, and structure of how we come together is the sampling device people use to determine the credibility of the strategy.

This means each consulting event needs to be a sample of the way we wish the larger change to proceed. Each moment becomes an example of the destination. If you are holding a meeting to discuss a new set of measures for a telephone call center, for example, this meeting on measures needs to embody major principles of engagement such as putting real choice on the table and dealing publicly with difficult questions.

## EIGHT WAYS TO ENGAGE

The elements of engagement look simple enough, but they are easier to list and to talk about than to practice. Here are eight practical ways for engaging people, regardless of the setting or the expectations they have on entering the room. Altogether these methods represent the key elements of engagement and lead to flawless implementation, for they confront the emotional and relationship-building work that this phase requires.

### Open with Transparent Purpose and a Level Playing Field

To open a conversation or gathering, describe the concerns that began the process, define where the change effort is at this moment, describe what the organization needs from us right now, and give some idea of the structure of this step.

Most of us are familiar with the need for this kind of information. The key is to tell the whole story. This includes weaknesses and failures. Don't protect people from bad news in the name of protecting them from anxiety. Anxiety is the natural state, best handled in the light of day. The only caution is to keep it short and informal, with more from the heart than from the head.

What is not needed are upbeat motivational blessings or homilies from managers or important sponsors who will not be part of the whole session. To have an executive show up for the beginning, express commitment to the process, and then leave is oxymoronic. To say, "I care, I am committed, and I'm gone," does not play well. It is regal and patronizing behavior, demeaning the proceedings and those who stay.

### Renegotiate Expectations About Participation

It amazes me how many new strategies or programs begin their implementation with a management/consultant lecture/presentation about goals, strategy, methods, and measures. I have watched a manager or consultant stand in front of the room for long periods of time—sometimes hours—stating vision, defining terms, giving the whole picture of what is to come. The structure of a meeting telegraphs our intention for the future and yet we keep operating out of habit rather than changing the technology to better meet our purpose. We base our meetings on the thought that when someone is confused or anxious by what we say, our response should be to repeat it again louder, as if turning up the volume will solve the confusion.

As participants, we go to meetings expecting something to happen to us. We are programmed for entertainment and wonder how good a meeting they are going to run. The forms we use to evaluate a meeting ask questions about its leaders: Were they prepared? Were their objectives clear and well met? What was the quality of the visual aids? How many evaluation forms have you filled out that asked you about your contribution to the meeting? Meeting leaders always say, "What we get out of the meeting is up to all of us," but they usually don't mean it—and we don't believe it—and few really act on it.

I was in a bar once and the entertainers began by saying, "We are the Southern County Rounders . . . and you are the audience." I thought that they understood something profound about the relationship between them up front and us in the cheap seats. By calling us out, they declared that we, the audience, had a job to do also: we had to join in creating the performance.

You may be thinking that the importance of the simple balance between presentation and participation is being overstated. Trust me: it has more meaning than we have realized. As straightforward as the concept is, most of the times when we come together, we put great energy on presentation and attend to participation as an afterthought.

The passive contract between leader and participant needs to be renegotiated early and dramatically. Having done this many times, I can assure you that something always changes. There is more life in the room. People ask more questions. Some people get irritated. Some would rather keep talking to their neighbor than return to the speaker. All are signs of life. How to do this is begun in what follows and outlined in more detail on the Web site.

---

Visit www.flawlessconsulting.com for questions to ask to renegotiate expectations about participation.

## Rearrange the Room

The shape of the meeting room and how we arrange the chairs shouts the message of our intentions. If we place participants in a circle, use a round table if tables are truly necessary, and do not have a clear front or podium, we make the point from the start that participation among peers is important. You may ask why make such a big thing out of a small activity like rearranging the room. The reason is that these particular

activities carry the message about the change in vision and culture that we have in mind. We are talking about them here as means of engagement, but they could easily be called the means of transformation or a change in culture. If we can change the room, and the way we inhabit it, we can also change the institution and the way we inhabit it.

The important point here is that there is not a right structure. There is no right way to arrange a room. Tables or not. Circle or square, or lined up like a chapel. Centralization or decentralization, functional or matrix or geographical organization. Is the leader at the front, behind a podium, on a stage, sitting in a circle? They all can work.

What matters is that everyone is engaged in adapting the structure to the task at hand. When we know that each of us can make the shifts to fit our own purpose and still serve the purpose of the larger organization, the world has shifted. We no longer need to live by the rules of the economist and engineer. We become the architects, designers, and authors of the institution in which we live. We have chosen to be accountable for the institution and no longer have to be held bound to it.

 Visit www.flawlessconsulting.com for more on the rationale for caring about the spaces in which we meet and things to do to make rearranging the room a metaphor for the change we have in mind.

## Create a Platform for Openness and Doubt

Freedom of speech and the right to assembly are constitutional guarantees. What is true for the streets, however, is less true for the offices and meeting rooms of our institutions. Part of our task as consultants is to bring the right of assembly and freedom of speech into organizations. In practical terms, this means creating assemblies where there is an opportunity for all voices and points of view to be heard. Reality in the words of the audience becomes as important as the reality spoken from the podium—perhaps more important. And those at the podium tell the truth about failure and uncertainty.

Creating this platform allows for a restoration of faith that is central to any change or improvement effort. Until we can speak in public, our sense of what is real—our doubts and reservations and our past disappointments—we are unable to invest in a different future. If we cannot say no, our yes has no meaning.

People do voice their doubts and tell the truth in organizations; it is just that they do it in private: in restrooms, at water-coolers, over a meal or a drink. If honest conversation stays private, the public conversations will be unreal and ultimately discouraging. The same is true in a large group meeting. If all the real discussions take place only in small groups, little faith will be built in the larger community.

The redistribution of power and accountability happens when honest, confronting conversations take place in public settings. There is a political power in having a wide range of viewpoints heard by everybody in the room, especially in larger group assemblies. If we believe the redistribution of power is critical to a shift in accountability, the shift will begin when the public conversations shift. Providing the physical and psychological space for this shift to happen is the first step in transforming a culture and implementing a change. It is the task of the consultant to help make this happen.

The key conversation that needs to go public is about people's doubts and reservations. If doubt and even cynicism cannot be publicly expressed, then internal commitment cannot be offered freely. Some doubts give guidance for improvement; others don't. The engineer in us wants to answer every doubt. When you are building a bridge or airplane, you need to know that all the doubts and questions have been answered. Human systems are not so orderly, and many doubts go unanswered. In creating high engagement, it is the expression of doubt that counts, not its resolution. We cannot construct a plan that eliminates all doubts, but we can always acknowledge them. We can acknowledge cynicism and make room for it without being paralyzed by it. The fact that the most alienated people in the organization are given a platform to speak does more to build commitment from those watching the conversation than any compelling presentation or financial incentive program ever can.

Openness and reciprocity need to occur each time we meet. It cannot be relegated to sessions we label "team building" or a "large-group intervention." Even when we are implementing a highly technical or business-oriented change, there has to be a relatively public platform for people's concerns to be voiced and viewpoints to be sought. Every technical and business change destabilizes the human system in which it is embedded. Relationships change, influence shifts, and boundaries are threatened; dialogue, widely held, is the only way to find new stability. Management reassurances don't help. Nobody believes them because it's management's job to reassure.

We waste meetings that are designed more to reassure, calm workers, and tell a story than to have a conversation. These are lost opportunities. The question in people's minds is whether they are getting the straight story. If the speaker does not speak of doubt and uncertainty, and talk about failure if it has occurred, there has been no straight story.

People will also not know whether they are getting a straight story until they have joined in the discussion. Too often in the effort to sell a strategy, problems are softened and positioned to promote confidence and win support. People's trust in management comes down not so much to whether management is right, but to whether it is willing to tell the truth.

The truth spoken in public is a rare commodity in most institutions. The success of an implementation strategy will depend on the quality of the conversation that begins it. And the more public the setting is, the more powerful is the impact. Change begins at the intersection of freedom of speech and the right of assembly. It is not only good for democracy, but it begins to turn rhetoric into reality.

Go to www.flawlessconsulting.com for more on the practice of creating a platform for truth and doubt.

## Ask, "What Do We Want to Create Together?"

There is no more profound question than this one, and none more difficult to answer in any meaningful way. It is the question on which real accountability hinges. There are two parts to the question: the question of creation and the question of together.

1. *Create?* "Do we want to create?" is the dangerous part of the question. If I answer yes, I am no longer reacting to what has been handed to me. I am now beginning to define a future that ultimately I will be responsible for. When we decide that we want to create, we are emotionally joining the organization in defining its future and in that way moving against the patriarchal part of the culture and our own habit. This may be why, when we ask people to define their vision, the first try is quite dull. When the question is, "What do we want to create?" the demand is for an answer that is unique to this group. That is the work: to ask each group to construct a unique future that is right for their function. This is another way we confront people with their freedom: asking them what they want to create forces the issue, even if the response may initially be pale.

2.   *Together?* The second part of the question, "Do we want to create something together?" is also difficult to answer. We may be used to creating something on our own or in our unit, but when you ask, in effect, "What can we create together that we cannot create alone?" you are asking for another level of collaboration. Most of the time when I have asked groups what they can create together, they return with a list of cooperative actions that each group can do alone.

To create something together, we have to cross boundaries and possibly yield territory. Most change efforts and implementation steps require this, and it is hard to do with any depth. This question opens us to the possibility and confronts us with the reluctance of attending to the larger institution first and our own unit second.

For a process and tip on asking, "What do we want to create together?" visit www.flawlessconsulting.com.

## Create a New Conversation

A change in action is preceded by a change in the conversation.* Old conversations lead to old actions. The challenge is to have a task-related conversation that people have not had before. Holding on to the old conversation, the old way of naming problems or describing possibilities, is a way of seeking safety and maintaining control.

Old conversations are a way of holding to a position that we know we can defend. We want people to take positions that they cannot defend. Then we know we are in new territory. Plus, optimism is born the moment we are surprised by what we say or what we hear.

The real cost of our habitual conversations is the cynicism they breed. It's not that the questions they raise have not been answered.

*Joel Henning was a friend and teacher of mine in understanding and articulating that you change the culture by changing the conversation.

For more on the telltale signs and costs of continuing old conversations, plus an activity for creating a new conversation, visit www.flawlessconsulting.com.

Rather, it is the staleness of the discussion that drains energy. Old conversations become a refuge, a way for us to find safety.

If changing the conversation does nothing else, it gives hope that each time we come together, we have the capacity to transform our experience. This is how culture changes in the moment, and if we do it often enough, we learn more, risk more, and move more quickly. Change and its cousins, surprise and unrest, are always within our reach. They are just waiting for us to design them into existence.

## Choose Commitment and Accountability

We build capacity when commitment and accountability are chosen. In society today, we have lost faith in our willingness to choose to be accountable. We think we have to legislate accountability or "manage accountability," or purchase accountability with incentive schemes. These low-faith strategies create their own deadweight, so we have to keep propping them up. They create a cycle in which the more management and legislation there is, the more resistance and loopholes are created, and this evokes a new wave of management and legislation. This is true of the workplace and the larger culture.

The alternative is to have faith that there are conditions in which people want to be accountable: they want to set high goals, care for the well-being of the larger organization, and know how they are doing. One of those conditions is a crisis. In a crisis the rules are suspended, status and self-interest are put aside, and the task and purpose override habit. The challenge is to find the same willingness without a crisis.

There are two conditions of accountability that support high-commitment implementation strategies. The first is that we need to be accountable to our peers first and our boss next. The second is that we need to commit without negotiation or barter.

### Peer Accountability

There is a power among peers that bosses can never approach. For one thing, we have a lifetime of practice in managing bosses. It begins with our parents. As children, we may have felt that our parents were in charge, but once we become parents, we know that was not true. Parents can give orders and administer consequences, but at the end of the day, the children decide when to clean their room or put the dishes away. We work hard at managing, and at times manipulating, those who have power over us. Over the years we become maze bright. We learn how to handle our parents, teachers, and finally bosses, so that we can do what we want and not have to pay a price for it. When our bosses are upset with us, we have learned how to say, "Thank you for the feedback," as a way of defending against their disappointment and not really having to change.

Our peers, however, are less likely to tolerate this sort of maneuvering. They see us more clearly, and they are around more, so they are harder to manipulate. This is one reason that being accountable to peers is a demanding proposition. Also, our interdependence lies with our peers, not our boss. It is their work that is eased when we do well and made difficult when we do poorly. They have to pick up the slack and operationally live with our mistakes. Peers are the ones we are functionally accountable to, no matter who conducts our performance review.

We already recognize this interdependence in our attention to teams, team building, and team pay schemes. The next step is to initiate more formal peer conversations about commitments and consequences. We want to adhere to the principle that accountability needs to be a voluntary act, and this has more power with peers.

Peer accountability also means that it is up to peers to speak for the well-being of the organization. It is not just the bosses' function. Peers need to tell us whether we have committed enough to meet the promises of the unit and larger system. This requirement to think of the interests of the whole system has as much impact on the peers who are listening to the commitments as on the person who is making them.

### Commitment Without Barter

A second element of implementation by consent is to explore what commitment and promise really mean. We are very much a negotiating culture. We like to bargain for goods and have the concept of quid pro quo deeply embedded in our relationships. The ideas about contracting outlined earlier in this book are a good example. There is an important distinction, though, between living up to our contractual agreements and making an emotional or personal commitment.

A personal commitment means that we agree to do something that is not conditional on the response of someone else. That is why the word *promise* is so appropriate. If we make our commitments conditional on the response from another, they are really not commitments; they are contracts or other forms of barter. They become conditional agreements that can be withdrawn if the other side does not deliver. Throughout this consulting process, we have been seeking the internal commitment required to get past the rhetoric and cosmetic change that surround us. A commitment is a promise or a pledge to do something. Even in its dictionary definition, there is no mention of anything the person making the pledge receives; it is only about the choice to be made.

If we commit in this spirit, the discussion about how the top needs to change, how other departments and people stand in the way, how systems and practices don't support the change: it all disappears. At the moment of commitment, the institution becomes ours to create, and in that act of committing, we can find our freedom. We now proceed on our own and with others we have freely joined. Something has shifted for us and the institution.

There will still be obstacles and disappointment, but they will not breed cynicism, for we were not choosing on the basis of another's action. If there is an affirmation or loss of faith, it will not be in others but in ourselves.

Visit www.flawlessconsulting.com for an activity that confronts and cements people's will to proceed.

## Focus on Gifts

There is a need to bring closure to each meeting that acknowledges the effort and care brought into the room. One good way to finish

is to focus on the gifts and value each participant brought to the proceedings. We live in a world that is much more interested in our weaknesses and deficiencies than in our strengths and gifts. This is so common that we have even come to believe that it is useful. Not so. Most of us have been working on our deficiencies for much of our life and look at the progress we have made.

If negative feedback were so useful, we would have it together by now, and we don't. The primary impact of focusing on weaknesses is that it breeds self-doubt and makes us easier to control. That is why it is so compelling and popular. We fear that if everyone really understood their strength and value, the system might not hold together. Everyone might exploit their free agency, become too expensive, and hit the road—or stay and become unbearable. If they stayed, what would they demand? And as employees, we are so used to looking at our weaknesses that it has become a comfort to us.

As adults, we have harvested all the learning we can from focusing on weaknesses. And we are blind to and embarrassed by our gifts, our capacity to forgive ourselves, our affirmation of the value we bring. Despite our shyness and the discomfort we feel in talking about gifts, successful implementation comes more quickly from capitalizing on our strengths. The conversation of gifts is how this happens. This is true for an organization as well as for an individual.

---

Go to www.flawlessconsulting.com for an activity to use to stimulate a new conversation to close a meeting in a way that acknowledges the gifts and values brought into the room.

## THE POINT

These elements and techniques are both a methodology and a metaphor for a more universal possibility. Each symbolizes the larger intent and in that way has more meaning than its momentary effect. Implementation is not a universal, clear path stretched out before us. It is more complex than the phases of contracting and discovery, for it is more particular to each situation. It is more emergent than amenable to a blueprint. The structures here are more a menu or a starting point than a series of steps to follow, and each is an example of how to treat engagement as the central issue in implementation. We all wish for a simpler path, as if decision were followed immediately by action, so we could see corrective action taken and then measured. This rational problem-solving conception of how ideas get embodied into a living system presents a world that does not exist.

People choose to commit to a decision based on emotion, feelings, intuition, trust, and hope. These become the playing field for change. Even the most concrete changes—such as restructuring, using a new information system, cutting costs—happen when individuals decide to support the recommendations and decisions and make the adjustments that are required at every step along the way. The decision to support change is not just based on logic and reason; we need to help our clients deal with attitudes and feelings as well. That is at the core of consultation as described in this book.*

Also people decide to commit to a decision based on the depth and quality of their relatedness to those around them. For this reason, the core strategy for building authentic commitment to implementation is to design new ways for people to engage each other. This may be more critical than the clarity or rightness of a decision. Results are achieved when members of a system collectively choose to move in a certain direction. It is this act of choice that is critical.

Leadership behavior is not as vital as membership behavior. It is difficult for a patriarchal society such as ours to accept this reality. We tenaciously hold on to the belief that leaders can induce others to act. Leaders can no more induce action on the part of their followers than consultants can induce action on the part of their clients.

No change, no matter how wise and needed, will help if there is not a widespread and deep sense that each individual exercising choice and working together must make this work. This is real accountability— the willingness to personally care for the well-being of the institution first and of my unit and self second. This is a personal choice, and it is most likely to happen when people feel attached to each other and have influenced the process.

I have talked throughout this book about how to bring responsibility and accountability into the interaction between ourselves and our

---

*I acknowledge how much I have learned about engagement from colleagues who have been part of the School for Managing and Leading Change. In particular, Dick Axelrod and the late Kathie Dannemiller understood engagement long before I took it seriously. They have been part of inventing the whole world of large-group methodology. Dick created The Conference Model with Emily Axelrod, and Kathie was a mentor for all in the realm of real-time, high-interaction strategic change. They offered their insights generously, and I am indebted to them.

client. The skills of expressing our wants, dealing with resistance, and navigating the contracting meeting are all ways of building responsibility. Creating high interaction among your clients is how to bring responsibility into the implementation phase.

If the goal is to build internal commitment, the means is to create connection, tell it all, have new conversations in habitable spaces, and finally offer people a choice over how they do business. The choice we give people is critical and argues against our wish to package the future. Effective implementation most often entails the redistribution of power. And this is much more subtle than redoing the matrix describing which people decide who advises, who offers input, at each point in the work process. A chart of decision rules does not shift power; it restrains it.

The redistribution of power needs to be present in how we live, not just in how we decide. That is the point of these structures.

For downloadable copies of Checklists #9 and #10 visit www .flawlessconsulting.com.

## Checklist #9: Preparing for Implementation

Here are some reminders on working the elements of engagement into a gathering during the implementation phase or any time in the consulting process.

1. What will you do during each gathering to tilt the balance away from presentation and more toward participation?

2. How are you planning to provide the space for people to voice their concerns and opinions? What will you do to promote openness and telling the truth?

3. Consider how you may be able to help define choices for the client. How could you help open opportunities for real choice at many levels of the organization? How can you structure time for serious dialogue on how things will change?

4. What will you do to help people get unstuck from the same old conversations and begin new ones about the hopes and doubts the proposed change generates?

5. How will you bring the power of place into your design for each event?

## Checklist #10: Reviewing an Implementation Event

Here are some questions to ask yourself after any meeting. Use them to assess your own learning from the meeting and to prepare for the next one.

1. Did the meeting produce energy in the participants or drain energy?

2. How was it alike or different from what you expected?

3. How did people choose to engage in the process? How active were they? What kind of risk taking did you observe?

4. If you rearranged the room, what difference did this make?

5. What doubts and reservations were expressed? How was the discussion handled? A rush to agreement? A search for solutions? Was it possible for the group to postpone decision making? Anyone spend a lot of time explaining themselves?

6. How did the group determine what they wanted to create together?

7. What did people do to make new conversations occur? How did you help? What did they learn?

8. What promises were people willing to make? Were they enough?

9. What did you do to end the meeting so that each participant's effort and contributions were acknowledged?

10. What effect on your relationship with the client did this meeting have?

# CHAPTER 18

# TEACHER AS CONSULTANT

WARD MAILLIARD IS A HIGH SCHOOL TEACHER who is exploring a different way of teaching in service of producing a different kind of learning. His pursuit of a more powerful way of teaching was inspired, in part, by reading *Flawless Consulting*. He decided that if he wanted to make more of an impact on student learning, something more dramatic or radical was required than trying harder with the traditional conversations about teacher performance, curriculum, consequences, or measurements. He determined that he needed to look at himself and reexamine the nature of the contract between him and his students. Using the approach and terminology from this book, he experimented with giving up the expert role of the teacher and moving toward a more consultative learning stance.

This journey took him beyond recontracting with the students. He embraced many of the practices explored in this book. He adopted a discovery and inquiry way of viewing student performance questions. He began to see difficult student behavior as a form of resistance, not rebellion or dysfunction. The class learning agenda shifted from a focus on deficiencies to a focus on gifts. The class meetings began to be structured in alignment with many of the whole-system principles. Every meeting of the class was designed for engagement as much as curricular content. He also rearranged the room.

This is why telling his story, mostly in his own words, seems like a good way to tie the ideas in this book together. Ward never called himself a consultant. He operates in the fire of the educational marketplace, in an arena where much of the conventional wisdom is not working for too many children. As a result of applying many of the "flawless" ideas, he got new, improved outcomes and did not have to spend more money to get them.

## THE STORY

Ward's story is about how a deep commitment to authenticity and the contracting, and discovery processes discussed here are making a difference in unexpected places. This example is not just about producing exceptional learning in a high school classroom. It is about a deep-seated shift in the way we educate children.

Like health care reform, the debate about education reform has been argued long and hard. The conversation has focused on class size, teacher performance, a variety of curriculum questions. On testing and measurement of student performance. As a nation, we have tried a variety of innovations like charter schools, private sector management of public schools, quality improvement methods, site-based management, high community control, hiring former military as superintendents, and more. It doesn't matter if you are not familiar with these approaches because they have not improved the overall learning of young people.

This chapter describes the process Ward used to radicalize education. He has chosen to bring a consultative stance, everything this book is about, into the classroom. This story of what one teacher created gives a clue as to what true reform may entail.

In a letter to me, he described his own thinking process and how he became committed to consultative learning. Here are his words.

> If we want to reform education, at the heart of the matter is a shift in
> thinking about teaching and learning. When we traditionally think
> of a teacher we conjure up someone who knows. Someone who

will impart knowledge. Conversely, when we think of a student, we think of someone who does not know and who needs to acquire knowledge.

We have active teacher and receptive student. The directional flow of information and decision making is from teacher to student.

In this context, the teacher is given a stage and assigned an audience. The teacher often works from a prepared lesson plan: clear teaching points, a sequence of activities, content and expected outcomes. We expect the students to grasp and often memorize that content, by a certain date, and we measure to assess performance. Teacher improvement usually means giving the teacher better tools and techniques to deliver the content and win on the measures.

## ASSUMPTIONS ABOUT MOTIVATING STUDENTS

The arrangement Ward is describing puts the challenge of motivating students in the hands of the teacher. Grades, a major tool for motivating students, are designed to maintain some control over an increasingly difficult and distracted student audience. Grades determine movement up and down the performance-and-achievement ladder. They control entrance to college, which, according to the conventional storyline, leads to well-paying jobs that provide security and purchasing power. The equation is simple: grades equal performance, which guarantees advancement, which delivers wealth, which offers security and is the key to happiness.

This is a reasonable theory of motivation; unfortunately it applies only to a minority of students. And if it does not work, it is viewed as the student's fault, or the family's, or the educator's. Why is it only partially successful? In Ward's words:

> There are very few levers of control for today's adolescents. They have money, mobility, and distractions galore: sex, drugs, entertainment, subcultures and sufficient freedom to sample everything out there. This is as true for suburbs and small towns as for urban centers.

> Young people also have a superb capacity for networking including text messaging, internet, live chat, socializing tools like Facebook,

MySpace and Twitter. Teenagers are organized, independent, creative and resourceful. They have their own culture and a code of ethics. You might say that school is where they meet to organize their weekends, afternoons and evenings. The cell phone is a major tool for this organizing task and is in use 24/7, especially where forbidden.

The result is that teachers don't have the attention or obedience necessary for the standard teaching and motivation model to work. The way the system tries to cope with this is to make grades the point and high performance on grades the bottom-line measure. This creates in the classroom essentially a power relationship between teacher and student based on fear. The teacher is left to cling to the last vestiges of authority: grades, threats, and the cultural shame of underperforming. It is all based on a value system that says education is about security and material success.

## THE REALITY

This equation creates a world where performance has replaced learning as the dominant purpose of education. To achieve the performance, as Ward tells it, teachers become entertainers, disciplinarians, alien beings, or overseers, or they begin to lower expectations, avoid conflict, and surrender to grade creep, giving higher grades for lower learning. Says Ward:

> There is a price to pay for the context that the teacher manages the future of the student through the grade equals performance equals success equation. The price is the humanity of the student as well as our own. What is lost is the pleasure of learning for the student and the joy of teaching for the educator. At the end of the day we are exhausted by the struggle. Teachers commiserate with each other, recounting the stories which have at the center the student as identified patient whom we are unable to heal.
>
> There are exceptions, but in fact most every teacher tries hard to get it right. I would posit most every teacher can relate to these forces that shape our daily experience and end up looking for a reason or to find someone, including ourselves, to blame.

What Ward began to search for and found was a shift in the context of his thinking about the classroom. For example, he wondered, *What if we shifted the stance of teacher as knower to teacher as learner?* The questions might be: "What could I learn from my students that would allow me to be more effective in the learning environment? What if I stopped thinking of myself as a teacher and started thinking of myself as a consultant to learning?"

Ward says he was inspired by the definition of a *consultant* in Chapter One of this book: "In its most general use, consultation describes any action you take with a system of which you are not part." He observed, "I hope that none of us as teachers are under the illusion that we are part of the system that is thriving below us and remains distinct from our plans and curriculum. As we all know, the youth culture is a separate system with its own associations, rules, intentions, language, entertainments, and purpose."

## TAKING A CONSULTANT'S STANCE

Ward decided to become a consultant to his students: he would stop controlling them and reach a point where they get some privacy and relief from the relentless pressure that they need to perform because it is useful and good for them. He saw this as a form of colonization from the adult world:

> This is a colonization, which like all colonial efforts, has little to do with what really matters to the colonized and does not consider their world as a viable, even competent, system.
>
> When we show up to "teach" them, we see them in terms of their future utility, not their present capacities. We have something in mind for them that is our notion of the good, much like the missionaries whose intention was to save the savages from ignorance, dismantle their culture, extract their resources, and use their labor for the sake of the dominant culture.
>
> If we just hold the notion we are not part of the students' social system, we can ask what we need to be a successful consultant to learning. Give up the idea of teacher as the driver or producer of learning. This helps us escape or extricate us from the question, "how do I teach my students?" At the very least it might make us curious about the student culture with which we are engaged.

## Context of Humanity and Abundance

His first step to implement these ideas was to work out of a new context. The essence of a new context was to see a class as a group of human beings, each with gifts in abundance, rather than as students with deficiencies or needs. Even in the face of real challenges, like dyslexia, attention deficit hyperactivity disorder, eating disorders, disabilities, behavior problems, or low motivation, students are learning, alive human beings, not, in Ward's terms, "identified patients."

Even when it seems that they are not learning, or not present, or unsupportive of what we adults have to offer, when we give priority to the restoration of their humanity, we will discover that they will learn what matters; we will see that given a chance, found on their own, they discover a pathway into their own future that neither we nor they could have imagined.

Given this context, when Ward took on a consultant role, he could not walk into a classroom and start telling students what to do without first taking the temperature of the room. Ward said:

> Teachers need to do the discovery work as described in *Flawless Consulting*. Inquire, interview, map, understand the dynamics, see how students are "managing the problem" of learning. Ask students about their intentions, goals, and challenges. We put what we do know, our expertise, at the service of the system by first learning everything we can about the system.

As Ward sees it, consultative teachers engage the three skills every consultant needs to get the job done: technical skills, interpersonal skills, and consulting skills. There is nothing about the consultative stance that denies the expertise of the teacher. We can assume that most teachers have the technical skills (they know their subject), and we also assume that most teachers have the basic interpersonal skills. Our focus is on the consulting skills that are key in this example.

## Renegotiating the Social Contract

The shared project or business objective of the classroom is exceptional learning for each person. The consulting challenge teachers confront is how to create a practice where learning occurs. This begins with contracting. The struggle that many students have with learning in the classroom might be best understood by considering that the learning project was faulty in the initial contracting stage.

In truth, the contracting stage in traditional teaching is pretty non-existent or at most implicit, fear based, and by no means mutual. This is so for many good reasons, the most prominent being that many students are not at school by choice. Where there is no choice, accountability and enthusiasm are hard to come by.

## Focusing on Trust Between Students

With a contract where power remains in the hands of the teacher and compliance is the response of the student, it creates a culture where there is little trust among the students. Often the most alienated, outlier students who are most disconnected become the most powerful. Within this dominant culture of compliance and resistance, there is a cost to the students who, for whatever the reason, show up to really learn. A sad truth is that students who show real caring about learning usually pay a high social price in their social realm. They are labeled and even ostracized. The dominant group has a stake in keeping expectations low. The question, says Ward,

> is about the relationship I want them to have with each other. How to contract for this? These are consultative questions. It takes time since they are so wounded by the traditional learning process that it takes half the semester to achieve some reconditioning. This has to be adapted to each group, to create a social system that values peer relationships and knows this is central to learning.

## Consultant Building Trust

The intent, then, is to consult with the youth in the room to help them build trust with each other. The teacher acts as a third party in a discovery mode. Not expert or even arbitrator. Here is one form that it took in Ward's experience:

> One kid was hurt by negative comments that were made about her in class. When it happened, I stopped the class and asked her for permission to use what happened as a learning. She gave a tentative yes. Then I asked her how she felt about the comment. She reported that it had hurt; it shut her down, made her feel like she was not liked. The offending students were asked to just listen. Not to defend themselves. When they just listened, something shifted at that moment in the class. Both sides eventually got to talk. It re-humanized the culture of the classroom.

## Conserving Trust and Relatedness

If the teacher chooses to act as a consultant to students' relationship with each other, the challenge, said Ward, is to create safety in the room:

> The question is, How do I get in the door when I am not welcome? I have to be willing to sacrifice covering content for the sake of the relationship. So what does my contract with the students entail?

> First of all I have to get interested in the lives of students. If a student shows up without her book, I have a choice to make. I can see a student who has not followed instructions, maybe for the fourth time and therefore is "student without a book." Or, instead of seeing a "student without a book," I see a person with a "story waiting to be told."

Margaret is a case in point. I called her over and asked what is going on. She said she is in the midst of her parents' difficult divorce. She was staying with her dad, it did not go well, so she ran out of her dad's house in anger and left her book there. When she got home there was no way she was going to call her dad and ask him to bring the book over.

When I got that, I let it go. Gave up punishment for the sake of connection.

In a very important way, the teacher gains power by choosing to act like a consultant, not a parent. Getting interested instead of making the student wrong. Ward continued:

The point is that if we engage as consultative partners we find a way for them to learn from their own experience. They will get something special out of this. If we focus only on the content of a class, or an assignment, or bringing in the book, then the student or the client will never understand the power of functioning like a partner and experience the engagement this produces.

What the consulting stance offers to teachers is a way of dealing with the fact that many students are not in school by choice. In the absence of choice, teachers get resistance in the form of students' saying, in essence, "Tell me what minimum I need to do to get what I want." Students become obedient and act as if they care because they think that obedience is worth at least a grade point. The compliance response works because teachers are seduced by interest and positive reinforcement like anyone else.

What Ward embarked on was an effort to renegotiate the contracting in the early phase of the class. It was not easy, he said:

If we do not have freedom of choice about being here, how do we claim our freedom or create in students a sense of real accountability?

There might be some possibilities that we as consultants might gain by creating a classroom that shares power and values learning over performing. For example, what if instead of arriving at the beginning of the year with a plan that we had prepared for our class, we instead made a plan with our class and took some time to explore the contracting questions first?

Ward began to have honest conversations with the students about these and other topics to begin to make the shift from, "How do I have power over my students?" to, "How do I have power with my students?" They actually opened up a conversation about trust. When he took the time to inquire about what might work differently, he was surprised to find caring under the mask of indifference.

## The New Contract

Here are some elements of the new contract he developed.

### Conserving Honesty Versus Defense

Ward had to ask himself what the cost is of telling the truth in his classroom:

> If you ask how many read the homework, what kind of an answer will you get? If 60 percent have not, do you want to hear it? When students tell you something you do not want to hear, how do you react? With criticism or curiosity? Are there subtle ways we teach them to lie? What do we do when they are not paying attention? Tell them to pay attention, or try to understand where their attention has gone? Lying is what they have learned, it is expected in traditional classroom.

### Failure Is an Option; Gifts Are the Point

One of the rules that emerged in his classroom is that failure is okay. Resistance is okay, and so is being wrong. Wherever they are is okay, because that is where they are starting from. As Ward recalled from reading *Flawless Consulting*, resistance is a sign that something important is going on. It is not a problem to be solved or overcome.

Agreeing not to have reprisals helped change the context of the classroom. There was no judgment for what others were doing, only on what students were choosing. Ward told them: "If you are tired, take a nap. When you are done with a task, go do something else. If we are doing a task as a group and what you are doing is not useful, find something else that is useful to do."

This is based on the reality that successful learning is random discovery. If the goal is learning, not teaching, each person needs permission to fail. That cannot happen without a stance that favors trying something new and being supported whatever the outcome, since if the goal is learning, "failure" is a big way it happens. So in effect, students who fail are on the way toward reaching the learning goal. This is what it takes, Ward says, to turn students who have become performers back into people who become learners:

> One way this gets implemented is by deciding to see the gifts in every student, even if it takes some serious reframing. Take Sandy as an example.
>
> Sandy is both dyslexic and has a great fear of going out. If you ask her to tell you something about herself, these are her lead stories: "I have a reading disorder and fear too much contact with the outside world." This is the dominant theme of her history and she has received a lot of professional help with these needs.
>
> It is quite visible that this child was challenged and dyslexic. She is bright but speaks and processes ideas very slowly. Sometimes the professionals call this a "delayed processor."
>
> I decided to see her as a "deep processor," rather than a "delayed processor." Let her pace be a gift: she holds depth over speed. Also, at one point I saw Sandy sketching and knew right then we had an artist on our hands. That was the final point where we stopped naming her for what she could not do. I decided to focus simply on what she could do. She is reflective, thinks deeply, and is an artist.
>
> Sandy and I both tested this premise when it came to an important part of senior year: a week-long class trip. As soon as the planning began, we learned Sandy was very afraid of the trip. She talked to me about it and considered not going. Her parents got involved. After a fair amount of conversation we decided together to work out a strategy. She agreed that instead of being controlled by the fear, whenever the fear showed up she would volunteer to go first.
>
> This became another gift for her to focus on: her capacity to show courage. She was still afraid, but not controlled by it. So we got her to agree that failing was okay, speaking up slowly was okay. She could still operate at her own pace, and this was not a problem. It gave

her the time she needed. While others might read more quickly, or do others things well, she was courageous, thoughtful, and an artist who knew all about sketching.

It was not until graduation that Ward found out how successfully Sandy had managed her own learning. All students had to give a three-minute speech about what the year meant to them. Sandy had benefited in ways few others would have guessed. The trip was a high point. Her confidence had changed. She was the one student who got a standing ovation after her speech.

### Conserving Not Knowing

Another big question Ward and his students asked themselves is, "What is the cost of not knowing?" "Usually it is shame on the part of the student," Ward says, "and disappointment on the part of the teacher":

> When we are disappointed or even irritated that they do not know, we are holding on to who we want them to be. We are not seeing who they are. We are also not setting up the conditions where failure and learning are friends to each other. Being wrong and fallibility have to be valued for learning to be about oneself. If not this, then performance becomes the point and learning about self is sacrificed.

### How Do We Measure Success?

In any discussion of education reform, we have to take up the question of measurement and have a thicker discussion than just grades. Success in learning and success in teaching may be different things. "As a teacher," Ward said,

> we are not just selling ideas, like selling a product. We are also promoting awareness of self. Awareness of what it means to be part of a community, a citizen. Students need to struggle with their own definition of success in this class. If we do not put the question of success on the table, then we will get stuck with the default position of student as consumer if they do well, identified patient if they do not. Too often we talk of students as someone to cure, fix, heal, or filled with information.

### How to Deal with Functions of Umpire (Grader) and Consultant (Facilitator) at the Same Time

This is the paradox inherent in the role of the teacher and consultant; the resolution is to present this as a community conversation. Teacher and student, contracting together, work to figure out how to meet the grading requirements of the larger society, yet not let that dominate the way they operate together. Ward said:

> It can begin by asking students what they want from this class. What wants do they have of themselves? What is their intention for themselves? The conversation could be about how they learn, how they work, how they operate as members of a team. Another contracting process.

He asks them what they want from him, the teacher. What can he, the teacher, do to support their intentions, achieve what they want from the experience? What role does the teacher play in supporting their definition of success and helping them measure that? These are all very consultative questions, Ward noted:

> This can play in very concrete ways. We can elicit the student vision of what defines success for each project or even each assignment. What is success and how do you know? The challenge is to get past what they are told to want. For example, on a reading or research assignment, ask them, "What struck you, what did you notice, what challenged you, what was interesting? What value did this book have for you?" These are different questions than asking what they remember, what was the storyline, what did the author have in mind?

### Conserving Learning Methods Versus Teaching Methods

If we reflect on how students learn, there is a continuum from listening, to reading, to seeing, to speaking, and to doing something. Most learning comes from speaking and doing. Yet we ask students to spend a lot of time listening and reading. This is a telling quote from a student in one of Ward's classrooms: "I like the small groups because when I talk to my peers I learn. When you the teacher speak, I don't listen."

If we really believe in their learning, we may have to give up a fair amount of our content, since what is the point of teaching or speaking if there is no listening? This is part of shifting the contract from teacher as curriculum provider to teacher as consultant. The strategy is that if we can engage and gain more investment from students, they will get something greater out of this. If focus is primarily on the content, then students, just like clients, will never understand the power of their own engagement.

## THE TRIP TO WASHINGTON, D.C.

What made these conversations and agreements about the ground rules of Ward's class noteworthy was that they were held around the curriculum for the class. At the first of the year, they took a look at the core project of the class, a trip to Washington, D.C., to interview government and nongovernmental organization leaders. Ward said,

> I have been doing this trip every other year since 1989. The trip has been very successful by most standards and has become a rite of passage for the 11th and 12th graders.

> Part of my old story was that the trip was successful because I managed it well. However I always felt there was more we could do and have a higher sense of engagement if the students had more of a sense of personal commitment. This is why I was interested in experimenting with the notion of shared power in the classroom. I thought, What if they defined success, established goals, and designed their own experience? What would it mean if I really became a consultant to their project rather than the students being participants in my project? I wondered what that might produce.

> I used the chapters on contracting in *Flawless Consulting* for the principles I might use. If I was going to do this project in this manner, then things like mutual consent, personal acknowledgment, exchange of wants, testing for control and vulnerability and a shared definition of the outcome or product needed to become topics of conversation.

In this beginning contracting phase and exploration of the shift from teacher to consultant, Ward discovered several things. The most important was that given the chance, the students would set goals that would meet or exceed anything he would have proposed. For the trip to Washington, even though they had never been there before, they were able to delineate and reveal everything Ward knew to be possible or important in almost twenty years of leading this journey to the nation's capital:

> Rather than my telling them what was important or describing the vision I had, I discovered that the vision was already in them and all I had to do was ask. Given a choice they chose more than what I would have chosen for them.

> It was essential that I be honest with my students. I told them that this process of having the students design their own journey was new to me and I was going to learn along with them. I was going to allow myself to be "caught learning." It was not easy. It felt at times like I was being peeled. I was no longer the expert.

My students could see that sometimes we got stuck in our process and I did not have the answer. I invited a friend, Vivian Wright, who is a very experienced consultant with Hewlett-Packard, to come into the classroom and help out. I called Peter Block and he did a phone conference where the students asked him questions. After engaging with both Peter and Vivian, the students felt better and had a clearer idea of the process. I was most often not the center of the learning experience, which felt like a big loss of control and more vulnerability.

The goal of shifting the story of ownership of learning from teacher to students is what sustained me.

On the trip in Washington, D.C., Ward noticed a qualitative shift in how the students participated:

I wasn't really able to define what it was. But after we returned we held our traditional school assembly where the students describe the meaning and learnings from the trip.

In the question and answer session that follows the presentation, the final question was asked, "What effect did having a choice in the design and experience of this trip have on you?"

The response was essentially that because they had had a choice, they often chose to engage even when they were not sure what they wanted. They took responsibility for their choices and were more present.

The shift from teacher as knower and judge to student as learner, producer, and center of the project can be frightening to contemplate. But as Ward's experience shows, that is when learning will take place for both. This is the intent of the consulting process discussed here. When we give up control and act as relative equals, we make ourselves vulnerable. It is admittedly a scary proposition, but it also creates trust. Most teachers know intuitively and by experience that relationship is the key to teaching and learning and relationship is based on trust. Without some level of mutuality in our classrooms, we will at best have moderate trust. The effect of this is that students will remain reluctant performers and a whole deeper level of learning will be sacrificed.

## THE CHOICE IN THE MATTER

One of the major shifts that occurs when we move from being teachers to becoming learning consultants is in our own perspective on where choice resides.

In the workplace world, a consultant knows the client has a choice. Part of the skill for the teacher becoming consultant is to acknowledge that even in school, where the student is required to show up, choice exists. According to Ward,

> Because we are passionate about our subjects and/or under mandate to provide certain results, we often act as if we and the student do not have a choice. Under the pressure of time and content delivery, we often use the power of the system to influence what is possible with students, all organized around the argument that their future will be impaired if they do not get with the performance-grade program.

> Developmentally, teenagers actually lack a fully developed capacity to understand the consequences of their actions. This does not fully form in the brain until the mid-20s. Perhaps that is why in our desperation to turn out successful children, we keep relying on threats as our tools of choice. We overplay the importance of performance with the argument that if you don't get good grades, you won't go to a good college, or any college, and it may affect your earning capacity and future financial security.

> The sad part is that many elements of successful learning essential to a life of meaning are suppressed. We desensitize our students to the more subtle accoutrements of an educated person such as citizenship, discernment, love of the creative process, passion, discovery, and surprise. All of these are sacrificed at the altar of the promise, perhaps illusion of future security.

So this example of education reform in the classroom is about choice, which is at the center of a consultative stance. It means we have to decide what values we want to embody, whether we believe a more consultative role is useful. Ward reflects on the experience:

We need to be conscious of what we want to conserve in our way of being in the classroom. There is one question we as teachers need to ask ourselves, and that is, "What am I conserving in my manner of living? In my manner of being with the students, what am I living? Am I conserving trust, intimacy, and cooperation. Or am I conserving fear, isolation and competition?"

These questions are at the core of education and teaching, just as they are at the core of how we consult and support others. They are the conversations that need to be at the heart of creating successful organizations and are the real foundation for the education reform so many seek.

# CHAPTER 19

# THE HEART OF THE MATTER

To say it one last time, MAYBE, consulting is primarily a relationship business. No matter how research-based or technical the project is, it will always reach a point at which the success of the work will hinge on the quality of the relationships we have with our clients. This relationship is the conduit through which our expertise passes.

The way we contact and engage people around our expertise is an applied art and takes a hundred forms. At times it is one-to-one coaching with an individual or team. It can be working with a group on strategy or technology, or running a training session. Underlying all the ways we work with clients is a set of beliefs about relationships, learning, and the nuances of how change occurs that ultimately define our practice.

While this book is threaded with thoughts about good, or flawless, consulting practice, I want to take a moment to be explicit about its foundational concepts. When I am lost, unsure how to proceed, which is most of the time, I return to a few ideas that ground me again and again and serve to reassure. Each of these ideas has as much to do with the heart as the head; in fact, finding and sustaining this connection may be the whole point. Consulting cannot be done well without genuine caring for the client, and the challenge is to find ways to embody our care in the way we do the work. Our care is expressed partly in our behavior and style, but it is also a matter of how we structure critical elements of the learning and change process.

In a sense, our job is to be a learning architect. At our best, we design social settings that lead to insight, resolution of differences, and change. What follows are some ideas that support conditions under which learning and change are more likely to happen. None is fail-safe, each contains elements of adventure, and all flow against the stream of the conventional wisdom and the dominant culture. That is what makes them useful.

## CHOOSING LEARNING OVER TEACHING

While we usually claim that we are in the business of helping our clients learn, most traditional educational or consulting efforts are more about teaching than learning. If you ask who is really learning at any

meeting, communication session, or training event, the answer is usually, "The person in charge."

The dominant models for learning come from our educational system. If you look at most of our classrooms, the teacher stands in front, and students line up behind or around tables, facing the front. The agenda, the objectives, and the method of learning are all specified by the teacher. The teacher is in effect the supervisor of learning. This is the world that Ward, in the previous chapter, is chipping away at. Similarly in consulting, the consultant is expected to be the change manager, even the change agent. The task of the client is to absorb what the consultant has to offer.

The classroom or consulting project run on this model is based on the need for predictability and control. Our need is to make the teacher or consultant central to the learning. It is partly a question of pedagogy and our desire to prescribe for others what we wish them to do. But we are not the only ones lured into an all-eyes-front approach. This classroom or meeting model is also demanded by the learners. If you decide to invite clients to define the agenda, create the learning process, and evaluate their own performance, you will probably face a revolt. Clients are so conditioned to be passive in the teaching-and-learning process that given the choice to manage their own learning, they will pass and turn the floor back to the consultant.

The result is that the teacher/consultant conspires with the participant or client to keep the teacher/consultant central and the student/client reactive. And one effect is that too often the consultant is the one who learns the most. Some of this is inevitable, for when we are forced to explain ourselves or teach others, we invest in the subject matter in a way that the client is not required to do. But some of it comes from our need to control what is presented and to specify what is learned and accepted. The symbol of this for me is the way we do much of our training. We have a passion for modeling videos in training, with predictable outcomes for participants. We promise a right way, make the way explicit by headlining the milestones and learning points, and then declare that the outcomes are predictable from the outset. We call it "good planning."

The cost is that we rarely see people engage their full capacity to learn. Just as Tim Gallwey, author and creator of the Inner Game method of learning, has suggested, in most training and instruction, there is a great deal of teaching and very little learning. In teacher-centered formats, the real learner is the trainer, and the participant is engaged in a sophisticated form of imitation and absorption.

The real learning is in the act of creating the online course, the modeling tape, the headlined points, and the lesson plan. It is in the struggle to create that we find value. It is in the effort to understand and create ideas and practices that the learning resides. The container for that teaching, the participant, often leaves the session little changed. We know this, which is why we talk so much about measurement. The talk is an expression of our anxiety about the relevance of the process.

## LEARNING AS A SOCIAL ADVENTURE

To bring value to the participant or the client, we need to design our efforts to support learning at the expense of teaching. As the education example shows, this means we need to build elements of surprise, discovery, and not knowing into our interaction with clients. We need to allow risk in the room, raise the stakes, engage in caring confrontation, offer strong support, and ensure affirmation of what each of us knows. These are what create learning.

Packaging an answer, putting it online, as we do with so many of our ideas and programs, interferes with learning. Granted, packaged consultation or training is faster, more digestible, more visible and predictable, and therefore more salable; it is a good short-term business strategy. But over time, it is like the alcoholic's hair-of-the-dog cure for a hangover. If high-control, predetermined thinking is the client's problem, we cannot fix it with high-control, predetermined answers.

If learning and change are truly our intent, a slower, more demanding, and more deliberative approach is required. We have to value struggle over prescription, questions over answers, tension over comfort, and capacities over needs and deficiencies.

## THE STRUGGLE IS THE SOLUTION

Most persistent problems that call for consultation have no clear right answer. This means we have to get used to facing the paradoxical nature of the workplace and the human beings we find there. Think about how you deal with situations where two opposing viewpoints are both true. Do we need more control, or less? More centralization, or more local control? Do people need more freedom, or will they abuse the privilege and go off in separate directions? Should we always tell the truth, or do we acknowledge the political nature of organizations? Will more technology and better information help, or is the problem one of motivation and lack of training?

Every consultation involves these kinds of questions. Even in very technical consulting, questions like these are embedded in the architecture of our solutions. We make a serious mistake if we choose one or the other, or even try to find a middle ground. We lose the benefit of the unique ideas at the two poles when we compromise for middle ground. The best outcomes emerge in the effort to understand the truth in both sides. The consultant's task is to evoke an exploration of the polarity, postpone the quick answers, and make sure that the complexity of the question is acknowledged before action is chosen. It is in the struggle to transcend both sides that a resolution is found.

For example, we need control, and we also need local choice. People need more freedom, and they will at times abuse it. More technology is vital, and motivation and skill are everything. It is the tension in these polarities that informs action that is based in reality and stays alive. If we can accept that this sort of tension is always present, then the action we take at a particular moment will in some ways not matter: whatever we choose, we will pay a price for it. So why not acknowledge this, see the struggle as the path, and resist the temptation of certainty and speed?

# THE QUESTION IS MORE IMPORTANT THAN THE ANSWER

What this means is that we have to learn to trust the questions—and recognize that the way we ask the question drives the kind of answer we develop.

We get stuck by asking the wrong question. The most common wrong question is that of the engineer in each of us who wants to know how we get something done. This question quickly takes us down the path of methodology and technique. It assumes the problem is one of what to do rather than why to do it or even whether it is worth doing.

The "how" question has several variations. Take them as warning signs.

- *How long will it take?* We want to make good time regardless of where we are going.

- *How do we get them to change?* If only they would change, we would be better off. The top thinks the bottom is the problem, the bottom thinks the top is the problem, and when they get together, both agree the middle is the problem.

- *What are the steps needed for . . . ?* Life can be reduced to a step-by-step plan. PowerPoint is the icon, points made for distribution to scale. Blueprints with milestones are the drug, and more discipline is the prescription that never cures.

- *How do we measure the effect?* This implies that there is no value in the invisible world. It is the measure of reality that becomes the point. Philosopher Alan Watts once said that we have reached the point at which we go to a restaurant and eat the menu. We have become more interested in the definition and measurement of life than in living it.

- *How do we communicate this?* The problem is they do not understand us. "A problem in communication" is the ultimate empty diagnosis. It denies real conflict and raises spin to the level of purpose. Our finest example of this is Washington, D.C., where the primary work of the political class is to manage image and the news. Questions of communication are most often the easy way out of questions of will, courage, and commitment.

- *What are other organizations doing or where has this worked?* We want to lead and wish to go second at the same time. There is some value in discovering what others are doing: it gives us hope. More often, though, the question is a wish for safety, for when we hear where it has worked, we then talk of how unique our situation is.

These questions are so appealing because they demand so little. They promise a world that is logical and predictable. They also externalize the problem and are focused on change from people who are not in the room. What's more, they shrink the problem to manageable size by treating it as a matter of skills rather than questions of purpose and the use of power.

## BEYOND HOW

"How" questions will take us no further than our starting place. They result in trying harder at what we were already doing. The questions that heal us and offer hope for authentic change are the ones we cannot easily answer. Living systems are not controllable, despite the fact that they evolve toward order and some cohesion. To move a living system, we need to question what we are doing and why. We need to choose depth over speed, consciousness over action—at least for a little while.

The questions that lead to a change in thinking are more about why and where than about how. Some examples:

- *What is the point of what we are doing?* We live in a world measured by wealth and scale. Are we here to make money, meet budgets, grow the operation? Is this enough? And who is the beneficiary of this? Who are we here to serve, and what price are we willing to pay to stay true to our answer?

- *What has to die before we can move to something new?* We want change but do not want to pay for it. We are always required to put aside what got us here to move on. Where do we find the courage to do this?

- *What is the real value of our product and service?* And in whose eyes? How valid is our promise, and what are the side effects of our delivery? Are our advertising and the way we present ourselves a picture we even believe is true?

- *What personal meaning do people find in what we are doing?* What intrinsic rewards exist for us? Do we show up voluntarily, or have we indentured ourselves simply to sustain our life outside work? Many people think work is just that, work, and to expect more is to be a fool.

- *What would happen if we did nothing?* When is change for its own sake? Maybe we should just get better at what we do now.

- *What are the capacities and strengths that we are not using fully?* Give up on fixing weaknesses; find out what more is possible. Sometimes we do not even know our gifts as individuals and as institutions. What strengths do others see in us? Years ago in our consulting firm, we asked clients why they hired us. They said that what they found attractive was our seeming disinterest and reluctance in working with them. We were shocked. We thought that if we seemed aloof, it was because we were disorganized; they saw it as a sign of integrity.

- *And what are we leaving for the next generation?* This question is for the second half of life, but it is still a useful focusing exercise. Our materialistic culture consumes its resources and bets on science or miracles to cope with what we leave for those after us. What will our legacy be?

These are difficult questions, ones that require faith and patience. They do not substitute for action, and at some point we do have to ask, "How?" But the why questions are designed for learning and change, and in that way they are very practical indeed. It is in the dialogue about these questions that change occurs. They are questions for the client to engage in at the top and bottom and in between; they are not questions for the consultant to answer.

It is hard for some to engage in this level of abstract dialogue, even though these are the questions we each privately ask ourselves. No matter how difficult, these are the questions our clients must deal with publicly, because the route to genuine change is less obvious than a list and some milestones; without some depth to our inquiry, our thinking will never change, and we destine ourselves to the pursuit of quick fix and fashion. And if a consultant cannot pose these questions, who will?

## INSIGHT RESIDES IN MOMENTS OF TENSION

To value struggle, entertain maddening questions, and live with paradox in the service of thinking differently is hard. Really hard. Our instinct is to move toward comfortable subjects, reach for the habitual way of working. If we consultants propose questions about meaning and demand an extended period of reflection, we will be blamed for not being practical, action oriented, and step minded.

If we view this tension as a flaw in the process, we will jump ship at the first salvo and retreat into comfort. Many of my mistakes have occurred when I became anxious about the process and reverted to the safe harbor of action plans and lists. Once the actions were listed, we all breathed a sigh of relief and smiled at the familiar feel of milestones in our hands. That was the good news.

When I would look back at those times, though, the changes that came out of those efforts were always disappointing. Follow-through was weak, optimism quickly faded, and even the effort to push the changes along left most people feeling that nothing had changed. We just had more action items on our plate. I let those clients down by yielding to the tension too easily. If I had persisted with the difficult questions longer, asked for more rethinking of the basics, I would have served the client better.

Another source of tension might simply be the strained relationships among those in the room. If resolving this strain were easy, they would have done it before we got there. We are often faced with tension that is historical and tenacious. Everyone feels it, but no one wants to name it. Do we dive into it or manage around it?

Here is an example that still rolls around in my mind. I facilitated a meeting of eleven agencies that had come together to cooperate with each other better. It was a good cause, and a big event, to even all be in the room together. Halfway through the meeting, after getting acquainted and hearing some ideas on possible mutual interests, the momentum for action and agreement started to build. I had planned for more open dialogue, more discussion of differences, more reflection, more time in mixed groups getting connected.

I felt the pressure build, the co-planners huddled with me in the corner, and I yielded on the original plan. We broke people into their natural teams and asked them to come back in an hour with ideas on what this whole group could do together that their organizations could not accomplish separately. It seemed reasonable; that was why we were there, after all. At the end of the hour, the teams reported. To a team, each reported what that team alone might do to move its agenda forward. They were not prepared to cross boundaries, yield on the positions they had come to the meeting with, or trust each other in new ways. A group that had been convened to seek new cooperation devolved into their history of firm boundaries and negotiation.

The tension that was expressed in the desire to get to an action plan was really a defense against the deeper conversation about ways they were apart and the caution they felt in yielding positions that would be required for significant movement to occur. And the worst part was that I had colluded with them out of my own anxiety about being practical and useful. I tried to recover the next morning, but it was too late; the moment had passed, and the energy that might have led to a shift had been drained.

The door to new ways of thinking does not open easily, and it is the tension in the room that actually becomes the key. The tension points to where the resistance or doubt resides. Discussing the tension makes insight and resolution possible. If we can see the tension as energy and go toward it, big insights will follow. If we manage around it, we risk losing the day, as I did.

When the tension surfaces, it needs to be named, discussed, and acknowledged. The consultant has to push the discussion into the difficult areas. We have to ask ourselves when we will be in a better position to move ahead. When will be a better time to discuss failure, conflict between individuals and groups, feelings of futility and doubt? More structure is not what is needed at these moments; it is courage that is in short supply. By naming the tension and supporting a discussion of what it means, we gain some learning about the emotional part of work.

This is what learning requires and what clients need from us. It is the patriarchal culture that wants to keep a lid on feelings, which is what running from the tension is about. The key is understanding that the expression itself is what is valuable, not the answer or resolution. If we can support both sides in expressing things they find hard to discuss, then the decisions made afterward will be of a different nature.

## CAPACITIES BEAR MORE FRUIT THAN DEFICIENCIES

Another element of change is the choice whether to focus on what is missing or on what is present. I once thought that my service as a consultant was to identify problems, and so I dedicated myself to figuring out what was missing. After capitalizing on weaknesses for years, I have changed my focus to seeing what gifts are there and where capacities lie.

There is a practical side to this choice. We should accept that we have harvested the yield available in the deficiency field. Why pursue a path of diminishing marginal returns? We already have the product of a lifetime of working on deficiencies. A lot more effort will yield few more results.

In terms of strategic work with clients, John McKnight, leading light in the world of understanding the nature of community, has articulated a wonderful case that focusing on deficiencies or needs only reinforces the power of the expert at the expense of the client or employee. In his language, it turns citizens, people with rights and power, into consumers, people with weaknesses and needs. He believes that in this shift from citizen to consumer, the one who benefits is the service provider—in our case, the consultant.

Focusing on deficiencies is also a question of how we treat the human spirit. Are we here to remind each other of what is missing or of what is possible? If what you see is what you get, then look for the strength, and you will find it. The problem with looking at strengths is that we are not used to it, and we don't know what to say, so we feel embarrassed. And we have dealt with weaknesses for years, so it is easy for us to decide not to change them. But to search for the divine in each of us, or in our communities, would confront us in ways that most of us are not prepared for.

Finally, if we persist in looking at needs and weaknesses, it becomes a political gambit, an expression of power. The one who defines the conversation and the needs is the one in charge. When we institutionalize the talk of weaknesses in others, it is a way of maintaining control over what we are talking about. We position ourselves above the fray, uniquely able to see what is wrong. When we look at what is missing in other people or other organizations, we put them in a lesser position, even if we do so with the claim that we just want to be helpful. Our attitude implies that they have work to do and we do not. We are the parents lovingly looking at the child.

This becomes a comfortable stance for the consultant, for we can stand next to the critics, joining them in their favored position. It is a way of being sheltered by their halo. It also affirms that we are needed. But comfort is only the easiest way, not the most fruitful. It is better for us to be present by virtue of choice rather than by need and let our gift be to affirm the best in what we see.

## WE ARE RESPONSIBLE FOR ONE ANOTHER'S LEARNING

That everything that happens in the room is every person's business is a radical thought. Why? Because we have such a history of competition that it has become the air we breathe. In our first exposure to institutional life, at school, our success came at the expense of others. I needed to get a D so someone else could get an A. If I got the A, then it needed to be balanced by another's failure. If you don't believe this, think what would happen if a teacher gave all A's. The teacher would have a problem. What happens if a boss thinks everyone is an outstanding performer? Think again, boss.

This is not a moral stance against competition; it is a question of how competition affects learning. Competition with our peers breeds isolation and leads to holding tightly to what we have. It is good, perhaps, for our ambition, but hardly for our institutions. If learning requires risk and not knowing, it will not happen if we see others as strangers with their own problems—problems that we do not share. The fact that so much of the culture thinks that individual competition is the key to motivation is a measure of how much our thinking has been defined by a marketplace mentality and its love of scarcity.

It always surprises me when I hear managers speak for the well-being of the whole and then see them participate in fostering competition among the parts. The challenge of organizational life is to connect people in common effort. Understanding my interdependence with all others connects me to the whole. And when each is responsible for the learning of the whole, then each shares a deeper sense of purpose with all members. Accepting this challenge demands cooperation and a willingness to acknowledge our connectedness. It is no small feat, but worth trying, for it is a significant way to ensure lasting learning.

If our goal as consultants is learning and change, we need to act as if all are responsible for it. This simple shift in thinking leads us to be more inclusive and to see that learning needs to come from all directions. If we are working in systems that breathe competition, we may not be able to change that, but at a minimum we can refuse to reinforce it.

## CULTURE CHANGES IN THE MOMENT

This is a tricky and potentially very powerful idea. In every encounter with the client, we hear concern about what will happen tomorrow. We rarely end a meeting without someone expressing doubts about whether their agreements will last and their optimism endure. In the first hour of our training sessions, someone will ask whether the world will be any different when we leave the session.

My response is that if we want to see change, we had better not wait to leave this session for it to happen. How can we have hope in tomorrow if today is not different? Each moment has to carry within it an element of the destination. This is why the way we come together is so important. It offers hope—at this minute—about how the future might look. It leads us to give great attention to how we design this moment, this meeting.

The moment also instructs us in methods. If we learn to watch what is happening now, this reflection will tell us what works and what doesn't. As a discovery method, it is understanding the universe in a grain of sand. It is understanding the organizational culture in the nature of this meeting or conversation. If you see nothing happening, either you are not watching or maybe there is "no thing" happening. To witness the absence of life, or action, or dialogue is as descriptive of a system as seeing the presence of something. If we would trust the moment, we would learn the power of reflection.

Also we would see that we can implement the future without having to wait for it. How long does change take? Well, are we ready to begin it at this moment? Want to bring trust, honesty, more or less structure, cooperation between units, clearer focus, alignment into the organization? Now is the time to begin. Our action plan is what we do in the next hour. It is not what we say but what we do together. This meeting becomes the tablet on which the future is written. Each intention of cultural change needs to find expression in the present, or it loses its credibility.

The moment fails us only when what we have in mind is a change in someone else. Those "someone elses" cannot be changed in the moment if they are not in the room. If they are not in the room, they cannot be party to the change. So why are we focusing on them anyway? Why do we always think that some other group is the problem? Why is it that in all these years of training, I have never had the right group in the room? Whoever is in the room is always the wrong person. Whoever gets the training asks whether others have received it yet. If I say they have, then they say it didn't take. If I say they haven't, then they ask, "Why do you expect us to change if they won't?"

Treating this moment as an example of what we seek in the future requires us to forsake the past, to let go of our guilt or resentment. Victims do not do well in the moment, and we have all been wounded. We create little room in organizational life for forgiveness—of ourselves and others. I have seen few learning exercises that are about forgiveness. Maybe this is one of the reasons we are so focused on weaknesses; they remind us of our unfinished business with our own history. If we have not forgiven the past, we will keep trying to fix it. Changing this moment, giving it importance, honoring it as a prediction of the future may be the way to heal the wounds and urge us into choosing optimism.

## IF CHANGE IS SO WONDERFUL, WHY DON'T YOU GO FIRST?

Another heart-of-the-matter notion is that change, transformation, and hope are all self-inflicted. Change faces us with human questions, and dealing with them is dependent on a certain kind of integrity and willingness to participate in what we have chosen for the larger system. We colonize each other when we define others as the problem. And the higher in the institution we go, the more we are cut off from our own need to change.

When we run an organization or achieve real success, we begin to think of ourselves as a finished product. The institution expects so much, and the employees project so strongly on its management, that people at the top begin to believe their own press. They begin to think there is no room for them not to know and they too each take the stance of certainty. When this occurs faith is weakened. They become the god-father, and their lot is to dispense justice to others, not to be the ones who strive for justice within themselves.

If you look at the great leaders through history, you see a conscious-ness of their own limitations that was essential to their greatness. From Confucius, Buddha, and Christ, to Lincoln, Gandhi, and Martin Luther King Jr.—all touched the lives of others because of their presence more than their position. They became archetypes for the right use of power, and one source of their power was their own humility.

Power that is used to distance ourselves from our prescriptions is power abused. In seeking a partnership with school administrators and communities, Robert Chase, past president of the National Edu-cation Association, often has said that the union has to be the one to blink first. It is an observation that we would be wise to take to heart. It would make us credible and offer an antidote to the patriar-chy embedded in our strategies of change.

But don't think that leaders are alone in thinking others should be the ones to change. The love of patriarchy is as strong in employees as in management. As consultants, we once thought that as soon as management changed, employees would follow. Not necessarily so. Employees create bosses. If we create high-control bosses, we consider ourselves entitled, and entitlement means that we are not the problem. Something is due us, and we owe nothing. We hold to the safety of our dependency, just as the boss does, and each of us thinks the other needs to be fixed.

All of these beliefs trust that there is a movement toward learning that has its own energy and own intention. The world will provide the events that will force movement. Life provides the disturbance. We do not have to induce change, drive it, or guide it. All we have to do is join it. The consultant is as much a learner as any client. We in fact are often more changed by our consultation than the client, and this is as it should be.

In the end, it is our authenticity, the way we manage ourselves, and our connection to our clients that is our methodology, our marketing strategy, and the fruit of our labor. The fact that we show up with a briefcase, a résumé, and a conceptual framework is more a function of habit than necessity. It will be enough if we simply show up. This requires an act of faith. And that may be at the heart of the matter.

# HANDY CHECKLISTS
# YOU CAN USE

Now that you have finished reading this book, you have a good grasp of consulting concepts and skills. These ideas and techniques offer a methodical, sequential structure for the preliminary events to heighten the probability of successful

action. You also have journeyed through the choices in the discovery phase, all designed to help clients fulfill their intentions.

The checklists in the online appendix will be useful to you as a continuing reference on how to do consulting. Suppose you have an appointment to see a prospective client and want to quickly refresh your understanding of what to do in contracting. Turn to the section on contracting there, and use it as an outline of what to cover in your meeting and what to pay attention to.

The appendix at www.flawlessconsulting.com is divided into sections: overview, contracting, data collection and discovery, feedback, resistance, and implementation. The checklist in each section is an outline of main points or a summary of the business of that phase and the skills required. You can simply read through the checklists to refresh your knowledge and understanding of the material in the book from time to time. Or you may use them to check off some of the points you may not be completely sure about, that you want to learn more about, or that you want to practice further. The checklists also function as a topic index, giving page numbers of text if you want to review a particular point in more detail in the book. There are also some great illustrations that bring the online appendix to life. Enjoy those too.

Thank you for making it to the end. Feel free to download what's online for your own use and let us know how it works out.

Visit www.flawlessconsulting.com for more suggested reading, tools, updates, and evolving commentary on the consulting process.

Alexander, Christopher. *The Timeless Way of Building.* New York: Oxford University Press, 1979.

Argyris, Chris. *Knowledge for Action: A Guide to Overcoming Barriers to Organizational Change.* San Francisco: Jossey-Bass, 1993.

Argyris, Chris. *Flawed Advice and the Management Trap: How Managers Can Know When They're Getting Good Advice and When They're Not.* New York: Oxford University Press, 2000.

Axelrod, Richard H. *Terms of Engagement: Changing the Way We Change Organizations.* San Francisco: Berrett-Koehler, 2000.

Axelrod, Emily M., and Axelrod, Richard H. *Collaborating for Change: The Conference Model.* San Francisco: Berrett-Koehler, 2000.

Bellman, Geoffrey M. *The Consultant's Calling: Bringing Who You Are to What You Do.* (Rev. ed.) San Francisco: Jossey-Bass, 2001.

Biech, Elaine. *The Business of Consulting: The Basics and Beyond.* (2nd ed.) San Francisco: Jossey-Bass/Pfeiffer, 2007.

Blake, Robert R., and Mouton, Jane S. *Consultation.* (2nd ed.) Reading, Mass.: Addison-Wesley, 1983.

Block, Peter. *The Empowered Manager: Positive Political Skills at Work.* San Francisco: Jossey-Bass, 1991.

Block, Peter. *Stewardship: Choosing Service over Self-Interest.* San Francisco: Berrett-Koehler, 1993.

Briskin, Alan. *The Stirring of Soul in the Workplace.* San Francisco: Berrett-Koehler, 1998.

Brown, Juanita. *The World Café: Shaping Our Futures Through Conversations That Matter.* San Francisco: Berrett-Koehler, 2005.

Bunker, Barbara Benedict, and Alban, Billie T. *Large Group Interventions: Engaging the Whole System for Rapid Change.* San Francisco: Jossey-Bass, 1996.

Bunker, Barbara Benedict, and Alban, Billie T. *The Handbook of Large Group Methods: Creating Systemic Change in Organizations and Communities.* San Francisco: Jossey-Bass, 2006.

Clapp, Neale. *Work Group Norms: Leverage for Organizational Change. Part I: Theory. Part II: Application.* Plainfield, N.J.: Block Petrella Associates, 1979.

Dannemiller, Kathleen, and Dannemiller Tyson Associates. *Whole-Scale Change: Unleashing the Magic in Organizations.* San Francisco: Berrett-Koehler, 2000.

Dannemiller, Kathleen, Dannemiller Tyson Associates, and Badore, Nancy. *Whole-Scale Change Toolkit.* San Francisco: Berrett-Koehler, 2000.

Gallwey, W. Timothy. *The Inner Game of Tennis.* (Rev. ed.) New York: Random House, 1997.

Henning, Joel P. *The Future of Staff Groups: Daring to Distribute Power and Capacity.* San Francisco: Berrett-Koehler, 1997.

Illich, Ivan, and others. *Disabling Professions.* New York: Marion Boyars Publishers, 2010. (Originally published 1977)

Koestenbaum, Peter. *Leadership: The Inner Side of Greatness: A Philosophy for Leaders.* (2nd ed.) San Francisco: Jossey-Bass, 2002.

Maurer, Rick. *Beyond the Wall of Resistance: Why 70% of All Changes Still Fail—and What You Can Do About It.* (Rev. ed.) Austin, Texas: Bard Press, 2010.

McKnight, John. *The Careless Society: Community and Its Counterfeits.* New York: Basic Books, 1995.

McKnight, John, and Block, Peter. *The Abundant Community: Awakening the Power of Families and Neighborhoods.* San Francisco: Berrett-Koehler, 2010.

Oshry, Barry. *Seeing Systems: Unlocking the Mysteries of Organizational Life.* (2nd ed.) San Francisco: Berrett-Koehler, 2007.

Owen, Harrison. *Open Space Technology: A User's Guide.* (3rd ed.) San Francisco: Berrett-Koehler, 2008.

Palmer, Parker J. *The Courage to Teach: Exploring the Inner Landscape of a Teacher's Life.* (10th anniv. ed.) San Francisco: Jossey-Bass, 2007.

Pascale, Richard, Sternin, Jerry, and Sternin, Monique. *The Power of Positive Deviance: How Unlikely Innovators Solve the World's Toughest Problems.* Boston: Harvard Business School Press, 2010.

Schein, Edgar H. *Process Consultation Revisited: Building the Helping Relationship.* Reading, Mass.: Addison-Wesley/Longman, 1998.

Steele, Fritz. *Consulting for Organizational Change.* Amherst: University of Massachusetts Press, 1975.

Walton, Richard E. *Interpersonal Peacemaking: Confrontations and Third-Party Consultation.* Reading, Mass.: Addison-Wesley, 1969.

Weisbord, Marvin. *Discovering Common Ground: How Future Search Conferences Bring People Together to Achieve Breakthrough Innovation, Empowerment, Shared Vision, and Collaborative Action.* San Francisco: Berrett-Koehler, 1992.

Weisbord, Marvin, and Janoff, Sandra. *Future Search: Getting the Whole System in the Room for Vision, Commitment, and Action.* (Rev. ed.) San Francisco: Berrett-Koehler, 2010.

Wheatley, Margaret J., and Kellner-Rogers, Myron. *A Simpler Way.* San Francisco: Berrett-Koehler, 1996.

Whitmore, John. *Coaching for Performance: Growing Human Potential and Purpose—the Principles and Practice of Coaching and Leadership.* (4th rev. ed.) London: Nicholas Brealey, 2009.

**Peter Block** was born in Chicago and spent most of his early years in the Midwest. After college, he went to New Jersey and was involved in the early days of creating the field of organization development. This entailed some years at Exxon Research and Engineering Company and then the formation of the consulting firm of Block, Petrella, Weisbord.

In 1980, Block started Designed Learning, a training company that continues to offer workshops based on the ideas in his books. It thrives and works to help support people in organizations to have more influence and impact. The primary products are the Flawless Consulting Workshops based on this book.

Block has written seven other books, including *The Abundant Community* (with John McKnight), *The Empowered Manager*, *Stewardship*, *Freedom and Accountability at Work* (with Peter Koestenbaum), *The Answer to How Is Yes*, and *Community: The Structure of Belonging*.

His work is now centered in Cincinnati, Ohio, where Block has been a citizen since 1998. He is involved in developing a civic engagement network called A Small Group, plus a series of other projects working on building the capacity of this urban community to value its gifts and see its own possibility.